Political Traditions in Foreign Policy Series
Kenneth W. Thompson, Editor

The values, traditions, and assumptions undergirding approaches to foreign policy are often crucial in determining the course of a nation's history. Yet, the interconnections between ideas and policy for landmark periods in our foreign relations remain largely unexamined. The intent of this series is to encourage a marriage between political theory and foreign policy. A secondary objective is to identify theorists with a continuing interest in political thought and international relations, both younger scholars and the small group of established thinkers. Only occasionally have scholarly centers and university presses sought to nurture studies in this area. In the 1950s and 1960s the University of Chicago Center for the Study of American Foreign Policy gave emphasis to such inquiries. Since then the subject has not been the focus of any major intellectual center. The Louisiana State University Press and the series editor, from a base at the Miller Center of Public Affairs at the University of Virginia, have organized the series to meet a need that has remained largely unfulfilled since the mid-1960s.

The Collapse of
the Grand Alliance
1945–1948

The Collapse of
the Grand Alliance
1945–1948

JAMES L. GORMLY

Louisiana State University Press
Baton Rouge and London

Designer: Christopher Wilcox
Typeface: Palatino
Typesetter: G&S Typesetters, Inc.
Printer: Thomson-Shore, Inc.
Binder: John Dekker & Sons, Inc.

A section of Chapter III has appeared, in different form, in *Red River Valley Historical Journal of World History*.

Publication of this book has been assisted by a grant from the Andrew W. Mellon Foundation.

10 9 8 7 6 5 4 3 2 1

Library of Congress Cataloging-in-Publication Data

Gormly, James L., 1946–
    The collapse of the Grand Alliance, 1945–1948.

    (Political traditions in foreign policy series)
    Bibliography: p.
    Includes index.
    1. World politics—1945–   . 2. World War,
1939–1945—Diplomatic history.   3. United States—
Foreign relations—1945–1953.   4. Soviet Union—
Foreign relations—1945–   . 5. Great Britain—
Foreign relations—1945–   . I. Title.   II. Series.
D842.G67 1987   327′.090444   86-27438
ISBN 0-8071-1320-4

Contents

Preface and Acknowledgments

O N MARCH 12, 1947, President Harry S Truman stood before the United States Congress and announced that the world was divided into two opposing camps: the free and the unfree. It was the responsibility of the United States, he said, to "support free people" who resisted subjugation "by armed minorities or by outside pressure." Truman did not mention the Soviet Union by name, but no one who listened to or read the speech failed to understand that Truman sought an accelerated American effort to prevent the further expansion of Soviet power.[1]

Often considered the beginning of the cold war, the Truman Doctrine speech is, more precisely, a part of the breakdown of the Grand Alliance. The alliance was based on common needs and goals of the United States, Great Britain, and the Soviet Union during World War II, when they collaborated despite mutual suspicions and differing world views and national goals. When the war ended, hopes and confidence were widespread that the wartime cooperation would serve as the foundation for a new international system and an enduring peace.

1. Harry S Truman, *Public Papers of the Presidents of the United States: Harry S Truman, 1947* (Washington, D.C., 1963), 176–80.

Conditions existed within each of the three powers that seemed conducive to a postwar Grand Alliance. Statesmen and citizens agreed that a lasting peace depended on understanding and cooperation among the powers. Despite some talk of returning to isolationism, the American people accepted the idea of the United States actively promoting a lasting peace. Walter Lippmann voiced the view of many "realistic" Americans when he suggested that rivalries between Britain and the Soviet Union were the major threat to postwar harmony and that Washington should play the honest broker between the two European nations.[2]

Similarly, a large segment of the British population, especially within the Labour party, believed that Britain and the United States should make special efforts to understand Russian suspicions. The British press, continuing a wartime policy, generally avoided criticizing the Russians.[3]

Russians, too, projected a desire to continue the Grand Alliance as the basis of peace. The state-controlled Soviet press presented favorable wartime images of the Western Allies and played down the differences between economic and political philosophies. As Russia prepared for peace, Stalin demonstrated Russia's willingness to participate in world affairs, and the Russian media reaffirmed Big Three cooperation as the road to lasting peace. Those who suggested hostility between capitalism and communism were condemned as fascists.[4]

Despite the hopes and support for continued cooperation, however, the Grand Alliance collapsed between the summer of 1945

2. Walter LaFeber, "American Policy-Makers, Public Opinion, and the Outbreak of the Cold War, 1945–1950," in Yonosuke Nagai and Akora Iriye (eds.), *The Origins of the Cold War in Asia* (Tokyo, 1977), 43–65; Ralph B. Levering, *American Opinion and the Russian Alliance, 1939–1945* (Chapel Hill, 1976), 39–199.

3. Paul Winteron, "Report on Russia," July, 1945, Foreign Office Memorandum, February, 1946, N 3859/605/38, in Foreign Office General Correspondence File 371, 1946, Public Record Office, London, hereinafter cited as document number, FO 371, year, PRO; Foreign Office Research Department (FORD) Paper, "Anglo-Soviet Relations Since 1934," December, 1948, N 10521/1/38, in FO 371, 1948, PRO; Bill Jones, *The Russian Complex: The British Labour Party and the Soviet Union* (Manchester, 1977), 58–120.

4. FORD Paper, "Anglo-Soviet Relations," N 10521/1/38, in FO 371, 1948, PRO; Victor Rothwell, *Britain and the Cold War, 1941–1947* (London, 1982), 97–99, 128–44; William Taubman, *Stalin's American Policy: From Entente to Detente to Cold War* (New York, 1982).

and autumn of 1946. In its place emerged a divided Europe and, eventually, a polarized world—the world of Truman's speech. The shift from Grand Alliance to cold war occurred because of major alterations of international and domestic behavior by the Big Three. In moving from collaboration to confrontation, each power first recognized that national interests were more important than continued cooperation. Second, the powers determined that "friendly" rivalry between East and West was unlikely and that real threats existed to national interests and security. Finally, each of the Big Three demonstrated publicly that collaboration was no longer possible, that enemies existed, and that the nation needed to be unified against the new foe.

The change from cooperation to confrontation took place in three stages. The first stage, from August, 1945, through March, 1946, constituted the interactions of the Big Three during and after the foreign ministers' conferences in London and Moscow. The ministers' inability to implement satisfactory agreements destroyed belief that the Grand Alliance could continue. Left unresolved, however, was the nature of the new relationship among the Big Three. Events and perceptions between January and September, 1946, the second stage, resolved that question, as the United States and Great Britain moved from policies of patience to those of firmness toward the Soviet Union and as their actions assumed more and more of a collaborative nature.

Unable to split the British and American alliance, the Soviets intensified their public attacks on British policy and initiated attacks upon the United States' policies. At the same time, the Soviet Union moved to strengthen its position within Eastern Europe and contributed to political instability outside of its immediate orbit. By the end of 1946, the Big Three were, in differing degrees, entering into the third stage of the transformation from Grand Alliance to cold war. The three powers each accepted the premise that hostile East and West blocs now existed, and they were developing a new international system based upon that assumption. Steps were taken to further strengthen influence where it existed and to put domestic affairs in order. Truman's March, 1947, speech, the formation of the Cominform (1947), and Ernest Bevin's Gatehead speech (1948) confirmed the third stage, in which gauntlets were publicly thrown down and picked up.

This study seeks to examine the causes and manner of the collapse of the Grand Alliance. In moving from collaboration to confrontation, the three powers often demonstrated hesitancy and confusion. None of the big powers had set concrete goals or policies, and they frequently reacted to each other, formulating explanations and policies as events overtook them. Compromises were made and rejected. As cooperation failed, as the Grand Alliance floundered, each decried the others' tactics, protested the estrangement, and proclaimed innocence. None was innocent; all were guilty.

Space does not allow a full accounting of the people and institutions that have contributed to my research and writing. Thomas G. Paterson criticized, suggested changes, and provided invaluable help with the manuscript. The staffs of the Harry S Truman and Franklin D. Roosevelt libraries, the staffs of the State Department and Modern Military branches of the National Archives, and the staff of the Public Record Office facilitated research. I owe a special debt to Sir E. I. C. Jacob of Woodbridge, Essex, for providing his notes and insights regarding the Washington and Moscow conferences.

Research and writing would have been impossible without the financial assistance provided by the Truman and Roosevelt libraries and the Faculty Research Council of Pan American University. I would also like to thank Elizabeth L. Carpelan and the staff at Louisiana State University Press for their professional editorial work and expertise. Most importantly, this book would not have been possible without the help and encouragement of my wife. Without her physical and moral support, her insights and numerous hours of proofreading, and, most of all, her faith, this work would not exist. Thank you, Sharon.

The Collapse of
the Grand Alliance
1945–1948

I

Winning the Peace

AUGUST 14, 1945. The second Great War was over. The Grand Alliance stood victorious over the Axis nations. The tasks of rebuilding a shattered Europe and fashioning an enduring peace lay ahead. Much of Europe was in physical ruin, its population depleted and its remaining economic capacity worn to the breaking point. Of the victorious Allies, the Soviet Union was, without doubt, the most devastated—a condition that Western statesmen believed would help ensure Soviet cooperation with the West. Politically, almost every nation touched by the war was undergoing major changes, with a shift occurring toward the left. Only the Soviet Union and the United States seemed immune to political and social change. Europe was a setting sun; the United States, the dawn.

Economically stronger than before the war, the United States experienced little of war's devastation and disruption. Psychologically and spiritually, Americans faced the future with great expectations and almost blind faith in American know-how. The war had brought about the end of American isolationism and fears of being corrupted by wily Europeans, and an image of the United States leading the European nations and the world along the path of progress and civilization emerged. Many Americans echoed the views of Henry Luce, who believed that the "American Century" had begun.[1]

American statesmen had been anxious to structure the peace from the time of America's entry into the war. "We are going to win the war, and we are going to win the peace that follows," President Franklin D. Roosevelt promised as the nation mobilized for war. Commitments to that promise found expression in the creation during wartime of a variety of commissions and committees designed to study postwar problems and recommend policy, and in the support given to the formation of the United Nations organization. In 1945, Americans everywhere were proud that the headquarters of the world organization was to be in New York City. President Truman concluded that the choice of the American site proved that the United States was the new heart of Western civilization. The Los Angeles *Times* stated that the United States should direct the establishment of a permanent peace because it had "no other direct interest."[2]

The Truman administration stood ready to assume the responsibility of making the peace, even if Truman was less than anxious to participate directly in international negotiations after his Potsdam experiences. Truman may not have been anxious, but his secretary of state, James F. Byrnes, was. Truman had selected Byrnes because he wanted a politician capable of dealing with Congress, and with experience as a tough negotiator. He wanted someone with obvious links to Roosevelt's policies but who had views similar to his own. Byrnes appeared to fill all the requirements, and he wanted the job. Convinced that Woodrow Wilson had lost the peace after World War I, Byrnes wanted to oversee the efforts to make the peace after World War II.[3]

Within hours of Roosevelt's death on April 12, Truman sought to find Byrnes by telephoning the bereaved Roosevelts at Hyde Park.

1. Lawrence S. Kaplan, "Western Europe in 'The American Century': A Retrospective View," *Diplomatic History*, VI (1982), 111–24.

2. John Lewis Gaddis, *The United States and the Origins of the Cold War, 1941–1947* (New York, 1972), 1; Los Angeles *Times*, September 12, 1945, Sec. A, p. 1.

3. James F. Byrnes, *All in One Lifetime* (New York, 1958); James F. Byrnes, *Speaking Frankly* (New York, 1947), 38–50; Lord Halifax to Anthony Eden, August 20, 1945, Microfilm roll 2, A4.410.4.5, in Lord Halifax Papers, Churchill College Library, Churchill College, Cambridge.

Byrnes was located in South Carolina, and a Navy plane was sent to bring him to Washington. On April 13, Truman and Byrnes met and discussed domestic and foreign issues, including the Yalta Conference. It was at Yalta that Byrnes had gained his experience in foreign affairs. Roosevelt had selected Byrnes to attend the conference largely for political reasons, to have him "do some persuading . . . of the Senate, with which he was popular." Byrnes did an excellent job of selling the results of Yalta to Congress and earned the reputation of being a first-rate diplomat, if not Roosevelt's right-hand man at the meeting. Truman accepted this view of Byrnes and asked him to assume the position of secretary of state. Byrnes accepted but said he would start only after the United Nations meeting in San Francisco, held in April, May, and June, 1945.[4]

The appointment did not receive unanimous acclaim in Washington. Henry Morgenthau, secretary of the treasury, said that he could not "get along" with Byrnes. Secretary of the Navy James Forrestal, Admiral William Leahy, and Senator Arthur Vandenberg doubted the wisdom of the choice. Vandenberg thought that "Jimmy Byrnes is a grand guy (for any other job down here)." Bernard Baruch suspected that the new secretary was "power crazy."[5]

State Department personnel were also dubious of the selection. Rumors circulated that Byrnes had a bias against career, "striped pants" diplomats. Some feared that he would dismiss or retire many of the older, more conservative, hands. Others worried that he would ignore department experts and heed the advice of a small coterie of handpicked advisers. Eugene Dooman, a specialist in Far Eastern affairs, speculated that the newly appointed counselor of

4. George Curry, *James F. Byrnes* (New York, 1965), 105–32; Robert L. Messer, *The End of an Alliance: James F. Byrnes, Roosevelt, Truman, and the Origins of the Cold War* (Chapel Hill, 1982), 1–93; James F. Byrnes to Harry S Truman, April 11, 1945, in Box 843:237, Official File, Harry S Truman Library, Independence, Mo.; Jonathan Daniels Oral History (Transcript in Carton 16, pp. 29–30), in Jonathan Daniels Papers, University of North Carolina Library, University of North Carolina, Chapel Hill, N.C.

5. Henry Morgenthau, Jr. Diary, April 16 and 17, June 1, 1945, in Henry Morgenthau, Jr., Papers, Franklin D. Roosevelt Library, Hyde Park, N.Y.; Arthur H. Vandenberg, Jr. (ed.), *The Private Papers of Senator Vandenberg* (Boston, 1952), 255; Cabell Phillips, *The Truman Presidency: The History of a Triumphant Succession* (New York, 1966), 82–86.

the State Department, Benjamin V. Cohen, would be Byrnes's primary adviser.[6]

Despite others' doubts about Byrnes's qualifications for the position, Truman trusted him, respected his opinions, and deferred to his judgment. The new secretary of state had unlimited access to the White House and, until at least January, 1946, enjoyed nearly unlimited freedom to formulate and conduct United States foreign policy. Truman rarely wired Byrnes for information, and when asked by the secretary of state for a decision, he usually replied, "I agree with your stand" or "Use your best judgment and I am sure things will come out all right." Byrnes's role was so well understood by the White House staff that State Department messages needing the president's signature were often dispatched by the staff over Truman's signature without his having seen them.[7]

Public and congressional opinion did not place any significant restrictions on Byrnes's conduct of foreign policy. The State Department monitored public opinion and the views expressed by major newspapers and leading commentators and found that domestic concerns far outweighed interest in foreign issues. Throughout the spring, summer, and autumn of 1945, State Department and other polls consistently found that more than half of those asked thought that Russia could be trusted and that the United States should work with Russia to ensure peace. The overall impression gained from the polls was that opinion was diverse and that most Americans trusted their policy makers to do the right thing.[8]

What Byrnes lacked in actual experience, he compensated for in

6. Balfour to Foreign Office, July 11, 1945, AN 2035/145/45, May 31, 1945, AN 266/145/45, both in FO 371, 1945, PRO; *Time*, July 16, 1945, p. 25; Morton Blum (ed.), *The Price of Vision: The Diary of Henry A. Wallace, 1942–1946* (Boston, 1973), 469; Eugene H. Dooman to Herbert Feis, December 7, 1960, in File D, Herbert Feis Papers, Library of Congress, Washington, D.C.

7. Tris Coffin, "Report from Washington," a CBS Radio News Program, December 30, 1945, Transcript in Carton 16, Daniels Papers; Balfour to Foreign Office, April 14, 1945, AN 1198/145/45, in FO 371, 1945, PRO; Messer, *End of an Alliance*, 77–85; Charles Bohlen, *Witness to History, 1929–1969* (New York, 1973), 224–25, 243–45; Robert L. Messer, "The Making of a Cold Warrior: James F. Byrnes and American-Soviet Relations, 1945–1946" (Ph.D. dissertation, University of California at Berkeley, 1975), 378–82.

8. LaFeber, "American Policy-Makers," 43–47; Thomas G. Paterson, *On Every Front: The Making of the Cold War* (New York, 1979), 113–38.

personal attributes, a global view of American interests, and judicious selection of advisers. Byrnes's negotiating ability, a colleague commented, rested "on his personal and political tact, his capacity for friendly relations with virtually everyone . . . [and] his skill and smoothness as a negotiator." Chester Bowles testified that Byrnes had a "way of settling a case so that everyone looked good, didn't look as though they had been weakened by it." Lord Halifax informed the Foreign Office in London that Truman required his officials to be "good American horse traders" and to emerge from "negotiations with an accretion of influence and concrete benefits" equal to America's power. The British and the Soviets believed that the secretary of state fulfilled Truman's dictum. Stalin called Byrnes the best horse trader he had seen.[9]

Confident in his negotiating skills, Byrnes sought to lay the foundation for an enduring peace. Like most Americans, the secretary of state identified two paths to peace and national security: military deterrence and a cooperative world. Halifax described the American view as one part humanitarianism and one part imperialism.[10]

To promote peace through deterrence, the United States sought to expand upon its obvious military capabilities, which included possession of the world's largest and strongest navy and air force as well as the atomic bomb. But military power based in the United States was no longer enough to fully protect American military and diplomatic needs. The United States was a global power and required the means to demonstrate its power around the world. Naval planners sought to dispatch naval squadrons, many of which included powerful battleships and carriers, to nearly every ocean and sea in the world. Bases were sought beyond the Western Hemisphere. By 1945, Iceland housed an American base, negotiations were underway with the British to use airfields in Iraq and India, and construction had begun on an American-operated airfield in Saudi Arabia. In addition, Byrnes hoped to buy Greenland from the Danes and acquire Clipperton Island from the British.

9. Lord Halifax to Foreign Office, July 11, 1945, AN 2136/245/45, in FO 371, 1945, PRO; Chester Bowles Oral History (Transcript in Box 78, pp. 136–37, Columbia University Oral History Collection, Columbia University, New York, N.Y.); Blum, *The Price of Vision*, 475.

10. Lord Halifax to Foreign Office, December 4, 1945, AN 3768/145/45, in FO 371, 1945, PRO.

Concerns about the high level of military expenditures projected for the fiscal year 1946 seemed to fall on deaf ears. The navy lobbied for new carriers and cruisers. The War Department wanted to develop jets and new tanks. Byrnes promised to secure necessary funding for the hydrogen "superbomb." Flanked by admirals and generals, Truman told a New York crowd in October that he had asked "Congress to adopt universal military training" to ensure that the United States would have the manpower necessary to "mobilize a powerful and well-equipped land, sea, and air force." [11]

Military strength, however, was not the only recognized means to ensure peace and national security. Edward R. Stettinius, who preceded Byrnes as secretary of state, said that the goal of foreign policy was to build an "enduring peace in a prosperous world." Global peace and prosperity went hand in hand, he told the Inter-American Conference on the Problems of War and Peace in February, 1945. [12]

In planning for peace, officials in Washington shared a widespread conviction about the causes of war and the necessity of peace. They drew their lessons from history. The international economic system of the 1920s and 1930s had gone bankrupt, resulting in instability and totalitarian rulers who lusted after power. Byrnes reflected that in prewar Germany and Japan there had been "no opportunity to appeal to the judgment of the millions" and, therefore, no restraints on the warlike designs of the leadership. State

11. U.S. Department of State, *Foreign Relations of the United States, 1945* (10 vols.; Washington, D.C., 1967), IV, 206–17, 233, hereinafter cited as *FR*, with date, volume, page; State-War-Navy Coordinating Committee (SWNCC) Minutes, March 2, 1946, SWNCC Files, National Archives, Washington, D.C.; Harold D. Smith Diary, September 19, 1945, in Harold D. Smith Papers, Roosevelt Library; George Harrison to Secretary of War, August 17, 1945, in Folder 77, Manhattan Engineer District Files, 1942–1946, NA; Richard G. Hewlitt and Oscar E. Anderson, Jr., *The New World, 1939–1946* (University Park, Pa., 1962), 417–18; Harry S Truman, "Recommendations to Congress for Universal Military Training," *Department of State Bulletin*, XIII (October 28, 1945), 660, hereinafter cited as *DSB*, volume, date, page.

12. Edward R. Stettinius, "Address at the Plenary Session of the Inter-American Conference on the Problem of War and Peace," *DSB*, XII (February 25, 1945), 277; Lloyd C. Gardner, *Architects of Illusion: Men and Ideas in American Foreign Policy, 1941–1949* (Chicago, 1970), 84–138; Thomas G. Paterson, "The Quest for Peace and Prosperity: International Trade, Communism, and the Marshall Plan," in Barton J. Bernstein (ed.), *Politics and Policies of the Truman Administration* (Chicago, 1970), 78–112.

Department expert on Asia John K. Emmerson blamed the war in the Pacific on Japan's "conquest mad military dictators." The view that citizens did not create war but that dictators did was shared by most Americans. A *Public Opinion Quarterly* poll in 1940 found that over 63 percent of those asked said that they did not blame the German people for the war. American officials had concluded that one step in ending war and in building a permanent peace was to remove the elites that caused war and replace them with representative government.[13]

To eliminate the dictators, the United States officials relied on unconditional surrender. This would, they believed, fix the responsibility for the war and its hardships on the rulers and clear the way for the emergence of new leaders and political groups not connected with the previous militaristic regimes. But new leadership was not enough to ensure peace. Postwar governments would need to be democratic, representative, and stable. Promoting this model meant combating not only the reactionary forces of rightist militarism but those of totalitarian "democracy" as well.

Many American political observers saw a worldwide, leftward political trend and believed that the leftward movement must be channeled along lines that would protect private ownership, capitalism, and civil liberties. The presidential briefing book for the Yalta Conference stated that the new governments of the liberated nations "must be sufficiently to the left to satisfy the prevailing mood . . . [but] sufficiently representative of the center and the '*petit bourgeois*' elements" to prevent "a Communist dictatorship." A special adviser to Byrnes, Charles Bohlen, wrote that the United States should promote "the democratic left" that based social and economic reforms on "the preservation of civil and political liberties." It was unfortunate, United States officials noted, that the removal of dictators and the promotion of democracy dealt only with the political process contributing to war. The true roots of peace and stability went deeper.[14]

13. Byrnes, *Speaking Frankly*, 5; Akira Iriye, *The Cold War in Asia: A Historical Introduction* (Englewood Cliffs, N.J., 1974), 76; *Public Opinion Quarterly*, IV (1940), 98–99.

14. Gaddis, *The U.S. and the Origins of the Cold War*, 8–13; Gaddis Smith, *American Diplomacy During the Second World War, 1941–1945* (New York, 1965); Department of State, *Foreign Relations of the United States: The Malta and Yalta Conferences, 1945*, (1955), 103; Charles Bohlen and Dr. J. Robinson, Draft Memorandum on United

American officials generally agreed that fascism had arisen in the Axis nations because of economic depression and resulting social and political instability. During the preceding decades, rampant economic nationalism encouraged trade barriers, currency speculation, hoarding, and inflation. The climax of these actions was international economic depression, political upheaval, the emergence of militaristic leaders, and eventually war. To ensure peace in the postwar world, depression and economic nationalism had to be forestalled. In August, 1945, Secretary Byrnes told Congress: "In the field of international relations we have joined in a cooperative endeavor to construct an expanding world economy based on the liberal principles of private enterprise, nondiscrimination, and reduced barriers to trade. The importance which we attach to this task derives from the firm conviction that a durable peace cannot be built on an economic foundation of exclusive barriers, autarchy, and economic warfare."[15]

Free, multilateral trade seemed to be the panacea. Unencumbered commerce would ensure international prosperity and stability, dispel distrust, encourage interdependence, and promote continued American economic growth. The last point, Truman and other officials frankly stated, was important for both world reconstruction and United States security. "A large volume of soundly based international trade is essential if we are to achieve prosperity . . . and attain our goal of world peace and security," Truman told one audience.[16]

The House of Representatives' Committee on Postwar Policy and Planning (the so-called Colmer Committee) emphasized the role of the United States in building a prosperous world economic system. The committee saw the United States as the fulcrum of international finance and trade and recommended that only through free trade

---

States-Soviet Relations, February 14, 1946, in File 711.61/2-1446, Department of State Records, NA, hereinafter cited as document, date, file or box number, DSR-NA; Ernest R. May, *"Lessons" of the Past: The Use and Misuse of History in American Foreign Policy* (New York, 1973), 9–12.

15. May, *"Lessons,"* 9–14; James F. Byrnes, "Statement to the Senate Committee on Banking and Currency: The Full Employment Bill of 1945," *DSB,* XIII (August 26, 1945), 279; Thomas G. Paterson, *Soviet-American Confrontation: Postwar Reconstruction and the Origins of the Cold War* (Baltimore, 1973), 1–34.

16. Paterson, *Soviet-American Confrontation,* 4; Harry S Truman, "The State of the Union Address, January 6, 1947," *DSB,* XVI (January 19, 1947), 279–80.

and unrestricted access to markets, raw materials, and investment opportunities could Washington rebuild the war-torn world. The creation of the International Bank for Reconstruction and Development at Bretton Woods, the United Nations Relief and Rehabilitation Administration, the Lend-Lease agreement, and postwar credits were a beginning, but much still needed to be done to place international economics on a multilateral basis. Washington expected the United Nations Economic and Social Council to play an important role in the further growth of economic liberalism. Stettinius labeled the council the "greatest opportunity to break once and for all the vicious circle of isolationism, depression, and war." His words were, perhaps, overstatement but expressed a hope shared by the first United States representative on the council, Eleanor Roosevelt.[17]

The United Nations was to promote political and social understanding as well but not necessarily to act as the guarantor of American national security or global peacemaking. The secretaries of war and the navy, Henry L. Stimson and James Forrestal, had long held serious reservations about the adequacy of the United Nations and collective security to protect the sovereignty and security of the United States. Like many within the State Department, they believed that, while the world organization would be useful in promoting Western, liberal traditions and free trade, world peace was best maintained by a strong, armed United States and big power cooperation. Byrnes held opinions similar to those of Stimson and Forrestal. He confided to the British that he hoped a permanent site for the world organization would be found in Europe, where it could be useful in mediating European squabbles.[18]

To handle the major problems facing the major powers and to begin the construction of the postwar settlement, Byrnes favored a smaller, more select organization—the Council of Foreign Minis-

17. U.S. Congress, House of Representatives, Special Committee on Postwar Economic Policy and Planning, "Economic Reconstruction in Europe," 11th Report, 79th Congress, 1st Session (December, 1945), 85; Edward R. Stettinius, "Radio Report on the San Francisco Conference, May 28, 1945," DSB, XII (June 3, 1945), 1012; FR 1946 (10 vols.; Washington, D.C., 1969), II, 131; Robert A. Pollard, Economic Security and the Origins of the Cold War, 1945–1950 (New York, 1985), 5–32.

18. Dean Acheson, Present at the Creation: My Years in the State Department (New York, 1969), 6; Thomas M. Campbell, Masquerade Peace: America's U.N. Policy, 1944–1945 (Tallahassee, Fla., 1973), 136–48; Foreign Office Note, October 21, 1945, U 8330/12/70, in FO 371, 1945, PRO.

ters. Benjamin Cohen explained to Truman that the council could
"handle the necessary peace negotiations and territorial settle-
ments in lieu of a general peace conference." During the Berlin
Conference, held from July 17 to August 2, 1945, Byrnes confided
to Soviet Foreign Minister V. M. Molotov that he wanted "to avoid a
general peace conference . . . of fifty-odd nations" with the accompanying endless discussions that accomplished little.[19] Meeting
with the foreign ministers of the Big Five (China, France, Great
Britain, the Soviet Union, and the United States) was better suited
for Byrnes's style of diplomacy. The secretary realized it would take
tough bargaining to convince Britain and Russia to accept the policies and views of the United States. But he was "emphatic and
firm" in his belief that both would eventually meet United States
terms. Byrnes knew that the Russians would be the more difficult
to convince and that control of Eastern Europe would be the most
difficult issue to resolve.[20]

The Far East and the Pacific were relatively secure and offered
few obstacles to the implementation of United States postwar objectives. Those objectives hinged on continued United States domination of Japan and the Pacific, a stable coalition government in China
under the direction of Chiang Kai-shek, the return of colonial areas
to their former guardians, and stability and free trade throughout
the area.

Discussing the United States' economic position in Asia with
Leahy, Truman said that he believed that in the future East Asia and
the Pacific would assume an economic relationship to the United
States like that of Latin America, and that he intended to "make
every practicable effort to preserve at least an equal opportunity for
American interests in the Western Pacific."[21]

United States domination of Japan and the Pacific was nearly a
fait accompli by September, 1945. A Soviet attempt to gain equal occupation and control rights in Japan was blocked. The British were
still asking for more command privileges in Asia and refusing to

19. Campbell, *Masquerade Peace*, 136–48; Minutes of Secretary's Staff Committee,
June 8, 1945, in Box 304, Secretary's Staff Committee Records, DSR-NA; Department
of State, *Foreign Relations of the United States: The Conference of Berlin (The Potsdam Conference), 1945* (Washington, D.C., 1960), I, 285–87, II, 354–56.

20. Campbell, *Masquerade Peace*, 159–93; Byrnes, *Speaking Frankly*, 70–71.

21. Admiral William Leahy Diary, September 12, 1945, in Box 5, William Leahy
Papers, LC.

cede some Pacific islands to the United States, but those obstacles were not expected to last long. On the Asian mainland the "open door" was supported by Chiang and Stalin, and the State Department was optimistic about bringing the Communist and Nationalist Chinese together in a coalition government.[22]

The State Department was also optimistic about maintaining and developing economic multilateralism in the Middle East. A policy memorandum spelled out the formula for United States economic activity, multilateralism, and peace. The United States could best promote "a peaceful evolution in the Middle East" by removing trade barriers and making credits and investment opportunities available. "A positive role assumed by the United States in furthering economic coordination" of the Middle Eastern states and other powers would remove "the causes of difficulties which might arise." Supporting the optimism were increased American military and economic involvement in the region and indications that Britain was weakening in its "dog-in-the-manger" tactic aimed at restricting American economic development in the Middle East and the eastern Mediterranean.[23]

In the Middle East and in Western Europe, the chief obstacles facing the United States were the nationalistic and imperial policies of Great Britain. Britain's political goals, especially in Western Europe, largely paralleled those of the United States. However, Britain's weakened military and economic condition permitted the United States to assume a position of leadership. Many within the State Department were referring to Britain as the "junior partner" of the United States. W. Averell Harriman told his staff: "England is so weak she must follow our leadership. . . . She will do anything that we insist and she won't go out on a limb alone."[24] The United States' main objections to British foreign policy centered upon Brit-

22. Herbert Feis, *Contest Over Japan: The Soviet Bid for Power in the Far East* (New York, 1968), 22–30; Iriye, *The Cold War in Asia*, 99–118; John Paton Davies, Jr., *Dragon by the Tail: American, British, Japanese, and Russian Encounters with China and One Another* (New York, 1972), 411–19; Christopher Thorne, *Allies of a Kind: The United States, Britain, and the War Against Japan, 1941–1945* (New York, 1978), 678–80.

23. *FR 1945*, VIII, 34, 954–56; Phillip J. Baram, *The Department of State in the Middle East, 1919–1945* (Philadelphia, 1978), 223–39; Barry Rubin, "Anglo-American Relations in Saudi Arabia, 1941–1945," *Journal of Contemporary History*, XIV (1979), 253–67.

24. Balfour to Foreign Office, December 5, 1945, AN 2851/763/45, in FO 371, 1945, PRO; David Dilks (ed.), *The Diaries of Sir Alexander Cadogan, 1938–1945* (New

ain's refusal to join the Far Eastern Advisory Commission, its protection of economic interests and political influence through restrictive trading practices, and its objections to the United States' atomic monopoly.

British efforts to protect its economic position in the Empire, the Sterling Bloc, and in the Middle East were deemed the most troublesome. Those efforts blocked economic multilateralism as well as specific American business interests. Britain's nationalistic economic policy, however, was not a new problem for American planners. It had existed from the beginning of the war, when the United States attempted to eliminate Britain's imperial preference system. Attempts to solicit Britain's consent to an unconditional pledge to promote free trade had complicated and delayed the creation of the Atlantic Charter. In drafting the Mutual Aid (Lend-Lease) agreement, the United States sought to remove British imperial discriminatory commercial practices as a condition for Lend-Lease materials. The British resisted what they termed "blackmail" until February, 1942, when they agreed to American terms. After the war ended, however, Britain found ways to circumvent the agreement and protect her interests and markets.[25]

The failure of the Lend-Lease agreement to eliminate Britain's restrictive trade practices might have worried officials in Washington were it not for Britain's postwar economic plight and its request for postwar credits from the United States. Byrnes supported granting Britain a generous loan, provided that "we get them coming clean on other things." Both the loan request and the Lend-Lease agreement offered the United States opportunities to penetrate Britain's economic spheres of influence and to spread the benefits derived from multilateralism and increased American activity. As the secretary of state sailed for the first meeting of the Council of Foreign Ministers in London, negotiations with the British on a loan were imminent, leaving only control of Japan and atomic energy and weapons as possible points of conflict. Byrnes saw little difficulty in dealing with the British on those issues.[26]

York, 1972), 778; W. Averell Harriman and Elie Abel, *Special Envoy to Churchill and Stalin, 1941–1946* (New York, 1975), 531.

25. Dilks, *The Diaries of Cadogan*, 431; Richard N. Gardner, *Sterling-Dollar Diplomacy: The Origins and Prospects of Our International Economic Order* (New York, 1969), 40–68.

26. Gardner, *Sterling-Dollar Diplomacy*, 64–100; Paterson, *Soviet-American Con-*

Byrnes and most American policy makers believed that the only real threat to an American peace came from the Soviet Union. Moscow's political and economic system—state-controlled trade and totalitarian "democracy"—differed markedly from the free trade and representative democracy of the United States. Russian actions in Eastern Europe indicated that the Soviets meant to follow their own policies in that region. Moscow appeared to favor economic nationalism, building trade barriers in Eastern Europe and eliminating Western economic interests. The State Department's chief of Eastern European affairs, Elbridge Dubrow, thought Soviet trade agreements affecting the region from Stettin to Trieste were "very restrictive and . . . apparently aimed at excluding free trade." He believed the agreements indicated an attempt to return to the old European pattern of power politics. In April, 1945, Harriman, ambassador to the Soviet Union, told Truman that Soviet actions in Eastern Europe were not only a threat to peace in the region but a threat to the United States and world peace as well.[27]

Still, United States policy makers assumed that Soviet officials were neither unthinking nor unalterably bound to their unilateral course of action. Bohlen believed that the Russians frequently agreed to "accept comprehensive plans presented to them by others." The Russians had broadened the Polish government and postponed Bulgarian elections, and it seemed likely that they would again alter their policies when faced with reason and firmness. Officials in Washington believed that the Soviet Union's leaders understood and respected strength. Byrnes intended to use both sword and purse to convince the Russians to change their ways.[28]

The atomic bomb would "make Russia more manageable in Eastern Europe," Byrnes told atomic scientist Leo Szilard, and before

---

frontation, 159–74; Memorandum of conversation between Henry A. Wallace and William Clayton, October 17, 1945, in Henry A. Wallace Papers, University of Iowa Library, Iowa City.

27. *FR 1945,* V, 852; Geir Lundestad, *The American Non-Policy Toward Eastern Europe, 1943–1947* (New York, 1975), 59–66; Lynn Ethridge Davis, *The Cold War Begins: Soviet-American Conflict Over Eastern Europe* (Princeton, 1974), 154–55, 218; Byrnes, *Speaking Frankly,* 316; Eduard Mark, "Charles E. Bohlen and the Acceptable Limits of Soviet Hegemony in Eastern Europe: A Memorandum of 18 October 1945," *Diplomatic History,* III (1979), 202–206.

28. Byrnes, *Speaking Frankly,* 316; Davis, *The Cold War Begins,* 154–55; Campbell, *Masquerade Peace,* 199–200.

leaving for the London Conference of the Council of Foreign Ministers, he informed Stimson that he looked forward to having the
"implied threat of the bomb in his pocket." Byrnes was not alone in
considering atomic weapons a means to achieve American goals.
The International Trade Policy Division of the State Department
noted: "The atomic bomb should serve to create an international
political environment conducive to enlarged international economic relations." The division did not explain exactly how or why
the atomic bomb would promote more trade, but, nevertheless, it
strongly linked the atomic bomb to trade and linked both to proper
international behavior. "If we tickle the palms of the foreigners with
a few billions," they will conduct "their international economic affairs according to the pattern we advocate," Joseph Coppock of the
International Trade Division stated. In London, Byrnes confided to
British Foreign Minister Bevin that the State Department had "control of credits for Russia . . . [and was] in a position to use them as
one of their diplomatic weapons." Bevin and the Foreign Office
thought the loan was an excellent lever to use against the Russians.
Bevin called it a "means of hidden pressure which should help us
in obtaining our political demands from Russia."[29]

The major target of Byrnes's diplomacy was Soviet influence in
Eastern Europe, where every Russian action mocked American
principles and goals. The United States seemed strong enough to
challenge Soviet assumptions about Eastern Europe, if not Soviet
influence there. The Soviets wanted stability in Eastern Europe, but
the continued British and American nonrecognition of Rumania
and Bulgaria offered only the prospect of increased political turmoil. The Russians desired defense in depth through an Eastern
European buffer zone, but air warfare and the atomic bomb made
the area ineffective as a buffer. The Soviets hoped to rebuild the nation's shattered economy and to raise the Russian standard of
living. However, even with war booty, the resources of Eastern Eu-

29. Leo Szilard, "Reminiscences," *Perspectives in American History*, II (1968),
127–29; Henry L. Stimson Diary, September 21, 1945, in Henry L. Stimson Papers,
Yale University Library, New Haven; Walter Johnson and Carol Evans (eds.), *The
Papers of Adlai E. Stevenson* (Boston, 1972), II, 258; Gregg Herken, *The Winning
Weapon: The Atomic Bomb in the Cold War, 1945–1950* (New York, 1980), 39–49; Record
of Byrnes-Bevin conversation of September 12, 1945, Foreign Office Minute, September 16, 1945, N 12377/18/38, in FO 371, 1945, PRO.

rope, and German reparations, the only real opportunity for a rapid economic revival seemed to depend upon American loans and technology.[30]

To Byrnes and most Kremlin observers, the Soviet Union had two alternatives: it could continue its extremely nationalistic approach, which offered only hardship and false security to the Russian people, or it could join in the cornucopia of prosperity and security offered and directed by the United States. The London conference presented an excellent chance to convince the Soviets of the advantages of a world reconstructed along American universalist principles. Byrnes sailed to London confident about the future. "The strongest and most powerful nation in the world," he stated, "must show the way to lasting peace."[31]

30. Lundestad, *The American Non-Policy*, 435–65; *FR 1945*, V, 845.
31. Byrnes, *Speaking Frankly*, 18–19.

II

Protecting National Interests

ARMED with sword and purse, Byrnes sought to convince the other powers to accept the American formula for global peace. The Allies noticed the nation's determination to achieve its postwar goals. The French foreign minister, Georges Bidault, was "struck during his visit [in August, 1945] by America's consciousness of superior power." He believed that "Americans saw themselves as [the] arbiters of the world's destinies." He was more than a little frightened by the prospect. The British were also concerned. The Foreign Office ascribed a "duality of motive" to United States foreign policy. John Balfour argued that the appointment of William Benton as assistant secretary of state was a perfect example of this duality. He explained that Benton was of the "American gentry" school, which was characterized by "a combination of genuine humanitarianism and desire for vigorous commercial and ideological penetration throughout the world."[1]

Lord Halifax, British ambassador to the United States, informed the Foreign Office that within the Truman administration there

1. Balfour to Foreign Office, August 26, 1945, Z 9943/514/17, Lord Halifax to Foreign Office, December 21, 1945, AN 3853/35/45, Balfour to Foreign Office, September 28, 1945, AN 2976/35/45, all in FO 371, 1945, PRO.

existed "a truculent new brand of 'America First,'" different from the earlier isolationism, that sought to promote American interests without regard to the interests of other nations or to long-range results. "Side by side," he wrote, with "the principles of Mr. Hull . . . there are found the aspirations of those special interests and industries which aim at staking out exclusive positions for themselves."[2]

This evaluation arose from Britain's experience with the United States in economic and commercial matters. The British did not accept the American view of the interlocking relationship between economic interests, free trade, worldwide prosperity, and lasting peace. The influential Chatham House Study Group reported on an American "tendency to exaggerate the value of an increase in prosperity as the factor making for greater security." The Chatham group concluded that there was "no certainty that prosperity must bring peace in its train."[3]

Lord Beaverbrook, a staunch supporter of the Empire and a close friend of and adviser to Churchill, noted that between World War I and World War II Britain had upheld free trade and that this policy had not strengthened Britain or averted war. He and the Chatham group believed that wars were the product of various causes, the two most common being national interests and prejudices. The Chatham group assumed that in a world composed of different nations, each with its own interests, all were "subject . . . to the temptation to make illicit use of strength" to achieve their objectives. Frequently, the result was conflict, and the Chatham group concluded that the best way to avoid war was to restrict or eliminate the illicit use of force. It recommended two approaches: the United Nations and British strength. It stressed the latter, stating, "This country can be a bulwark of peace only if she is strong."[4] The British government agreed.

The primary objectives of British foreign policy were national security and the promotion of political, diplomatic, and economic interests abroad, especially in Western Europe and the Middle East. To accomplish these goals, officials in London supported the United

2. Lord Halifax to Foreign Office, December 21, 1945, AN 3853/35/45, in FO 371, 1945, PRO.
3. Chatham House Study Group, *British Security* (London, 1946), 16–17.
4. *Ibid.*, 16–18; A. J. P. Taylor, *Beaverbrook* (New York, 1972), 570.

Nations, urged cooperation between the major powers, and sought to develop and maintain British resources and influence. The United Nations was viewed as a useful organization in which some international disputes could be arbitrated. But many within the government, most importantly Foreign Minister Ernest Bevin, held that the usefulness of the United Nations depended largely upon continued cooperation between Britain, the United States, and the Soviet Union. Bevin referred to the United Nations and the earlier League of Nations as "international talkshops" that accomplished little. United States Ambassador to the United Nations Stettinius found that Bevin believed that the current and future emphasis of international relations would remain "power politics."[5]

The Post Hostilities Planning Staff, a subcommittee of the British Chiefs of Staff, echoed Bevin's point of view in a report stating that the United Nations "would foster international cooperation" and might even civilize the Russian bear, but it would not remove "the responsibility of taking measures to safeguard . . . security" from Britain, the Commonwealth, and the Empire. The planning staff recommended a "policy of military preparedness" as the best means to prevent aggression and to defend Britain's interests.[6]

In its evaluation of the postwar world and Britain's strategic needs, the planning staff believed that only the United States and the Soviet Union were powerful enough to pose external threats. Bevin agreed. He told a colleague, "I have no intention of being taken on bit by bit by either Russia or the U.S.A." For the foreign minister and the Foreign Office, the major problem was how to influence and resist stronger international rivals. There were no easy or simple solutions, although it was widely held that a combination of British intelligence, a British-led Western Europe, and a policy that would "make use of American power" would serve to promote and protect British goals.[7]

5. Elisabeth Baker, *Britain in a Divided Europe, 1945–1970* (London, 1971), 1–25; Thomas M. Campbell and George C. Herring (eds.), *The Diaries of Edward R. Stettinius, Jr., 1943–1946* (New York, 1975), 417; Rothwell, *Britain and the Cold War*, 1–20, 222–80.

6. Post Hostilities Planning Staff (PHPS), "Security of the British Empire," October, 1945, in File 81, War Cabinet Papers, PRO.

7. Comment by Ernest Bevin, September 28, 1945, AN 3121/3121/45, in FO 371, 1945, PRO; Terry H. Anderson, "Britain, the United States, and the Cold War, 1944–1947" (Ph.D. dissertation, Indiana University, 1978), 12–20; Peter G. Boyle,

The United States was not considered a military threat. Rather, the main British concern was that the Americans seemed to be more interested in expanding their economic and political interests, often at Britain's expense, than in promoting Britain's role as a major power. There was too much talk in the United States about Britain being a junior partner. The Foreign Office feared that the Truman administration might use the United Nations "to unload undesirable responsibilities," especially if such responsibilities included supporting British interests against Moscow. Officials in London were particularly mindful of the opinion of liberals like Walter Lippmann, who suggested that America should act as a neutral mediator between the two European powers.[8]

To promote and protect British interests, the Foreign Office sought to emphasize Britain's position and experience as a world power. As the war ended, the British media effort in the United States shifted from presenting England as a wartime ally to picturing a strong Britain as a vital part of an "enduring peace." It recommended that British officials "ceaselessly" stress Big Three cooperation and Britain's role as spokesman for Western European and Middle Eastern interests as a means to "compel" treatment as "an equal." The British also believed that American inexperience in world affairs would permit London's input into American policy. Truman was described as "a bungling if well-meaning amateur." This lack of knowledge and expertise would allow British statesmen to show the Americans the proper directions for their policy to take. A verse circulated throughout the British foreign service at the time read: "In Washington Lord Halifax / Once whispered to Lord Keynes / 'It's true *they* have the money bags / but *we* have all the brains.'" American desk officer Bernard Gage believed that the United States would be forced to ask for British assistance to demonstrate "the proper application of their power."[9]

"The British Foreign Office View of Soviet-American Relations, 1945–1946," *Diplomatic History*, III (1979), 308–10.

8. Anderson, "Britain, the U.S., and the Cold War," 300–20.

9. *Ibid.*, 308; Rothwell, *Britain and the Cold War*, 145; Gardner, *Sterling-Dollar Diplomacy*, xvii; Boyle, "The British Foreign Office View," 308–309; Foreign Office Note, July 17, 1946, N 9816/140/38, in FO 371, 1946, PRO; Caroline Anstey, "The Projection of British Socialism: Foreign Office Publicity and American Opinion, 1946–1950," *Journal of Contemporary History*, XIX (1984), 417–51.

No matter how confident British statesmen were that the Americans would rely on British experience, they placed a high priority on developing Britain's own power in areas traditionally of British concern. Close cooperation with Western European nations was required to create a Western bloc. Bevin recommended "the closest possible collaboration with the Commonwealth and with overseas territories, not only the British, but French, Dutch, Belgian and Portuguese." To Chancellor of the Exchequer Hugh Dalton he was optimistic: "If we only push on and develop Africa we could have the United States dependent on us, and eating out of our hand in four or five years." The Truman administration seemed to be less anticolonial than the Roosevelt administration. In November, 1945, Arthur de la Mare, Foreign Office Asian officer, reported on the "relatively sympathetic attitude" shown by the Americans toward colonial problems in the Netherlands East Indies and in French Indochina.[10]

The Foreign Office correctly credited the American retreat from anticolonialism to a growing apprehension of Russian motives and a desire to strengthen Western European nations, especially France. James Dunn of the State Department's European Division confided to Balfour that the United States hoped to strengthen France, making it an "'outpost' of Western influence." Bevin and Dalton hoped such actions would encourage the formation of a British-led Western bloc.[11]

Bevin foresaw the world being divided into three spheres of influence: the American orbit (the Western Hemisphere and Pacific sphere), the Soviet orbit (Eastern European and Mongolian sphere), and the British orbit (Western European and "middle-of-the-planet" sphere). In December, 1945, at the meeting of foreign ministers in Moscow, he broached the idea of dividing the world into "three Monroe Doctrine" areas. Byrnes rejected the idea, denying that the United States had a sphere of influence in either Latin America or

10. R. B. Manderson-Jones, *The Special Relationship: Anglo-American Relations and Western Unity, 1947–1950* (London, 1972), 5–10, 20–25; Hugh Dalton Diary, October 15, 1948, in Hugh Dalton Papers, British Library of Politics and Economics, London School of Economics and Political Science, London; Foreign Office Memorandum, November 15, 1945, F 10156/1394/23, in FO 371, 1945, PRO.

11. George C. Herring, Jr. "The Truman Administration and the Restoration of French Sovereignty in Indochina," *Diplomatic History*, I (1977), 97–117; Lord Halifax to Foreign Office, July 9, 1945, U 5559/5559/70, in FO 371, 1945, PRO.

the Pacific. Despite the rejection, Bevin and the Foreign Office continued to believe the Americans would alter that opinion as fears of Soviet behavior increased.[12]

The Russians, of course, were expected to strongly protest any semblance of a Western bloc. To reduce criticism, the Foreign Office denied Germany a role in any Western grouping and officially contended that any Western bloc would be aimed at controlling Germany and not the Soviet Union. Further, the impact of Soviet objections to a Western bloc would be reduced by Soviet efforts in Eastern Europe to construct an Eastern bloc.[13]

The United States posed a threat to Britain's economic and political influence in the "middle-of-the-planet" sphere. Foreign Office officials were particularly concerned about American economic activities in the Middle East. As those interests increased, so too would Washington's political influence, and Britain's traditional leadership of the region would be threatened. One disgruntled Foreign Office officer lashed out at what he regarded to be American "manifestations of diplomatic gangsterism in the service of an unscrupulous economic imperialism."[14]

Despite distaste for American methods, the British decided not to vehemently resist American efforts to establish economic bridgeheads. Concerned about the loan from the United States and interested in developing postwar cooperation between Britain and America, the Foreign Office sought to reduce points of confrontation. British officials hoped that in time the Truman administration would realize the importance of Britain's role in maintaining global security and peace and would support London's policies. The

12. Manderson-Jones, *The Special Relationship*, 21; PHPS, "Security of the British Empire"; Bevin to Foreign Office, December 17, 1945, U 10134/6550/70, John Ward, "Future of British Interests Forecast for 1960," April 18, 1945, U 2885/2885/36, both in FO 371, 1945, PRO.

13. Ward, "Future of British Interests," April 18, 1945, U 2885/2885/36, Foreign Office Memorandum, "Western Bloc," August 6, 1945, Z 9639/13/7, both in FO 371, 1945, PRO; Joseph Frankel, *British Foreign Policy, 1945–1973* (London, 1975), 124–30, 150–60; D. C. Watt, *Britain Looks to Germany: British Opinion and Policy Toward Germany Since 1945* (London, 1965), 28–98.

14. James L. Gormly, "Keeping the Door Open in Saudi Arabia: The United States and the Dhahran Airfield, 1945–1946," *Diplomatic History*, IV (1980), 202; John A. DeNovo, "The Culbertson Economic Mission and Anglo-American Tension in the Middle East, 1944–1945," *Journal of American History*, LXIII (1977), 913–36.

Americans were anxious to share in Britain's economic and political position in the Middle East, and the Foreign Office wanted to induce the United States to share in political and military responsibilities in the region as well. For "strategic and political reasons" the Foreign Office in late 1945 instructed Saudi Arabia to accept an American aviation concession.[15]

Unlike the United States, the Soviet Union represented a military threat, and there was little likelihood that Stalin or the Russian people could be persuaded to promote British interests. Although the Foreign Office called Soviet foreign policy the "great enigma," most officials accepted the premise that Moscow based its policy on nonideological considerations. British intelligence sources concluded, in the autumn of 1945, that Russian policy was above all realistic. Although the Russians were opportunistic and anxious to stake out territory and to extend their influence, they would not seek conflict with the West and would follow policies aimed at "avoiding any major war." The Soviets recognized their economic weakness and sought to rebuild their economy and develop an atomic bomb before they risked alienating the West.[16]

The Foreign Office conceded Soviet influence in Eastern Europe but was unsure as to whether Moscow would attempt to extend it to other parts of Europe, the Middle East, and Asia. Some members of the Reconstruction Department hoped that Soviet actions would be limited to "strategic frontiers" and therefore create few points of conflict between the Soviet and British spheres. Others were less optimistic. Many speculated that Moscow sought to extend its influence into the Middle East and the Mediterranean region. Sir Orme Sargent, deputy undersecretary of state, recommended abandoning Eastern Europe and building up British power in Western Europe and the eastern Mediterranean. There was overall agreement within the Foreign Office with the view of the Chiefs of Staff and the Post Hostilities Planning Staff, who stated that "common prudence . . . dictates that we should take full account of the potentialities of the U.S.S.R." The Soviet Union presented a poten-

15. Gormly, "Keeping the Door Open," 200–203.
16. Ward, "Future of British Interests," April 18, 1945, U 2885/2885/36, in FO 371, 1945, PRO; Boyle, "The British Foreign Office View," 307–10; Memorandum, Chiefs of Staff, October 6, 1945, (45) 601 (o), in File 80/97, Cabinet Papers, PRO.

tially "grave" military threat to Britain and the Empire, a planning staff report stated.[17]

The British believed that displaying strength and determination to uphold their national interests were as important as promoting Big Three unity in dealing with the Russians. The Russians respected strength, Bevin concluded, and viewed even conciliatory gestures as signs of weaknesses to be exploited. Soviet rulers were "infinitely more flexible than those of Germany," and there was "infinitely less danger of sudden catastrophe with the Russians than with the Germans." Bevin phrased it succinctly: "We shalln't reach any agreements, but we shall live together."[18]

Like his American colleague Byrnes, rotund, ruddy-faced Bevin was new to his job and had little experience in international relations and diplomacy. Bevin was by vocation a labor leader. Truman considered him to be a "crude and uncouth" John Lewis. Before becoming foreign minister in July, 1945, Bevin had served the Churchill coalition government as minister of labor and supply. Prior to joining the government in 1940, he was the secretary-general of the Transport and General Workers' Union—the largest union in the world and the backbone of the Labour party's strength.[19]

Bevin's selection as secretary of state for foreign affairs caught many observers by surprise. Most had expected him to be named chancellor of the exchequer by Prime Minister Clement Attlee. Members of the Foreign Office knew little about him and responded with guarded silence to his selection. A previous foreign minister, Anthony Eden, offered the Foreign Office his opinion: Bevin "was the best man" the Labour party had to offer. He said that he thought the new foreign minister would "harken" to the "experience" of the Foreign Office. Eden's words were welcome news to

17. Ward, "Future of British Interests," April 18, 1945, U 2885/2885/36, in FO 371, 1945, PRO; Paterson, *On Every Front*, 33–45; PHPS, "Security of the British Empire"; Rothwell, *Britain and the Cold War*, 136–50, 236–39.

18. Roberts to Foreign Office, March 17, 1945, N 4196/97/38, in FO 371, 1945, PRO; Manderson-Jones, *The Special Relationship*, 21.

19. Eben Ayers Diary, November 1, 1945, 124, in File 124, Box 26, Set II, Pt. II, Eben Ayers Papers, Harry S Truman Library; Avi Shlaim, Peter Jones, and Keith Sainsbury, *British Foreign Secretaries Since 1945* (London, 1977), 35–68.

members of the Foreign Office, who had suffered as research assistants and file clerks under Churchill.[20]

As foreign minister, Bevin quickly assured the Foreign Office that he had no intention of altering British foreign policy or catering to the Russians. In fact, he believed that Churchill had sacrificed too many British interests. Upon being briefed, he could only murmur, "My God, my God, what a mess, my God." The previous government had thrown too many "baubles to the Soviets." He was determined to avoid giving away any more British concessions. This was to prove difficult, however, as Bevin faced not only the need for continued harmony between the Allies but a large segment of British opinion that called for British cooperation with the Soviet Union.[21]

During the war, government propaganda had presented a positive image of the Soviet Union and the necessity of alliance with Russia as a cornerstone of victory and peace. As the war ended, despite some dissatisfaction over Soviet policy in Eastern Europe, popular support for Moscow was still strong, especially within the Labour party. Michael Foot suggested that before the government condemned Soviet behavior in Eastern Europe it should consider British policies toward Greece and Turkey. Bevin's election statement, "Left understands left," confirmed to many that Britain would have closer relations with Moscow and cooler relations with Washington. Member of Parliament W. G. Cole expressed a popular view when he wrote, "Socialism will perish in Britain if a Labour Government ties herself to America."[22]

Labour's victory in July, 1945, demonstrated the reality of a leftward political shift throughout Europe and offered the possibility that socialist Britain could assume leadership of the movement. As early as 1942, Bevin had recommended that the Foreign Office work more closely with world socialist organizations and be more sympathetic to the needs of the common man. Many in the center and left of the Labour party agreed with spokesmen of the British Communist movement who favored the Soviet Union and Britain work-

20. Dilks, *The Diaries of Cadogan*, 773; Lord Strong, *At Home and Abroad* (London, 1956), 287–301; Shlaim, Jones, and Sainsbury, *British Foreign Secretaries*, 33–38.

21. Foreign Office Minute, August 8, 1945, Z 9501/13/7, in FO 371, 1945, PRO; Frankel, *British Foreign Policy*, 91–92, 124–30, 157–58.

22. Jones, *The Russian Complex*, 58–74, 103–21.

ing together to foster socialism around the world. However, Bevin, Attlee, and other Labour government leaders held a different outlook, a more traditional view of British interests and goals. They believed that Britain should assume leadership of the international socialist movement, but not on Soviet terms or by supporting Soviet-style totalitarian regimes. Bevin distrusted the Soviets and intended to meet them no more than halfway. He also wanted to protect and extend British national interests, even if they conflicted with international socialist principles.

Bevin demonstrated the continuity of British foreign policy and the thrust of his personal policy almost immediately upon taking office, when at the Potsdam Conference he advanced positions at odds with Soviet goals and denounced the Soviet-sponsored regimes in Romania and Bulgaria. To Truman and Byrnes, he seemed more anti-Soviet than Churchill. Molotov later commented that Bevin was no gentleman compared to Churchill. Bevin's policy toward Moscow was restrained. On certain issues, he conducted foreign policy without consideration of public opinion. In trying to establish general policy toward Russia, however, Bevin did consider pro-Soviet public opinion in England and on many occasions rejected requests from political representatives in the field and Foreign Office personnel to launch a more combative policy toward Soviet Communism and the Soviet state.[23]

Realizing Britain's immediate lack of diplomatic leverage and domestic restraints, Bevin relied on what many thought was best about British diplomacy: its pragmatic, patient professionalism. An official in the Foreign Office stated that British policy toward Russia should be correct, courteous, patient, and discreet. Bevin hoped to protect British interests through practicing steady diplomacy, balancing one ally against another, and offering intelligent alternatives. Bevin agreed with the view once expressed by a former foreign minister, Lord Palmerston: "When people ask one . . . for what is called a policy the only answer is that we mean to do what may seem best upon each occasion as it arises, making the interests of one's country one's guiding principle."[24]

23. Rothwell, *Britain and the Cold War*, 222–25; Jones, *The Russian Complex*, 103–21; Peter Weiler, "British Labor and the Cold War" (Paper presented at the annual meeting of the Southern Historical Association, November, 1983).

24. H. C. F. Bell, *Lord Palmerston* (London, 1936), ii, 161.

THE SOVIET PERSPECTIVE

Opposing Bevin and Byrnes was one of the most tough-minded and patient statesmen of the period, V. M. Molotov. "His signature is as good as a portrait, completely closed in a circle, like his personality," wrote Oscar Berge. Some British and American diplomats gave him the nickname Stonebottom because of his obstinacy and impervious bearing. Although not liked by Western statesmen, Molotov was respected as an intelligent well-prepared hard bargainer. "God made Molotov to be Molotov," one State Department official told a reporter.[25]

Molotov's diplomatic style was characterized by orderliness, thoughtfulness, and a disciplined intellect. His demeanor was often pontifical. When confronted with strong opposition, he would either refuse to discuss the issue or counterattack with another topic. When angered, his face twitched. State Department experts warned Byrnes that the Soviet foreign minister was a cold and calculating adversary who "never hesitated to make the power of the Soviet Union felt." By 1945, many Kremlin watchers in London and Washington believed that Molotov was the second most powerful man in the Soviet Union. He was Stalin's close friend and the likely successor to the Russian dictator. Many speculated, including Ambassador Harriman, that Molotov formulated much of Soviet policy himself.[26]

The overarching goal of the Soviet Union's foreign policy in 1945 was national security. Vladimir G. Denkansov, a member of the Central Committee of the Communist Party of the Soviet Union, told a British official that Russian policy was "clear and consistent" but that Western policy seemed "changeable and confusing." He added that Soviet policy was based on military, economic, and geo-

25. Oscar Berge, "The Big Three Off Guard," *New York Times Magazine*, December 8, 1946, p. 15; *Time*, April 3, 1945, p. 32; Department of State Briefing Paper, "Molotov," September 1, 1945, in File 740.00119 (Council)/9–145, DSR-NA; *Time*, August 23, 1945, p. 16; M. N. Roy, *Men I Met* (Bombay, 1968), 97–102.

26. Department of State Briefing Paper, "Molotov," September 1, 1945, in File 740.00119 (Council)/9–145, DSR-NA; Philip E. Mosley, "Some Techniques of Negotiations," in Philip E. Mosley (ed.), *The Kremlin and World Politics* (New York, 1960), 3–41; John C. Campbell, "Negotiations with the Soviets," *Foreign Affairs*, XXXIV (January, 1956), 305–19; Stephen D. Kertesz, "Reflections on Soviet and American Negotiating Behavior," *Review of Politics*, XIX (January, 1957), 3–36.

graphic imperatives and not on concepts of idealism, morality, and ideology.[27]

Most Western observers agreed that Soviet foreign policy had been guided by nonideological considerations since the 1930s. Throughout World War II, and in earlier relations with Nazi Germany, Moscow's foreign policy was characterized by the realities of strength and territory rather than Communist ideology. Believing themselves to be isolated against a stronger Germany in 1939, Soviet leaders chose to negotiate rather than risk war. The Ribbentrop-Molotov nonaggression pact followed, and served, as Stalin told the Russian people, to keep Russia out of the war for a year and a half.[28]

The German invasion dictated a new course in Soviet policy, but one that still reflected military and economic realities. In June, 1941, Stalin announced collaboration with the capitalistic foes of Hitler's Germany. For the rest of the conflict, Soviet relations with the Western Allies fluctuated from trust and accommodation to suspicion and obstinacy, depending on military exigencies and on real or perceived British and American actions. At the end of the war, no major shift appeared in the nature of Soviet foreign policy, except that Soviet officials were demanding full recognition of the Soviet Union as an international power.[29]

To most Soviet officials in the autumn of 1945, national security meant the creation of "friendly" neighbors along Russia's borders, economic reconstruction, and continued cooperation between the major powers. The desire to ensure cooperative neighbors was evident in Russian military strategy, when, instead of massing its armies for a direct assault on Germany across Poland, the Soviet high command instructed its forces to overrun Eastern Europe. The

27. Foreign Office Memorandum, September 23, 1945, U 8071/559/70, Roberts to Foreign Office, September 27, 1945, U 7471/5559/70, both in FO 371, 1945, PRO.

28. Roberts to Foreign Office, March 18, 1946, N 4157/97/38, in FO 371, 1946, PRO. For studies of Soviet foreign policy during and after World War II see: Adam B. Ulam, *Expansion and Coexistence: The History of Soviet Foreign Policy, 1917–1967* (New York, 1968); Vojtech Mastny, *Russia's Road to the Cold War: Diplomacy, Warfare, and the Politics of Communism, 1941–1945* (New York, 1979); William O. McCagg, Jr., *Stalin Embattled, 1943–1948* (Detroit, 1981); Taubman, *Stalin's American Policy.*

29. Roberts to Foreign Office, March 18, 1946, N 4157/97/38, in FO 371, 1946, PRO; William H. McNeil, *America, Britain, and Russia: Their Cooperation and Conflict, 1941–1946* (New York, 1953), 575–76; Paterson, *On Every Front,* 148–49.

message that accompanied the liberating Red Army was clear, although not always heeded. Once freed from Fascist rule, the new governments of Romania, Austria, Czechoslovakia, Hungary, Poland, and Bulgaria were expected to look to Moscow for guidance and leadership.

Governments led or dominated by Communists were not deemed necessary by the Soviets, but they wanted local Communists to be represented. As Eduard Beneš of Czechoslovakia realized, the Soviets required "real friendly and loyal cooperation." The Russian desire for such cooperation was understood by General Bela Miklos of Hungary and Dr. Karl Renner of Austria, who, like Beneš, were able to establish governments that included Communists but were not dominated by them. In Romania, where the regimes of General Constantín Sanatescu (August to December, 1944) and Nicolai Radescu (December, 1944, to March, 1945) failed to meet Soviet expectations, Moscow intervened to create a more cooperative and "friendly" government.[30]

In justifying actions in Eastern Europe, especially in Romania and Poland, Soviet officials repeatedly linked Soviet actions to security needs. On May 4, 1945, Stalin wrote to Churchill that because Poland was a neighbor, through which the Soviet Union was twice invaded, it was "essential" that the Polish government practice friendly relations with Moscow. The Russian premier emphasized that he would continue to "insist that only people who . . . demonstrated by deeds their friendly attitude to the Soviet Union, who are willing honestly and sincerely to cooperate with the Soviet Union, should be consulted on the formation of a future Polish Government."[31]

Izvestia applied the same criteria to Romania and Bulgaria in an editorial on the eve of the London conference, and a Soviet political commentator candidly told the British that Russia intended to take advantage of the present military and political conditions in East-

30. Lundestad, *The American Non-Policy*, 115–21, 149–53, 435–62; Paterson, *On Every Front*, 143–51; Eduard Beneš, *Memoirs of Dr. Eduard Beneš: From Munich to New War and New Victory* (London, 1954), 239–40.

31. Ulam, *Expansion and Coexistence*, 383; Lundestad, *The American Non-Policy*, 436–37; Ministry of Foreign Affairs of the U.S.S.R., *Correspondence Between the Chairman of the Council of Foreign Ministers of the U.S.S.R. and the Presidents of the U.S.A. and the Prime Ministers of Great Britain During the Great Patriotic War of 1941–1945* (Moscow, 1957), I, 331, 347.

ern Europe to secure its vital interests and to strengthen its defense. He maintained that the governments of Romania and Bulgaria were both "democratic," although the Romanian regime was not representative. He added that Russia needed more than friendly words from countries like Romania to prove friendly intentions.[32]

Aware of British and American dissatisfaction with many of the governments promoted by the Soviet Union in Eastern Europe, Ivan M. Maisky attempted to explain the Soviet definition of democracy. He suggested that one of the major issues dividing the Allies was the West's misunderstanding of the term *democratic*. He stated that British and American demands for political democracy rather than the Soviet-style social democracy only served to increase friction between East and West. He suggested that for the sake of international harmony, Britain and the United States should drop their objections to those Eastern European governments that practiced social democracy and were friendly to the Soviet Union. *Pravda, Izvestia,* and *New Times* presented similar arguments. On a more practical level, several Soviet spokesmen drew a parallel between Russian policy in Eastern Europe and British and American policies in Italy. They pointed out that Moscow did not object to the lack of social democracy in Italy.[33]

To Soviet leaders, Eastern Europe was not only an important "strategic frontier" but a valuable part of Soviet economic reconstruction. Russia's economy had been shattered by the German invasion and retreat: prime agricultural land in the Ukraine and southern Russia was in ashes, over 30,000 industrial plants were in ruins, and over 40,000 miles of railroad track had been destroyed. The vital coal fields in the Don Basin were in disarray. Iron production stood at 65 percent of the prewar level. Economic reconstruction was closely related to national security.[34]

To rebuild the Soviet Union, Moscow sought to use all available means: reparations, favorable trade and business agreements, and

32. Roberts to Foreign Office, September 8, 1945, R 15270/38/37, September 22, 1945, N 13100/10/38, both in FO 371, 1945, PRO.

33. Roberts to C. F. A. Warner, June 30, 1945, N 9416/13/38, September 1, 1945, N 13185/78/38, both in FO 371, 1945, PRO; A. Sokolov, "Again on Democracy," *New Times*, October 1, 1945, pp. 7–14; Lundestad, *The American Non-Policy*, 81–86; Cyril E. Black, "The Start of the Cold War in Bulgaria: A Personal View," *Review of Politics*, XLI (1979), 163–67.

34. Paterson, *Soviet-American Confrontation*, 33–43, 46–56; Adam B. Ulam, *The Rivals: America and Russia Since World War II* (New York, 1971), 6–9; U.S. Congress,

even loans from the capitalist world. With the loan from the United States still in question, reparations, war booty, and favorable economic agreements with Eastern Europe became more and more important in Soviet plans for economic development. The Soviets called these the "rightful fruits of victory" and deemed them necessary "to protect Soviet security . . . reconstruction and industrialization." George F. Kennan, American Soviet expert, reported in a quarterly evaluation that the Russians were intent upon making the Soviet Union, "in the shortest time possible, the most powerful economic unit in the world." A Foreign Office evaluation concluded that the Soviets placed the highest priority on integrating the economies of Eastern Europe with their own and did not care about Western objections.[35]

Another important Soviet foreign policy objective was recognition as an international power equal to the United States and the United Kingdom. Being a victor in 1945 meant not only sharing the spoils of war but having opinions listened to and desires met. From the strutting Russian soldier in Vienna, to the lowliest Soviet official, to the Generalissimo, being victorious meant receiving special favors and considerations previously denied. S. A. Golunsky, a minor Soviet official, told an American delegate to the International Waterways Conference, "In 1856 we were a defeated state. In 1919 we were not asked to be present. . . . Now we are a victorious Power. It may be that matters should be arranged somewhat differently now." On the same theme, Stalin told Bevin that Hitler's mistake was to not recognize the power and importance of the Soviet Union. Molotov boasted to a Moscow audience that Russia was "among the most authoritative of the world powers" and that no international problem could be solved without the "participation of Comrade Stalin."[36]

House of Representatives, Special Committee on Postwar Economic Policy and Planning, "Economic Reconstruction in Europe," 11th Report, 79th Congress, 1st Session (December, 1945).

35. Paterson, *Soviet-American Confrontation*, 94–102; Foreign Office Minute, October 25, 1945, N 15085/18/38, in FO 371, 1945, Foreign Office Memorandum on Soviet Economic Policy in Eastern Europe, January 14, 1946, N 605/605/38, both in FO 371, 1946, PRO; Kennan to State Department, August 15, 1945, in File 861.50/8–1545, DSR-NA; *FR 1945*, V, 928–36.

36. *FR 1945*, II, 1381; V. M. Molotov, *Problems of Foreign Policy: Speeches and Statements, April, 1945–November 1948* (Moscow, 1949), 28.

To demonstrate the Soviet Union's arrival as a major power, Soviet officials wore colorful and distinctive uniforms and bore titles that obscured their proletarian credo. The British chargé d'affaires in Moscow, Frank Roberts, wrote to C. F. A. Warner, the Foreign Office's chief of the Northern Department, that the "whole Soviet Union is being brought up to think in terms of past national glories associated with . . . Peter the Great." Stalin also displayed broader interests at the Potsdam Conference, where he asked for a Soviet role in the international control of Tangiers and Japan and in determining relations with Spain and how and when British and French troops would be removed from the Levant.[37]

Stalin's desire to participate in solving international issues reflected the Soviet view that the best way to maintain peace was continued harmony between the major powers. Multilateral organizations were effective only if the "Great Powers" worked together "in a spirit of unity." Stalin warned that the United Nations would "not be effective if this necessary condition is absent." The formation of the Council of Foreign Ministers signified British and American agreement that peace depended on the Big Three. At Potsdam, after Stalin listened to Byrnes describe the composition and function of the council, he asked only that its scope be enlarged to include any matter referred to it by a member nation.[38]

As the first meeting of the Council of Foreign Ministers neared, the Soviets felt confident. The creation of the council confirmed the principle of Big Three cooperation, while Russian armies occupied those neighboring areas thought to be vital to Soviet security. In a message to Western observers on the eve of the meeting in London, the Soviets applauded the "vivid affirmation of the . . . Anglo-Soviet-American coalition" that had made the Potsdam Conference a success. The message concluded that the success of the London conference would depend "upon the extent to which the Governments in the countries concerned are inspired by the spirit of Yalta."[39]

37. Roberts to C. F. A. Warner, April 25, 1945, N 4919/165/38, in FO 371, 1945, PRO; Charles L. Mee, Jr., *Meeting at Potsdam* (New York, 1975), 80–83.

38. Ulam, *Expansion and Coexistence*, 412; Campbell, *Masquerade Peace*, 26–57, 176–93; FR, *The Conference of Berlin*, II, 354–56; Mastny, *Russia's Road to the Cold War*, 295–96.

39. Roberts to Foreign Office, September 1, 1945, N 13185/78/38, in FO 371, 1945, PRO.

That spirit, however, was a consequence of the necessities of war. In London, the participants would no longer be concerned with defeating the Axis powers. Instead they would try to structure a postwar settlement. Each nation had its own ideas on what the best structure would be to ensure national interests and peace. With their own formulas for peace and their differing national needs, the foreign ministers arrived in London in early September, 1945, to deal with the issues referred to the council at the Potsdam Conference and additional matters raised by the surrender of Japan.

III

Points of Disagreement

THE PROCESS of making peace and establishing a pattern for postwar international relations started in September, 1945, as the foreign ministers gathered in London. There, Georges Bidault of France and Shih-chieh Wang joined Bevin, Byrnes, and Molotov for the first meeting of the Council of Foreign Ministers. The council was to be the primary vehicle through which the major powers structured the peace. The prescribed goal of the first meeting was to establish general policy on major issues. The writing of finished proposals would be left to the ministers' deputies. Agreement on the approach to major issues would signal the continuation of the Grand Alliance and establish conditions for an enduring peace. If the foreign ministers failed to agree on general guidelines, however, the door would be open for a return to traditional power politics.

The most important issue facing the council was the drafting of peace treaties for Italy, Romania, and Bulgaria. Consensus on the treatment of these allies of Hitler would solidify the Grand Alliance, almost guaranteeing the stability of Europe, and would also facilitate agreement on other issues looming in the background: Iran, Japan, and atomic energy and weapons.

Optimism was high that the foreign ministers could agree, but tough bargaining was expected. Justice Felix Frankfurter wrote that "the road to peace is long and hard" and that the problems were "only starting." No one, however, expected the negotiations to fail. The success of the conferences at Yalta and Potsdam seemed to confirm the view of former Secretary of State Stettinius that agreement among the major powers was stronger than their differences.[1] High on the agenda of the council were the peace treaties for Italy, Romania, and Bulgaria. Disagreements soon outweighed agreement.

ITALY

The future of Italy was of primary importance to the United States and Great Britain. An integral part of Western Europe, it occupied a prominent geographical position in the Mediterranean region. As the war ended, Italy rested firmly under British and American control. The Soviet Union conceded dominant Western influence in the region. British and American statesmen believed that Italy could become a showcase of Western reconstruction. A stable, prosperous, and democratic Italy would strengthen British and United States influence and prestige throughout Europe and provide useful points of comparison with conditions found in Soviet-controlled Eastern Europe. This influence would suffer, however, if Italy succumbed to economic chaos and the Italian Left gained political power. To ensure that Italy remained within their orbit and developed in accord with their designs, British and American officials agreed that any Russian influence must be eliminated, the Italian Left controlled, and the Italian economy incorporated into Western trade patterns. The advantages of an easy peace with Italy were evident. A "gentler treatment of Italy will bring Italy willingly and joyfully into the British orbit," a Foreign Office memorandum stated. American officials agreed that if "Italy's influence" was to support "stability and peace" the terms of the treaty would have to please the Italian people.[2]

The Italians realized their importance to Britian and the United

1. Justice Felix Frankfurter to Benjamin V. Cohen, August 19, 1945, in Box 45, Frankfurter Papers, Library of Congress.

2. Foreign Office Memorandum, "U.K. Policy—Italy," September 20, 1945, U 7597/50/70, Noel Charles to Foreign Office, June 26, 1945, U 5163/50/70, both in FO 371, 1945, PRO; SWNCC 155/1, September 6, 1945, in File 740.00119 EW/10–645, DSR-NA; *FR, 1945*, IV, 1034–47.

States and hoped to use it as a diplomatic lever to gain concessions from them. Alberto Tarachiani, the Italian ambassador in Washington, told Undersecretary of State Joseph Grew that an acceptable treaty would support the democratic elements and "persuade the Italian people that their friends lay to the West and not the East." He warned that an unacceptable treaty would "play directly into the hands of the communist elements and . . . Soviet Russia." British and American statesmen knew that the Italian response to the treaty would depend largely on the disposition of three issues: the Italian-Yugoslav border, the Italian colonies, and the Italian armed forces.[3]

In early August, 1945, British and American officials involved in Italian affairs could congratulate themselves on their successful policies. Conservative and moderate Italian political groups governed with the aid and consent of British and American occupation authorities. Italian socialists and Communists seemingly had abandoned their demands for immediate social and economic reforms in order to participate in the political system.[4]

However, British and American officials assigned to draft the Italian peace treaty were not complacent. They realized that the Soviets were interested in reparations and Italy's African colonies. The rejection of a Russian role in Italian affairs needed to be made carefully because the Soviets would use precedents in the Italian treaty to further their position in Eastern Europe. As R. Hayter-Miller of the Foreign Office's Western Department informed the Italian embassy in London, the Soviets took "the line that there was no cause to show any favors to Italy which should not be extended to Bulgaria, etc."[5] Further, the Soviet Union was expected

3. Memorandum of conversation between S. Alberto Tarachiani and Undersecretary of State Joseph Grew, August 9, 1945, in File 740.00119 EW/9–4445, DSR-NA; Norman Kogan, *Italy and the Allies* (Cambridge, Mass., 1956), 132–57; "People and Liberty," Association of Americans of Italian Descent letter to Truman, September 4, 1945, in File 740.00119 EW/9–445, DSR-NA.

4. F. Catalano, "The Rebirth of the Party System," and G. Warner, "Italy and the Powers, 1943–1949," both in S. J. Woolf (ed.), *The Rebirth of Italy, 1943–1950* (London, 1972), 30–36, 43–44, 57–94; Kogan, *Italy and the Allies*, 56–66; Donald L. M. Blackmer, *Unity in Diversity: Italian Communism and the Communist World* (Cambridge, Mass., 1968), 12–17.

5. Foreign Office Memorandum, August 9, 1945, U 6319/50/70, in FO 371, 1945, PRO; Warner, "Italy and the Powers," in Woolf (ed.), *The Rebirth of Italy*, 43–44.

to strongly support Yugoslav efforts to obtain the Venezia Giulia and the cities of Trieste, Zara, and Fiume.

By August, 1945, the Italians stated that they were willing to divide the Venezia Giulia along the ethnic Wilson Line that had been drawn in 1919, if Trieste remained a part of Italy, Fiume became a free city, and Zara became an autonomous part of Yugoslavia. British and American statesmen carefully weighed the Italian positions against their own goals and Yugoslav requests. Americans writing the draft Italian treaty agreed that it was "foolish to debate whether the Italians . . . [were] justified in their position" and concluded that the United States' desire to keep Italy in the Western orbit necessitated that the Italian viewpoint be "accepted." As a result, the United States was willing to meet Italian expectations regarding the Venezia Giulia and the contested cities. The Foreign Office came to the same conclusion.[6]

British and American officials were willing to agree to Italian desires concerning reparations and the military as well. The Italians asked that reparations be kept to a minimum and that the Italian military be allowed to rebuild. In support of keeping their armed forces intact, the Italians stressed that their arms helped defeat the Germans. They asked that their military force not be reduced below its strength at the end of hostilities, or an army of not fewer than 236,000 men and an air force of about 360 planes.[7]

The United States State-War-Navy Coordinating Committee recommended that the military clauses of the Italian treaty "be constructed more from the standpoint of the European and Mediterranean areas than the narrow standpoint of any possible threat by Italy itself." The committee disapproved of any attempts by other nations to limit the size and weapons of the Italian armed forces. In addition to making the Italians angry, such limits would weaken "a prospective friend in southeastern Europe and the Mediterranean." The committee's decision on Italian armed forces was made easier by the belief that Italy would never be a military threat to

6. State Department Memorandum, August 8, 1945, in Council of Foreign Ministers London Notebook, Vol. II, pt. II, in John Foster Dulles Papers, Firestone Library, Princeton University, Princeton, N.J.; Chiefs of Staff Memorandum (45) 534 (o), August 15, 1945, in File 80/96, Cabinet Papers, PRO.

7. Chiefs of Staff Memorandum (45) 534 (o), August 15, 1945; Kogan, *Italy and the Allies*, 130–32.

Western interests. Italy could not by itself support a modern war. The Americans postulated that as the United States became a major supplier of "basic materials," it would "be in a position to influence the direction . . . the Italian economy will take." This view dovetailed perfectly with the American assumption that economic preeminence would give the United States a central role in structuring the postwar world.[8]

Foreign Office agreement with American views on Italy's importance did not mean that the British totally forgave the "stab in the back" represented by Italy's declaration of war on France and Britain in June, 1940, or was willing to accept every Italian request. The British favored limiting the Italian armed forces, especially the navy. Their views on the disposition of Italy's colonies also differed from those of the Americans. Aware of some differences between British and American views, the State Department asked John Balfour, the British chargé d'affaires, for a copy of the Foreign Office's draft Italian treaty. Balfour responded that the United States should not be too concerned about minor differences because such discrepancies would prevent the Soviets from thinking that Britain and the United States were "ganging up" on them.[9]

Although American planners easily reached agreements on Italy's borders and armed services, officials in the State Department were divided as to what to do about Italy's colonies in Africa. The Near Eastern and African Department, more attuned to Arab and anticolonial sentiments, asked that the colonies be placed under a United Nations trusteeship until independence was granted. Officials in the State Department's Special Political Affairs Branch believed that the United Nations was too new and disorganized to assume such duties and recommended that an international trusteeship composed of representatives of the Big Five and Italy be created. It recommended that the colonies be administered by a select commission of experts and administrative officials. Italy's right to be a lone trustee was strongly supported by the Eu-

8. SWNCC 155/1, in File 740.00119 EW/9–645, DSR-NA.

9. Foreign Office Minute, May 28, 1945, U 3986/50/70, Foreign Office Minute, July 11, 1945, U 5474/5397/70, "Future Policy Toward Italy," ORC (45) 23, August 30, 1945, ZM 4588/1/22, Foreign Office Minute, August 27, 1945, U 6499/50/70, Balfour to Foreign Office, August 29, 1945, U 6604/50/70, Balfour to Foreign Office, September 5, 1945, U 6731/50/70, all in FO 371, 1945, PRO.

ropean Department and the military. James Dunn, an expert on
European affairs, wrote: "Our military are not very keen about hav-
ing several countries interested in the trusteeship there on the
Mediterranean."[10]

The internal debate continued throughout August and into September. Those watching the State Department's debates closely
found that support for Italy was high. During the last week in August, Balfour predicted that the final decision would be to name
Italy as the United Nations trustee. He added that the decision
seemed directly related to Russian interests in an African trusteeship. Actually, the final decision resembled the recommendation
made by the Special Political Affairs Branch and was not made until
after the London conference began.[11]

The future of Italy's African colonies was of special interest to
Britain. Vital imperial communication and supply lines passed
through the Mediterranean and the Red Sea, and the British wanted
to establish military bases in Libya. On August 18, 1945, the Foreign Office recommended that Britain take the "lion's share" of
Italy's colonies as a trustee. The Foreign Office believed that neither
the French nor the Americans would object because both seemed
unwilling to assume any responsibilities for the administration of
the colonies. Only the Soviet Union posed an obstacle to the British
trusteeship, and, unless Soviet objections could be overcome with
strong support from the United States and France, the Foreign
Office saw no other alternative but to give the colonies to Italy as a
trustee.[12]

Despite some differences, British and American officials agreed
on the importance of Italian friendship and the need to keep Italy
within the Western orbit. Russian initiatives were to be resisted.
The problem was how to increase British and American influence
in Italy while reducing Soviet influence in Eastern Europe.

10. Memorandum for the Secretary, "Disposition of Italian Colonies in Africa,"
August 16, 1945, Memorandum by Office of Special Political Affairs, August 30,
1945, Memorandum by Secretary of State, August 31, 1945, all in Council of Foreign
Ministers London Notebook, Vol. I, pt. I, in Dulles Papers.

11. Balfour to Foreign Office, August 24, 1945, U 6472/50/70, Balfour to Foreign
Office, August 27, 1945, U 6499/50/70, Balfour to Foreign Office, August 29, 1945, U
6604/50/70, Balfour to Foreign Office, September 5, 1945, U 6731/50/70, all in FO 371,
1945, PRO.

12. Foreign Office Memorandum, "Italian Peace Treaty—Colonies," August 18,
1945, U 6368/50/70, in FO 371, 1945, PRO.

EASTERN EUROPE

Both Romania and Bulgaria lay within the Soviet Union's inner circle of interest. The Russians believed that both nations needed to look toward the Soviet Union for leadership. Of the two, Romania posed the more complex and troublesome problem for the implementation of Soviet policy. The Romanians had a long history of close relations with Western Europe, particularly France, as well as a long tradition of being anti-Russian.[13]

Between World War I and World War II, the Romanians, with French, British, and German support, sought to close themselves off from Soviet Russia. Roads led to the Romanian-Russian border and ended. Railroad lines stopped at the border, with passengers and cargo having to be unloaded to await the arrival of a Russian train. Armed guards patrolled both sides of the border. Within Romania, King Carol had all but eliminated the Left (socialists and Communists) from political participation prior to World War II. Later, under the fascist regime of Ion Antonescu and the Iron Guard, the Left was slowly removed from Romanian social life as well. In 1941, when Germany invaded Russia, the Romanians reacted by eagerly joining their German allies. But in 1944 came, in the words of Cloyce Huston, the State Department's chief of southern affairs, "the greatest imaginable catastrophe" for the Romanians: military defeat and Russian occupation. The occupation only increased Romanian hatred for Russia and the Communist "liberators." Huston predicted that as soon as the Red Army departed "the Rumanians would begin immediately and frantically to rebuild the wall [between Romania and Russia] like ants hurry to repair a disturbed anthill."[14]

The terms of the Soviet armistice for Romania were actually temperate. The constitutional monarchy of King Michael I remained, and the conservative government of General Constantin Sanatescu continued to function. Even the amount of reparations owed Russia, $300 million, seemed within Romania's ability to pay. Prime Minister Churchill was surprised at the terms and told President

13. Henry L. Roberts, *Rumania* (New Haven, 1951), 250–63; Cortlandt V. R. Schuyler, "The View from Romania," in Thomas T. Hammond (ed.), *Witnesses to the Origins of the Cold War* (Seattle, 1982), 123–60.

14. Memorandum by Cloyce Huston, "Suggested Extension of American Policy on Eastern Europe," October 21, 1945, in File 711.61/10–2145, DSR-NA.

Roosevelt that they seemed "very reasonable and even generous."[15]

State Department officials were also initially pleased with Soviet policy toward Romania. The leader of the Peasant party, Iuliu Maniu, expressed fears of Russian domination, but the State Department believed he was overly alarmist. American officials planned for a quick resumption of diplomatic relations with Romania.[16]

Soviet acceptance of conservative rule in Romania changed, however, as local Communist and Socialist groups demonstrated in January, 1945, for a larger role in the government and for social and economic reforms. The Russians were also suspicious of Western statements of approval of the Sanatescu government and the increasingly friendly relations between British and American representatives in Romania and the leaders of the traditionally anti-Communist parties. In late February, 1945, Andrei Vyshinsky, Soviet deputy foreign minister, flew to Bucharest to oversee the reorganization of the Romanian government. For a week Vyshinsky pressured King Michael to appoint as prime minister the noncommunist, leftist leader of the Ploughmen's front, Dr. Petru Groza. On February 28, the king appointed Groza prime minister.[17]

Britain and the United States immediately protested the direct intervention of the Soviet Union in the internal affairs of Romania. The two Western nations invoked the Yalta Declaration. They held that the Groza government was unrepresentative and undemocratic, asked for tripartite consultations, and refused to recognize the new regime. Further British and American reactions were restrained. The American political representative to Romania, Burton Y. Berry, cautioned the king that it would be dangerous to ignore Vyshinsky's demands. Roosevelt and Churchill exchanged letters giving possible reasons for Soviet actions and explanations of why they were not inclined to protest too vehemently. Churchill wrote,

15. "The Armistice with Romania," *DSB*, XI (September 17, 1944), 252–89; Lundestad, *The American Non-Policy*, 226–28; Winston S. Churchill, *Triumph and Tragedy* (Boston, 1953), 66; *FR, 1944*, IV (9 vols.; Washington, D.C., 1965), 251–52.

16. Churchill, *Triumph and Tragedy*, 286–87; Lundestad, *The American Non-Policy*, 232–333; James L. Gormly, "Plots and Tactics: The United States, Britain, Russia, and Rumania, 1944–1947," *Red River Valley Historical Journal of World History*, IV (1980), 269–92.

17. Ghita Ionescu, *Communism in Rumania, 1944–1962* (New York, 1964), 105–107; Robert Bishop and E. S. Crayfield, *Russia Astride the Balkans* (New York, 1948), 97–98, 291–92; Mastny, *Russia's Road to the Cold War*, 256–57; *FR, 1945*, V, 489–90.

"I am not anxious to press this to such an extent that Stalin will say, 'I did not interfere in your actions in Greece, why do you not give me the same latitude in Rumania.'" He also pointed out that for diplomatic and military reasons Romania was a poor test case. Roosevelt agreed that it was "difficult to contest the [Russian] plea of military necessity and security." The president added, however, that he did not intend to let the event slip by unnoticed.[18]

Whatever plans Roosevelt had for contesting Russian actions in Romania apparently died with him. In the months between his death and the Potsdam Conference, the United States maintained its policy of nonrecognition toward the Groza government. At Potsdam, President Truman, without enthusiasm, repeated the American objection to the undemocratic regime in Romania. In Bucharest, however, the American attitude was different. There, Berry and his assistant, Roy M. Melbourne, recommended that the United States take a more assertive policy toward the Groza government. They personally encouraged opposition leaders to resist Groza, and American intelligence sources reported that the Communists were losing support and that the opposition remained active and popular. In early August, Berry reported that the opposition was anxiously "awaiting as a vital and urgent factor" in its plan to gain "Rumania's independence an Allied declaration that the Groza Gov't under the Potsdam Declaration is not considered a 'recognized democratic govt.'"[19]

The time seemed opportune for an attempt to oust Groza. Using Truman's statement at Potsdam as evidence of American support, Berry and Melbourne encouraged King Michael and the opposition to force the prime minister to resign. The scheme was simple. Using his constitutional authority, giving as justification the prime minister's obvious inability to gain recognition from the United States and Great Britain, King Michael would demand that Groza resign.[20]

18. FR, 1945, V, 493–94, 505–506, 509–10.

19. Bennett Kovig, The Myth of Liberation: East-Central Europe in U.S. Diplomacy and Politics Since 1941 (Baltimore, 1973), 33–39; Lundestad, The American Non-Policy, 233–36; FR, 1945, V, 524–25.

20. Melbourne to State Department, August 16, 1945, in File 871.00/8–1645, DSR-NA; Burton Y. Berry Diary, August 9, 1945, in Burton Y. Berry Papers, Lilly Library, Indiana University, Bloomington, Ind.

On August 16, Melbourne reported to the State Department that the king was calling a meeting of all the political parties "to ask if they thought the present regime could secure a peace treaty" and that upon receiving a negative reply, the king "would formally . . . ask Groza for his Government's resignation." Four days later the State Department received word that Groza had been asked to resign and had refused.[21]

Groza scoffed at the king's reasoning and said that the issue of recognition by the United States "was of little significance" and that the Soviets would eventually "secure Anglo-American agreement to a peace treaty." The prime minister's logic did not impress King Michael or alter his request for Groza's resignation. The king promptly retired to his mountain retreat and refused to sign legislation. Without the king's signature, all legislation was invalid, forcing a political stalemate and constitutional crisis.[22]

The Foreign Office was aghast. On August 10, D. L. Stewart, East European desk officer, wrote: "The Americans are intervening vigorously in Roumanian internal affairs. . . . In fact they have begun a full scale plot against . . . the Russians' favorite puppets." On August 14, John H. La Rougetel, the British political representative in Romania, reported to the Foreign Office that Melbourne and others were encouraging dissent, meeting regularly with anti-Groza forces and pledging United States support. Officials in London instructed La Rougetel to offer no support to the plot or any American actions. "I want the Greek elections through first," Bevin explained. Sir Orme Sargent, permanent undersecretary and Soviet expert, warned that "if they are not careful, the Americans are going to involve themselves in a humiliation and the King in a disaster." Fearful of Soviet support for Greek rebels and of Russian intrigues in Turkey, Iran, and India, the Foreign Office informed the State Department that it considered the actions in Bucharest ill-timed and useless. British officials believed it extremely unlikely that the Russians would accept tripartite consultations or share responsibilities in Romania.[23]

21. *FR, 1945*, V, 574–75.
22. Berry Diary, August 1–28, 1945, in Berry Papers; Melbourne to State Department, August 19, 1945, in File 871.00/8–1945, DSR-NA.
23. *FR, 1945*, II, 103; Foreign Office Minute, August 10, 1945, R 13740/28/37, La Rougetel to Foreign Office, August 14, 1945, R 13282/28/37, Bevin's Comment, un-

Britain's adverse reaction may have surprised the State Department, but it did not deter American hopes for toppling the Groza government and introducing United States influence in Romanian affairs. State Department officials had realized that there was only the remotest chance that Groza would be forced to resign and had planned accordingly. An August 25 State Department memorandum outlined a course of action to be followed once King Michael made his request for Groza's resignation. The United States would support the king while at the same time formally requesting that the signatories of the Yalta Declaration act to resolve the political impasse between king and prime minister. When, as expected, the Soviets refused to consider tripartite consultations, the State Department would publicly announce its deepest regrets, protest that the Yalta Declaration did apply, and suggest that the foreign ministers discuss the matter during the upcoming London conference. The memorandum further recommended that the king and Groza work together until the three powers found a solution. The State Department memorandum concluded that such a course "would involve no abandonment of . . . announced principles and purposes and would hold open the possibility of reaching agreement with the Russians at London in a calmer atmosphere."[24]

On September 4, a week before the start of the London Conference, Ambassador Harriman informed Molotov that the United States suggested "an arrangement whereby [Groza] could continue the routine business of administration" until the Allies could resolve the question of Groza's resignation. Harriman added that he believed the London meeting would provide an excellent opportunity to deal with the Romanian imbroglio.[25]

Molotov rejected Harriman's arguments. In his opinion, there was nothing wrong with Groza or his government, and he saw no

dated, R 13282/28/37, Foreign Office Minute, August 16, 1945, R 13282/28/37, Comments by D. L. Stewart and Sir Orme Sargent, August 28 and 30, 1945, R 14591/21/7, all in FO 371, 1945, PRO; Harrison to State Department, September 8, 1945, in File 871.00/9–845, DSR-NA; Berry Diary, August 19, 1945, in Berry Papers.

24. State Department Memorandum, August 25, 1945, in File 871.00/8–2545, DSR-NA.

25. Harriman to State Department, September 10, 1945, in File 871.00/9–1045, DSR-NA; *FR, 1945*, V, 606–608.

reason to discuss the issue in London. Molotov hinted that perhaps after the conference the powers might discuss the Romanian political impasse. Despite the disappointing response from Molotov, Byrnes vowed to discuss the issue in London even if he had to incorporate it into discussions on the Romanian peace treaty. The British, knowing of Byrnes's resolution, placed Romanian internal political affairs on their draft agenda for the London meeting.[26]

Romania's politics, however, was not the only example of Soviet influence in Eastern Europe that the Americans hoped to reduce. Byrnes also expected to discuss Bulgarian internal affairs in London in an attempt to obtain Soviet approval for the breakup of the Communist-dominated Fatherland front government.

The Fatherland front was a popular front movement that developed in Bulgaria during World War II in opposition to the pro-German government of Constantine Muraviev. The majority of the front's members belonged to the conservative-moderate Agrarian party. However, the front was controlled by the smaller Communist and Zvero parties. The Fatherland front enjoyed the support of the majority of the Bulgarian population, many of whom traditionally looked to Mother Russia for support and direction. The British and Americans maintained a diplomatic silence and watchful eye on the pro-Soviet government of Kimon Georgiev.[27]

Their silence lasted from September, 1944, until the end of March, 1945. In March, those in the State Department supporting a more assertive role for the United States in Bulgarian affairs finally obtained permission to issue a formal protest about the forthcoming Bulgarian national elections. On April 5, Harriman informed the Soviet Union that the United States objected to the single list of candidates offered by the Fatherland front and that the United States favored individual parties offering their own lists of candidates. The Soviets rejected Harriman's protests.[28]

26. "U.S. Proposals for Drafting the Peace Treaties with Rumania," undated, in Council of Foreign Ministers London Notebook, Vol. II, pt. I, in Dulles Papers; *FR, 1945*, V, 603–604, 614–15; *FR, 1945*, II, 116.

27. Black, "The Start of the Cold War," 163–76; Nissan Oren, *Revolution Administered: Agrarianism and Communism in Bulgaria* (Baltimore, 1973), 98–100; *FR, 1945*, IV, 167; William E. Houstoun-Boswell to Foreign Office, August 6, 1945, R 14453/723/7, in FO 371, 1945, PRO; Michael M. Boll, *Cold War in the Balkans: American Foreign Policy and the Emergence of Communist Bulgaria* (Lexington, Ky., 1984), 1–51.

28. *FR, 1945*, IV, 167–68; Lundestad, *The American Non-Policy*, 262–64; Boll, *Cold War in the Balkans*, 77–102.

Worried that Bulgaria was falling under Soviet domination, General John A. Crane, the American representative on the Bulgarian Allied Control Council, urged that the State Department apply diplomatic pressure on the Soviets and threaten to withhold economic aid unless the Soviet Union supported changes in the election law. The American political representative in Bulgaria, Maynard Barnes, meanwhile worked closely with politicians opposed to the front, particularly Nikola Petkov, general secretary of the Bulgarian Agrarian party. Barnes and Petkov hoped to build resistance to front control of Bulgaria. Preoccupied with the situation in Poland, the State Department was slow to respond to the recommendations of its personnel in Bulgaria. Finally in June, 1945, the department approved Voice of America broadcasts into Bulgaria in support of those political groups favoring individual lists of candidates. Still, American support fell far short of applying the type of pressure recommended by Crane and Barnes.[29]

After the Potsdam Conference, the United States began to assume a more active and publicly critical attitude toward the Fatherland front. On August 9, Truman announced that Bulgaria should not be part of any nation's sphere of influence. The announcement was followed shortly thereafter by an official note to the Bulgarian government stating that the United States could not "overlook the preponderance of . . . evidence that a minority element in power" was using "force and intimidation" to keep the larger democratic elements from fully participating in the political process.[30]

Barnes used these and similar statements by United States officials to encourage Petkov and his Agrarian dissidents to resist the front. Heartened by Barnes's support of the Voice of America broadcasts, Petkov broke completely with the Fatherland front during the week before the Bulgarian national election, scheduled for August 26. He formed his own independent political party and began to print his own candidate list. The Fatherland front government responded by passing an election law barring all splinter parties from the election. When Petkov broke with the front, the major-

29. Black, "The Start of the Cold War," 178–83; State Department Manual, "Bulgaria," in File 711.00/12–145, DSR-NA; FR, 1945, IV, 168–69, 212–13, 268–71, 272–73, 297–98, 303; Boll, Cold War in the Balkans, 103–35.

30. FR, 1945, IV, 282–83; Boll, Cold War in the Balkans, 135–39.

ity of the Agrarian party joined him in forming the Independent Agrarian party. The Fatherland front, claiming that the minority still within the front was the true Agrarian party, declared the Independent Agrarians a splinter party and barred them from the election. Barnes warned that the barring of Petkov's party ensured a complete Communist victory. He urgently requested the State Department to support him in an effort to have the election postponed and a new election law written.[31]

The State Department returned a negative reply: "Department is not making representation to Moscow nor can it support your action." Nor did the department intend to ask for a postponement of the election. The reply came too late or was ignored by Barnes. He and Generals Crane and W. H. Oxley, the British representative on the Allied Control Council, presented their complaints to the Bulgarian government and asked for a delay in the national elections. To everyone's surprise, on August 25, the day before the scheduled elections, the Georgiev government announced that the election would be postponed. Barnes gloried in his victory. He called it a "great moral victory" over an "aggressive foe" and made plans to travel to London so that he could be on hand to advise Byrnes at the foreign ministers' meeting.[32]

From Washington, Byrnes issued a mild statement congratulating the Bulgarians and expressing hope that the new election would result in a truly representative government. Despite the minor success at Sofia, the State Department and Byrnes intended to work their Eastern Europe policy at the London conference, where the United States would stress the unrepresentative nature of the Romanian and Bulgarian governments and its inability to recognize the governments. Byrnes hoped to justify the formation of a special commission of inquiry to investigate Balkan internal affairs while moving forward on the peace treaties.[33]

Another line of attack on the Soviet position in Eastern Europe

31. Black, "The Start of the Cold War," 184–86; *FR, 1945*, IV, 298, 302–303, 308–309, 317–18; Boll, *Cold War in the Balkans*, 139–43.

32. Black, "The Start of the Cold War," 184–86; *FR, 1945*, IV, 308–309, 317–18; Lisle A. Rose, *After Yalta: America and the Origins of the Cold War* (New York, 1973), 117; Oren, *Revolution Administered*, 92; Boll, *Cold War in the Balkans*, 143–55.

33. Memorandum of Bevin-Byrnes Conversation of September 13, 1945, Foreign Office Minute, September 16, 1945, R 15122/15122/67, in FO 371, 1945, PRO.

would be the peace treaties. The goal was to write into the treaties specific, multilateral economic and commercial clauses and to internationalize the Danube. The economic clauses were carefully designed to promote "American interests," and they included "special paragraphs, not included in the . . . treaty with Italy," that would ensure "non-discrimination" for Western interests. The special paragraphs were intended to bring Romania and Bulgaria into "a multilateral trading and financial system."[34]

Internationalizing the Danube would also encourage Western influence in Eastern European economic patterns. The Americans believed that if the countries of Eastern Europe were to be spared integration into the Soviet economic bloc it would be necessary to ensure that every nation had free and equal access to the Danube and the adjoining markets. Not only would multilateral trade in the region be protected but Eastern European trade patterns could again, as before World War II, be established with Western Europe and the United States. "If we are going to live in a world of international cooperation, certainly there must be international control of these waterways," wrote Norman J. Padleford, the State Department's expert on inland waterways and a delegate to the London conference.[35] If successful on all points of his strategy regarding Eastern Europe, Byrnes could break the Soviet hold there, both politically and economically.

For the British, who along with the French had largely influenced the area prior to the war, the assertive American diplomacy toward Eastern Europe presented two alternatives: either join with the United States in attempting to roll back Soviet and Communist influence or take a position somewhere between the Americans and the Russians. Prior to American actions in August, 1945, the majority within the Foreign Office favored concluding the peace treaties with Romania and Bulgaria, waiting for the removal of the

---

34. "U.S. Proposals for Drafting the Peace Treaties with Rumania," undated, in Council of Foreign Ministers London Notebook, Vol. II, pt. I, in Dulles Papers; Lord Halifax to Foreign Office, July 28, 1945, W 10201/142/803, in FO 371, 1945, PRO; State Department to Byrnes, September 18, 1945, in File 740.00119 (Council)/9–1845, DSR-NA.

35. Padleford to Walter Brown, October 12, 1945, in Folder 551, Byrnes Papers; Paterson, *Soviet-American Confrontation*, 108–19; New York *Times*, August 14, 1945, Sec. 2, p. 4.

Russian Army, and beginning normal political and economic relations with the two nations in hopes that over time British influence
would be reestablished. After assessing the benefits and draw-
backs, Bevin and others in the Foreign Office decided in late August to wait to see whether the American successes and asser-
tiveness were only temporary.[36]

Of the various tactics to reduce Soviet influence in Eastern Europe, the Foreign Office believed that economic diplomacy offered
the best chance for long-range success. A Foreign Office memorandum concluded that "a substantial resumption of trade between
the United Kingdom and South Eastern and Central Europe would
do much to open these countries to Western influence, to relax
the cramping restrictions on movement and publicity imposed by
the Soviet Government, and to soften the line between the Soviet
sphere of control and the sphere of the Western Powers."[37] By this
reasoning, the British willingly supported the internationalization
of the Danube (to the point of wanting to internationalize the Oder
and Elbe as well) and the inclusion of provisions for free trade and
multilateral trade in the Romanian and Bulgarian peace treaties.
The British, however, decided not to support American attempts
to alter the internal political affairs of the two nations. Fearful
of Soviet reactions in Greece, Orme Sargent wrote on the eve of
the London conference that "during the . . . conference it might
strengthen our position if we could play occasionally peace-makers
between the U.S. . . . and the Soviet Government." Sargent believed the dispute over Romania provided an excellent opportunity.
Sir Alexander Cadogan commented that while Sargent's suggestion
had merit, Britain would have "to be careful not to give the Americans the feeling that we're letting them down."[38]

Bevin preferred to wait to meet privately with Byrnes to see if the

36. FORD Memorandum, undated, R 19325/19325/37, Foreign Office Minute,
September 2, 1945, R 15122/15122/37, Foreign Office Minute, September 2, 1945, U
6795/5559/70, Comment by William Hayter, September 13, 1945, R 15119/21/7, all in
FO 371, 1945, PRO.

37. Foreign Office Memorandum, "Trade with South, Eastern, and Central Europe," August 23, 1945, UE 4032/79/54, in FO 371, 1945, PRO.

38. Cabinet Overseas Reconstruction Committee Report, ORC (45) 32, September 5, 1945, W 16355/142/803, Foreign Office Minute, September 10, 1945, R
15867/120226/37, both in FO 371, 1945, PRO.

Americans were earnest in their attempt to contest Soviet political control in Eastern Europe. If Byrnes indicated any hesitation, Britain was considering following the Russian lead and concluding the peace treaties—provided that the Soviets accepted the British treaty for Italy.

Britain and the United States sought to reduce Soviet domination in Eastern Europe and to further their influence in Italy. It was expected that the Russians would attempt the opposite. Hard bargaining was expected. It also seemed likely that the issues of Japan, atomic energy and weapons, and Iran would be raised by the Soviets to further complicate the pattern of negotiations. On these three issues there was little consensus between the British and the Americans, and it was possible that a wedge might be driven between the two English-speaking powers.

JAPAN

United States policy stood most isolated on the issue of control over Japan. The Soviet Union and Britain both objected to unilateral American occupation and control there. For the United States, World War II started in the Pacific. There was nearly unanimous agreement across the nation that for security reasons the United States should control the Pacific and the home islands of Japan. In July, 1945, policy makers in Washington concluded that the United States had a "paramount interest in peace and security in the Pacific" and should unilaterally control Japan. Such control became official policy on August 10 at a high-level cabinet meeting with Truman. "I felt it was of great importance to get the home islands into our hands before the Russians could put any substantial claim to occupy and help rule it," Secretary of War Stimson told his colleagues. Byrnes agreed fully and stressed that the "top commander over Hirohito" must be an American in order to "avoid any chance of misunderstanding as in Europe." When the cabinet adjourned it was clear to those present that America's allies in the Pacific war were now relegated to advisory status.[39]

On August 21, the United States formally offered advisory status

39. Stimson Diary, August 10, 1945, in Stimson Papers; Blum, *The Price of Vision,* 474; *FR, 1945,* VI, 608; Feis, *Contest Over Japan,* 22–28.

to the Allies as members of the Far Eastern Advisory Commission. Because of their countries' roles in the war against Japan, officials in Britain, China, and the Soviet Union could have taken issue with the American policy and demanded a larger occupational and policy making role. China and the Soviet Union gave their acceptance of advisory status. Britain, however, refused to accept the secondary position and asked that an Allied Control Council be established to rule Japan and share command responsibility with the Supreme Allied Commander, General Douglas MacArthur.[40]

The British rejected membership on the Far Eastern Advisory Commission because they believed their efforts in the war in Asia entitled them to an equal, or near equal, role in directing Japan's future. They also feared American domination of Asian trade and fully expected to discuss these matters with Byrnes when he arrived in London. Bevin concluded that "the Americans will act as independently as possible in controlling Japan" and that it was in Britain's best interest to "put forward as soon as possible a plan to insure maximum participation [for Britain] in Japanese affairs." The Foreign Office's request for an Allied Control Council for Japan was presented to the State Department on August 21.[41]

Byrnes was unimpressed. He reacted by announcing that Hong Kong's status might also be discussed at the London meeting. This was a clear warning to the Foreign Office that Britain too was vulnerable on Asian matters. At the same time, James Dunn told Balfour that the formation of an Allied Control Council for Japan was unthinkable and that the issue was closed. The Foreign Office replied that Hong Kong was not a matter for discussion in London and that it formally rejected membership on the Far Eastern Advisory Commission. The Foreign Office also sent its proposal for an Allied Control Council to the Soviets and the Chinese. The replies were encouraging. Molotov said that there seemed to be "room for agreement" between the British and American positions and that he expected to discuss the matter at the meeting of the Council of Foreign Ministers. The Chinese said they welcomed the proposal.[42]

40. *FR, 1945,* VI, 678, 683, 699, 712.

41. Cabinet Meeting, August 9, 1945, F 5743/364/23, "U.S. Policy for Japan," August 16, 1945, F 5378/364/23, both in FO 371, 1945, PRO; Thorne, *Allies of a Kind,* 678–81.

42. *FR, 1945,* VI, 678, 696–98; State Department Record of Conversation, August 30, 1945, in File 740.00119 (Control) Japan/9–3045, DSR-NA; Clark Kerr to Foreign

Japan was a potential diplomatic lever for the Soviets in London. It would be difficult for the United States to deny Russia a commanding position in Eastern Europe while demanding such a position in Japan. The Soviets could trade their support for the American position on Japan for American support for Soviet policy in Eastern Europe. Or, the Soviets could use their support for Britain's position to open doors into Italy. Aware of the possible advantage the Japanese issue might give the Russians, Bevin concluded only days before the London conference that it would be in Britain's best interest not to introduce the Japanese issue without first consulting with Byrnes.[43]

ATOMIC ENERGY AND WEAPONS

Control of atomic energy and the atomic bomb offered diplomatic problems as well. The United States held a monopoly over both as World War II ended. In speeches prior to the London conference, Truman made it clear that he intended for the monopoly to remain in American hands. The British feared that the United States would not continue the atomic partnership that existed during World War II, and they had reason to worry. American thinking was moving in a direction away from that of the British and their newly created Atomic Advisory Commission.[44]

Unlike Churchill and Truman, Prime Minister Attlee and a majority of his advisers wanted the atomic bomb placed under the control of the United Nations. They also wanted atomic scientific and technical knowledge to be shared not only with the United Kingdom but with the Soviet Union. To do otherwise, they reasoned, would create an environment conducive to an arms race and further impair relations between the West and the Soviets. Writing for the Chiefs of Staff, General E. Ian Jacob informed the Foreign Office

---

Office, September 7, 1945, F 6498/364/23, Memorandum of Conversation between Bevin and T. V. Soong, September 17, 1945, F 7205/186/10, both in FO 371, 1945, PRO; *FR, 1945*, V, 712–13.

43. Foreign Office Memorandum on the Control of Japan, September 11, 1945, F 6699/364/23, in FO 371, 1945, PRO.

44. Herken, *The Winning Weapon*, 9–42; Edward Francis-Williams, *A Prime Minister Remembers: The War and Post-War Memoirs of the Right Honorable Earl Attlee* (London, 1961), 97–101; John W. Wheeler-Bennett, *John Anderson, Viscount Waverley* (New York, 1962), 330–33; Dalton Diary, July 12, 1945, in Dalton Papers.

on August 22 that although "a weapon of war," the atomic bomb should "be left to the World Organization . . . to decide in what way to deal with [it] . . . for the benefit of mankind." John Ward, commenting for the Foreign Office, noted: "General Jacob's line . . . is very sensible."[45]

On August 28, Attlee circulated his views on the question to those involved with the formation of Britain's atomic policy. He suggested that information about and control of the bomb be shared with the Russians. "The only course which seems to me to be feasible and to offer a reasonable hope of staving off imminent disaster for the world is joint action by the U.S.A., U.K. and Russia based on stark reality." He proposed that the case for sharing knowledge and control with Russia be put as soon as possible to Truman and Stalin. He concluded: "The time is short, I believe that only a bold course can save civilisation."[46]

Bevin disagreed. He "did not think the question should be raised with Truman and Stalin in isolation from the many different subjects at present under discussion between the Three Governments." He wanted to see whether, as the Americans thought, the bomb would have an impact on Soviet policy. The Foreign Office believed that the Americans were overestimating the effect of the atomic bomb. The British embassy in Moscow warned that the Russian silence on the bomb was ominous and supported the theory that "the bomb had not changed Soviet policy . . . but has only intensified Soviet suspicions and existing trends." Bevin's position was incorporated into Attlee's message to Truman on September 25, in which Attlee expressed his hopes for international control and information sharing but made no mention of an overture to Stalin.[47]

The Russian response to the atomic bomb was studied silence. Stalin, in his victory speech to the Russian people, totally ignored the bombings and claimed that the Japanese surrender was caused by the entry of the Soviet Union into the war. Despite the calculated

45. General E. I. C. Jacob to Foreign Office, August 22, 1945, U 6717/6550/70, in FO 371, 1945, PRO; Margaret Gowing, *Policy Making* (New York, 1974), 20–23, 64–65.

46. Gowing, *Policy Making*, 63–65.

47. Francis-Williams, *A Prime Minister Remembers*, 100–101; Gowing, *Policy Making*, 65–81; Clark Kerr to Foreign Office, September 6, 1945, N 12165/165/38, Roberts to Foreign Office, September 9, 1945, R 15270/28/37, both in FO 371, 1945, PRO.

silence of Soviet authorities, however, Western observers in Moscow reported that private speculation about the atomic bomb and atomic energy was widespread. Notice was also made of the arrival of a Yugoslav atomic scientist in Moscow.[48]

Speculation was equally evident within the Russian orbit in Eastern Europe. General Cortland V. R. Schuyler, head of the United States delegation to the Romanian Allied Control Council, reported a popular joke heard in early January, 1946:

FIRST PERSON: Could a country be destroyed by atomic bombs?

SECOND PERSON: Yes, if they are dispersed correctly and enough were used.

FIRST PERSON: Well, how many would it take to destroy England for example?

SECOND PERSON: Oh, about 35.

FIRST PERSON: Well, how many would it take to destroy France?

SECOND PERSON: About 60.

FIRST PERSON: How many would it take to destroy the Soviet Union?

SECOND PERSON: 103!

FIRST PERSON: How many atomic bombs does the United States have?

SECOND PERSON: 103![49]

From Bulgaria, Maynard Barnes informed the State Department that the Communist-supported Fatherland front, in its campaign speeches, was boasting that it did not fear the Americans or the atomic bomb.[50]

Official Soviet silence was broken on September 1, 1945, when *New Times* denounced those in the West who advocated using the bomb and atomic energy as diplomatic weapons. *New Times* advocated international control. "The invention of the atomic bomb renders it still more imperative to mobilize all the forces of progress for the maintenance of enduring peace and reliable security for nations, big and small. At the same time it should be clear to all thinking men that this discovery cannot solve political problems, either nationally or internationally." In the United States, *Time* magazine

48. Joseph L. Nogee, *Soviet Policy Toward International Control of Atomic Energy* (Notre Dame, Ind., 1961), 3–6; New York *Times*, August 14, 1945, Sec. 1, p. 10, August 17, 1945, Sec. 1, p. 5, August 18, 1945, Sec. 1, p. 1.

49. General Courtland V. R. Schuyler to State Department, Annual Report, January 1, 1946, in File 871.00/1–146, DSR-NA.

50. *FR, 1945*, IV, 308.

aptly summarized the prevailing attitude among other nations: "Those who had the power favored keeping it; those who lacked it favored sharing it."[51]

Byrnes could be counted as one having it, and he was opposed to sharing it with any other nation. He was fully aware of the possible diplomatic advantages that the bomb brought and realized that possession of atomic energy and control of the atomic bomb would be discussed, at least privately, during the London conference. In preparation, he carefully reviewed not only the status of American atomic research and production but estimates of the time Russia would need to produce an atomic bomb. The pacts and agreements that governed British and American atomic collaboration were also examined. Byrnes expected to be ready to counter Soviet and British efforts to gain access to atomic information, and to use American control as his own diplomatic weapon. Stimson wrote at the time: "I found that Byrnes was very much against any attempt to cooperate with Russia. His mind is full of his problems with the coming meeting for the foreign ministers and he looks to having the presence of the bomb in his pocket, so to speak."[52]

IRAN

If the issues of atomic energy and weapons and control of Japan were not enough to cloud the negotiations involving the European peace treaties, there remained the problem of Iran, which was already firmly established on the agenda of the London conference. Iran was primarily a British and Soviet question. Both nations had long traditions of involvement in Iranian affairs, and as World War II ended both nations had large military forces stationed there. The United States had a small force in Iran to handle Lend-Lease shipments to Russia and had only recent experience dabbling in Persian affairs.[53]

51. M. Rubenstein, "The Foreign Press on the Atomic Bomb," *New Times*, September 1, 1945, pp. 12–17; *Time*, August 27, 1945, p. 23.

52. Memorandum for Record, August 29, 1945, in British Committee Folder 71, Harrison-Bundy Files, Manhattan Engineer District Files, NA; Stimson Diary, September 4, 1945, in Stimson Papers.

53. Bruce R. Kuniholm, *The Origins of the Cold War in the Near East: Great Power Conflict and Diplomacy in Iran, Turkey, and Greece* (Princeton, 1980), 130–282; Benjamin Shwadran, *The Middle East, Oil, and the Great Powers* (New York, 1973).

During the Potsdam Conference, Truman claimed that he did not even realize the United States had troops in Iran and that he intended to remove them as soon as possible. British efforts to establish a timetable for British and Soviet troop removals failed as Stalin would confirm only that Soviet troops would be removed in accord with the treaty signed with Iran. He also told Truman that the Soviet Union planned no actions against Iran. It was agreed that the foreign ministers would plan troop withdrawals at the meeting of the Council of Foreign Ministers. The ministers were to use as their guide the 1942 Tripartite Treaty of Alliance, which specified that all foreign forces would be removed six months after the end of World War II. To many Iranians, who wanted to see all Soviet and British troops immediately evacuated, the Potsdam decision was a disappointment.[54]

Between the end of the Potsdam Conference and the first meeting of the Council of Foreign Ministers, events in Iran heightened the importance of removing Soviet troops. In northern Iran, occupied by Soviet forces, a nationalistic rebellion against the Tehran government seized power and demanded autonomy. Most Western observers believed that the Soviets were behind the movement, and they feared that Russia might attempt to use the rebellion either to overthrow the Iranian government or to annex the region into southern Russia. Just as American interest in Iran was increasing, many Iranians were attempting to get the United States more deeply involved. The Iranian chargé d'affaires in Washington complained to the State Department that the United States was acting as if the matter were solely an issue between the Soviets and the British. He said that Iran depended "entirely on the US" to help remove British and Russian troops from its soil.[55]

Despite the rebellion and the pleas from the Iranian chargé d'affaires, American policy makers were not anxious to become involved. Byrnes decided to make Iran a minor issue and to try only to obtain British and Soviet agreement that on September 2, 1945,

54. Kuniholm, *The Origins of the Cold War in the Near East*, 271–73; *FR, The Conferences of Berlin*, II, 1477; Pierson Dixon, *Double Diploma: The Life of Sir Pierson Dixon, Don and Diplomat* (London, 1968), 163; State Department to Byrnes, September 26, 1945, in File 740.00119 (Council)/9–2645, DSR-NA.

55. Kuniholm, *The Origins of the Cold War in the Near East*, 273–80; Gary B. Hess, "The Iranian Crisis of 1945–1946 and the Cold War," *Political Science Quarterly*, LXXIV (1974), 117–46; *FR, 1945*, VIII, 301–11, 372–75, 387–91.

World War II officially ended. Six months following that date, if Britain and Russia respected their treaty obligations, all foreign troops would be removed from Iran. Byrnes hoped that this straightforward solution would not be a bone of contention between the powers.

For Byrnes and the American delegation, it appeared possible that the United States could avoid issues like Japan that might prove embarrassing and those like atomic energy and weapons and Iran that might detract from the main goal of drafting the peace treaties for Italy, Romania, and Bulgaria. Byrnes was confident, but he was not alone. British and Soviet policy makers had also formulated positions that they believed would, after some negotiation, be accepted. The foreign ministers had the difficult task of defending their nations' decisions and interests while trying to maintain harmony between themselves. The site for this foreboding task was a fourteen-foot long, plywood, green-covered table at Lancaster House, St. James's Park, London.

IV

The London Conference

I N LANCASTER HOUSE, St. James's Park, London, at half past three in the afternoon of September 11, 1945, Ernest Bevin called the first meeting of the Council of Foreign Ministers to order. A massive marble and gilt monument to Victorian architecture, Lancaster House was an ideal setting for the council. It served both as a visual reminder of Britain's past glories and as a symbol of the present Britain—damaged by war but still solid and proud.[1]

The initial session began without fanfare as the ministers quickly agreed upon the mechanics of the conference. With hardly a flicker of debate, they agreed to Byrnes's suggestion that the French and Chinese play an equal role in drafting the peace treaties. Byrnes believed that he could expect almost total support for his proposals from the French and Chinese and sought to have them in his corner. To reduce possible Soviet objections, the secretary of state added that France and China did not necessarily have to be given the right to vote on the finished treaty.

Byrnes's recommendation altered the decision made at the Potsdam Conference that deliberately eliminated France and China from drafting the peace treaties for Germany's allies. The alteration

1. John Charlton, *Lancaster House* (London, 1957); Dixon, *Double Diploma*, 183.

of the Berlin Protocol offered the United States and Britain a possible four-to-one advantage in debating provisions for the various
treaties. Nevertheless, Molotov accepted the reversal of the Berlin
Protocol almost without reservation. He asked only if he were correct in understanding that all council members could "attend discussions" while "decisions could be made only by the representatives concerned." Bevin and Byrnes said that his understanding
was correct—both apparently believed that it would be virtually
impossible to divorce the debate from agreements.[2]

The ministers next turned to the draft agenda circulated by the
host British delegation. The agenda contained those issues referred
to the council at the Potsdam Conference and those questions the
Foreign Office believed the other nations wanted to discuss. Almost immediately the facade of cordiality began to peel away. There
was no debate on the referred issues. However, debate erupted on
two of the other questions offered on the agenda and on one question that was not on the agenda. Molotov raised objections to two
proposals listed as American: item seven, discussion of the Bosporus and the Dardanelles; and item ten, discussion of the internal
affairs of Romania.[3]

Almost before Molotov raised his objection, Byrnes announced
that neither item seven nor item ten were American intentions. He
asked that both be removed from the agenda. But before Molotov
could enjoy his "victory," the secretary of state added that both
issues did concern the United States and could be discussed in con-
junction with inland waterways and the Romanian peace treaty
that were among the referred items on the agenda.[4]

As Byrnes was finishing his jab at Molotov, the Soviet minister
countered. Molotov said that he understood that there was to be
a question about Allied control of Japan on the agenda. He won-
dered why it was missing. Bevin braved the explanation that because no nation had officially requested its addition, the Foreign

2. *FR, 1945,* II, 114–16; Foreign Office Memorandum, August 10, 1945, U
6135/559/70, in FO 371, 1945, PRO; *FR, 1945,* IV, 721–22.

3. *FR, 1945,* II, 116–18; Excerpts U.S. Minutes, First Meeting, September 11,
1945, in Byrnes Papers; Foreign Office Minute, September 16, 1945, R 15122/28/37, in
FO 371, 1945, PRO.

4. *FR, 1945,* II, 118; Excerpts U.S. Minutes, First Meeting, September 16, 1945, in
Byrnes Papers.

Office had naturally left it off the agenda. Before anyone could suggest that it should be added to the agenda, Byrnes moved to cut off debate. He flatly stated that his delegation believed that the addition of Asian issues would greatly hamper progress on the subjects already before the council. Realizing that Byrnes did not intend to allow the issue of Japan to be discussed, but after making his point that the United States refused to discuss Japan while wanting to discuss Romanian internal affairs, Molotov politely said that he was not asking to place the question on the agenda. He merely was asking why the British had left it off.[5]

The Soviet foreign minister was less polite when he asked about Greece. Directing his remarks at Bevin, Molotov icily announced that he wished to discuss Greek internal affairs. Bevin snapped back that "he declined to discuss" the subject. Undaunted, Molotov asked Bevin if the British government was happy with the political conditions in Greece. Having already refused to discuss the matter, Bevin asked the Soviet minister if he realized the contradiction between refusing to discuss Romanian internal affairs and wanting to discuss Greek internal affairs. Bevin sat back content with having put the Russian in his place. However, the British foreign minister had played into Molotov's trap. The Russian then proceeded to tie together Romanian and Greek affairs by requesting that both matters be submitted for consideration.[6]

The Soviets were willing to argue their actions within their sphere of influence, provided the British and Americans acknowledged and argued their actions in their spheres. As Molotov no doubt expected, Bevin refused to discuss Greece. Seeing tempers rising, Byrnes interceded. It solved nothing, he said, to haggle over subjects not yet submitted. Instead, the ministers should begin work on the matters already on the agenda and save the others for later. Byrnes's advice was taken, but not before Molotov added that "he hoped they would . . . agree to discuss" Greece and Romania later. The first meeting of the Council of Foreign Ministers was over.[7]

The initial meeting was instructive and indicative of events to

5. *FR, 1945*, II, 121; Excerpts U.S. Minutes, First Meeting, September 16, 1945, in Byrnes Papers.
6. *FR, 1945*, II, 121; Excerpts U.S. Minutes, First Meeting, September 16, 1945, in Byrnes Papers.
7. Excerpts U.S. Minutes, First Meeting, September 16, 1945, in Byrnes Papers.

come. Each power had set out its positions and applied its double standard, discussing other powers' spheres of influence but not its own. Bevin revealed his temper and Britain's vulnerability regarding Greece. Molotov proved his strength as a negotiator while downgrading Moscow's concern about Allied interest in Romania. Byrnes had played the patient lawyer and indicated United States strength by refusing to discuss Asian matters. As for the French and Chinese delegations, they only sat and watched.

The second day of the conference proved to be more rancorous than the first. Bevin introduced the first item on the agenda, the Italian peace treaty, by offering a British draft treaty. A squabble immediately broke out over which nations to invite to the conference to express their views on the proposed treaty. Bevin wanted to have each of the Dominions represented as well as India. Molotov opposed Greek participation "so long as there was not in Greece a Government which he could regard as representative," and he used the opportunity to attack the political situation in Greece. The bickering continued until Byrnes suggested that "none of them was in a very good mood" and they should adjourn.[8] All agreed and quickly left Lancaster House to prepare for an official dinner at the House of Lords.

The ministers, assorted British officials, foreign dignitaries, and their wives attended the gala affair. The king and queen were not present. For Byrnes it was more than a social event, for it provided an opportunity to practice his best personal brand of diplomacy. Using his Irish charm and wit, the secretary of state accosted Molotov. Walter Brown, Byrnes's aide at London, described the encounter:

> JFB goes over after Molotov in typical Senatorial fashion. Wants to know when Molotov is going to get his sightseeing completed and "let us get down to business."
>
> Molotov asks JFB if he has an atomic bomb in his side pocket. "You don't know Southerners," Byrnes replied. "We carry our artillery in our hip pocket. If you don't cut out all this stalling and let us get down to work, I am going to pull an atomic bomb out of my hip pocket and let you have it."

8. *FR, 1945*, II, 127–28; Excerpts U.S. Minutes, Second Meeting, September 12, 1945, in Byrnes Papers.

Molotov laughed, but the seriousness of the atomic issue certainly was not lost on anyone. Later, Byrnes again kidded Molotov about getting to work: "Mr. Molotov, I don't think that vodka you drink agreed with you. What you need under your chest is two or three Kentucky Bourbons. I know they would make you feel better and then we might get down to work."[9]

When the conference resumed on September 14, the rancor dissipated. Brown attributed the change to Byrnes: "A different atmosphere prevailed at the Council today. Apparently the talks last night the Justice had with Molotov and Bevin at the House of Lords had good effect."[10] Quickly and cheerfully, the foreign ministers agreed on whom to invite to express views on the Italian treaty and moved on to discuss Italy's African colonies. At issue was an American proposal regarding the colonies.

Italy's African colonies—Libya, Eritrea, and Italian Somaliland— had little economic value but were of great strategic importance in controlling shipping and communications through the Mediterranean and the Red Sea. The British were especially concerned about their disposition and favored placing the colonies under a British trusteeship. On September 12, the official United States position had not been decided, and the Soviet position was unknown. The British suspected that the United States would support an Italian trusteeship and that the Russians would want some role in governing the colonies. On the last issue, American officials were inclined to agree, and they also agreed with their British counterparts that any Soviet role should be prevented.[11]

The United States proposal on Italian colonies introduced on September 12 was surprisingly harsh toward Italy. It condemned Italy's colonial record, recommended that Italy be stripped of its African colonies, and asked that the colonies be placed under a collective United Nations trusteeship. Byrnes had decided upon this policy during a midnight conference only hours before the council meeting. In outlining the collective trusteeship concept to the surprised ministers, Byrnes explained that the trusteeship would be

9. Walter Brown's Book, September 13, 1945, in Byrnes Papers; Janet A. Dulles, "Journal of London Trip," September 12, 1945, in Janet Avery Dulles Collection, Dulles Papers.

10. Walter Brown's Book, September 14, 1945, in Byrnes Papers.

11. Byrnes, *Speaking Frankly*, 94.

governed by an administrator appointed by the Trusteeship Council of the United Nations and a special advisory committee composed of representatives from Britain, France, the United States, the Soviet Union, and Italy, as well as a European and native representative of the territory involved. This system, he argued, would prevent the misuse of a territory by a single trustee and prove to the peoples of the world that the powers would give the colonies their eventual independence.[12]

Only the Chinese immediately accepted the American proposal. The ministers from France, Britain, and Russia each commented on the newness of the concept of a collective trusteeship in which none of the powers would have a dominant position and asked for time to consider the proposal. Each reserved his right to consider alternatives. Georges Bidault was the first to take exception to Byrnes's proposal. The French foreign minister first disagreed with the United States characterization of Italy as an unfit colonial ruler and finished his comments by ardently supporting Italy's right to be named the United Nations' single trustee for the colonies. Molotov, on the other hand, heartily agreed with his American colleague on Italy's history as a colonial ruler but, like Bidault, recommended a single trustee for each colony. Molotov suggested that the colonies be divided among the four powers, with the western half of Libya, Tripolitania, going to Russia. Fearing a Soviet foothold in the Mediterranean, Bevin made no mention of the Foreign Office recommendation that Britain receive all the Italian colonies and only stated that he needed time to consider all the alternatives.[13]

Byrnes now faced two problems: the defense of collective trusteeship, and the rejection of the Russian request for individual trusteeships. In a private meeting with Molotov, the secretary of state emphasized the merits of his plan and the difficulties with the Soviet request: "It would be extremely difficult for the Council to agree which States should administer particular colonies." Molotov disagreed. He believed it would be easier to divide the colonies among the four powers than to select administrators. Throwing the

12. Excerpts U.S. Minutes, Third Meeting, September 14, 1945, in Byrnes Papers; Memorandum for Secretary of State, September 14, 1945, in File 740.00119 (Council)/9–1445, DSR-NA; FR, 1945, II, 162–65.

13. FR, 1945, II, 160–75, 179–81; Excerpts U.S. Minutes, Fourth Meeting, September 14, 1945, in Byrnes Papers.

weight of the Russian victory over Germany into the debate, the Soviet foreign minister reminded Byrnes that Russia was not an average member of the United Nations but a victorious power that "had the right to play a more active part [in] the fate of the Italian colonies than any rank and file member of the United Nations."[14]

After his meeting with Molotov, Byrnes met with Bevin. The British minister learned that the idea of the collective trusteeship arose from American efforts to keep the Russians from establishing themselves in either the Mediterranean or the Red Sea. Although Bevin was in agreement about preventing a Soviet presence in the regions, he did not give Byrnes any sign of support. Rather, he immediately huddled with Foreign Office experts to evaluate both the American and Soviet positions. Foreign Office opinion differed on Molotov's reason for asking for a Soviet trusteeship over Tripolitania. Pierson Dixon, Bevin's private secretary, thought the request was made in seriousness and that it indicated Molotov's hostility toward England and the Empire. Sir Orme Sargent and Sir Alexander Cadogan did not believe that Molotov actually thought Russia would be awarded a trusteeship on the Mediterranean and concluded that the request was a negotiating ploy—a ploy designed to solicit British and United States concessions on issues like Italian reparations, Trieste, Eastern Europe, and the Bosporus and the Dardanelles. After a full night of discussions, however, everyone agreed that common prudence dictated that Molotov's request for an African colony be taken seriously and that Britain must reject it.[15]

The United States proposal, the British concluded, had definite merit. It would bar any direct Soviet role in administering a colony, and it would be attractive to the public and avoid possible outcries of British territorial aggrandizement. But it also meant that Britain would not be able to use the eastern half of Libya, Cyrenaica, for desired military installations. Bevin recommended that the British "play for time and avoid taking too definite a line" on the United States proposal. The British cabinet, in a special meeting, sup-

---

14. *FR, 1945*, II, 164–66; Byrnes, *Speaking Frankly*, 95; Excerpts U.S. Minutes, Fourth Meeting, September 14, 1945, in Byrnes Papers.

15. Dixon, *Double Diploma*, 183; Foreign Office Minute, September 15, 1945, U 7574/51/70, in FO 371, 1945, PRO.

ported Bevin's recommendations to delay supporting the American position while rejecting the Soviet position.[16]

When the council renewed its discussion on the issue of Italy's African colonies on September 15, the lines were drawn. Officials from Britain, France, China, and the United States firmly resisted the Soviet bid for a trusteeship. Bevin went so far as to say that he was "very much surprised" by the Russian request, considering Britain's well-known "vital interests" in the region. Afterward, he supported the United States proposal "with the view of avoiding friction between the Great Powers in these areas." Ignoring the rejection of his proposal, Molotov continued to give reasons for a Soviet trusteeship based on the Soviet Union's newly acquired role as world power. According to Molotov,

> The Soviet Government claimed the right to active participation in the disposal of the Italian Colonies, because Italy had attacked, and had inflicted enormous damage upon, the Soviet Union. . . . The Soviet Government had no intention of restricting in any way the facilities available to the British Commonwealth for maintaining communication with all parts of the world. But Britain should not hold a monopoly of all communications in the Mediterranean. Russia was anxious to have bases in the Mediterranean for her merchant fleet. World trade would develop and the Soviet Union wished to take her share in it.

He assured Bevin and the rest of the council that the Soviet Union would not introduce "the Soviet system" in Tripolitania but promote democracy—though not, he added, "on the lines which had recently been followed in Greece."[17] Bevin failed to appreciate Molotov's logic or humor.

Molotov next turned to Byrnes. He asked if the United States intended to apply its principle of collective trusteeship in the Pacific. The secretary immediately replied that collective trusteeship "could be applied to the Kuriles and other strategic areas." Craftily, Byrnes skirted the issue of a single United States trusteeship for many of the islands in the Pacific and drew into focus the still unclarified status of the Kuril Islands and the strategic importance of those islands to the Soviet Union. With no solution to the question of Italy's colonies in sight, and anxious to move on to other segments of

16. Cabinet Minutes, C. M. (45) 32nd, Conclusions, September 15, 1945, U 7574/51/70, in FO 371, 1945, PRO.
17. *FR, 1945*, II, 188–89.

the Italian treaty, the ministers asked their deputies to work on a trustee plan.[18]

By September 20, the deputies were instructed to draft the entire Italian peace treaty. Hoping to slant the draft toward Western interests, Byrnes had asked Molotov to support the view that the deputies' draft be formulated "on a majority view." The request, seemingly made offhand, carried important consequences. If Molotov accepted, it would mean that in case of disagreement on provisions of the treaty, the majority view would be the one incorporated into the draft treaty for discussion at the ministerial level. In most cases, the majority view would be that of the United States, Great Britain, France, and China. The Russians would be placed at a diplomatic disadvantage. Even if the Soviets rejected the "majority view," their refusal could be used to mobilize public opinion against the Soviet Union. Molotov, however, refused to be rushed into a decision. He noted it "was an interesting but new suggestion and he would like a day or two to consider it."[19]

Molotov's reply came two days later. He not only rejected the "majority view" of the deputies but sharply attacked the British and American position on Eastern Europe, reversed his support for French and Chinese participation in discussions on the treaties, and introduced the issue of American control over Japan. Before looking at Molotov's comments of September 22, however, it is necessary to review the unfolding of the American strategy on Eastern Europe.

Byrnes came to London intending to take a firm stand against Soviet policies in Eastern Europe and the Russian-supported regimes in Romania and Bulgaria. On September 13, he outlined his strategy to Bevin. He planned to introduce a proposal to create a special commission of inquiry to investigate political affairs and civil liberties in Eastern Europe. The commission would be composed of the representatives of the United States, Britain, France, and the Soviet Union and be responsible to the council. The Council of Foreign Ministers would act upon the recommendations of the commission. Bevin was at first hesitant but finally agreed to

18. *FR, 1945*, II, 191–92; Walter Brown's Book, September 15, 1945, in Byrnes Papers; John J. Stephan, *The Kuril Islands: Russo-Japanese Frontier in the Pacific* (Oxford, England, 1975), 156–61; *FR, 1945*, II, 193–94.

19. *FR, 1945*, II, 202–16, 225–36, 239–61.

support the formation and operation of the commission of inquiry. He offered to allow the commission to first investigate alleged political repression in Greece.[20]

Discussion of the peace treaties for Hungary, Romania, and Bulgaria began on September 12 when the Soviet Union introduced draft peace treaties. Within two days, Byrnes's advisers had carefully examined the drafts and found them unacceptable. Cavendish W. Cannon, James Dunn, Burton Berry, Maynard Barnes, and Leslie Squires "agreed that urgent steps would have to be taken to impress the Secretary and his advisers with the reality of the Soviet 'trap' and the necessity of preventing acceptance of the Soviet proposals." According to Squires, the problem with the treaties as written by the Russians was that they "would eliminate American participation in the reconstruction of the Balkans and would guarantee to the USSR an even more important role than her physical position and power would insure." Cannon explained to Byrnes that to accept the Soviet drafts would mean "the abandonment" of democracy and "equality of economic opportunity" throughout the region. Byrnes needed little convincing. On September 16, he told his close friend Walter Brown that "the time had come . . . to let Molotov know that the U.S. would remain firm in its stand on the Balkans."[21]

That same afternoon, Byrnes met with Molotov in private and raised the State Department's objections to the regimes in Romania and Bulgaria. Byrnes tried hard to assume the role of an objective, reasonable elder statesman. He assured the Soviet minister that the United States wanted only governments friendly to the Soviet Union on Russia's borders but added that he could find no reason why those friendly regimes could not also be truly representative. A solution to the political impasse in Romania was needed, and Byrnes suggested that the Polish precedent might be applied. Soviet aid in broadening the Romanian government, Byrnes said, would receive widespread congressional and public approval and would enhance the prestige of Russia around the globe.[22]

20. Foreign Office Minute of September 12, 1945, Meeting with Byrnes, September 16, 1945, R 15122/28/37, in FO 371, 1945, PRO.
21. Walter Brown's Book, September 16, 1945, in Byrnes Papers; Memorandum to Byrnes, September 14, 1945, in Council of Foreign Ministers London Notebook, Vol. II, pt. I, in Dulles Papers; FR, 1945, II, 182–85.
22. FR, 1945, II, 194–220.

Molotov was not moved by Byrnes's earnestness. He "categorically" rejected any attempt to reorganize the Romanian government. According to Molotov, the Polish example did not apply; if it were applied, "civil war" might result. As for Bulgaria, the Soviet Union had already "met the wishes of the United States and Great Britain" in postponing Bulgaria's national election.[23]

Byrnes was equally forceful, and he adopted a tougher position. He told Molotov that the United States "could not conclude treaties with the existing governments" of Romania and Bulgaria until they were truly representative. The Soviet minister concluded that Byrnes meant that the United States was unwilling to even consider the draft treaties before the council and lashed out at the secretary of state. American refusal to discuss the treaties would force the Soviets to think that the Americans wished "to see governments unfriendly to the Soviet Union" established in Romania and Bulgaria. Molotov emphasied that such a belief would create "a very bad impression . . . in wide circles of the Soviet public opinion."[24]

Before the meeting ended, Molotov also attacked the American proposal on Italy's colonies. Molotov claimed that former Secretary of State Edward Stettinius "had assured Ambassador Gromyko that the United States was prepared to support the Soviet Government in its request to receive a territory for administration under trusteeship." Therefore, Molotov was surprised when Byrnes rejected Moscow's request for a trusteeship over Tripolitania. Although Byrnes was aware of Stettinius' written commitment to "support in principle" Soviet administration of a trusteeship, the secretary stated he was unsure as to what Stettinius had said to the Soviet envoy. Byrnes added that he was sure that no specific area had been mentioned. Molotov agreed that the American pledge referred to no specific territory but pointed out that this council meeting "was the only opportunity" the Soviet Union had of getting a trusteeship. Russia was willing to accept any of the former Italian colonies, and it appeared, Molotov concluded, that "the United States did not wish the Soviet Union to have any territory under trusteeship."[25]

23. *Ibid.*, 194–97.
24. *Ibid.*, 195–200.
25. *Ibid.*, 200–202; State Department to Secretary Byrnes, September 26, 1945, in File 740.00119 (Council)/9–2645, DSR-NA; Foreign Office Memorandum, September 21, 1945, U 7839/51/70, in FO 371, 1945, PRO.

Byrnes left the meeting disheartened. Molotov had not wavered on the question of the Bulgarian and Romanian governments, and he had even confronted the United States on the issue of a Soviet trusteeship in Africa. Disheartenment turned to discouragement and gloom during the functions of the next day. Walter Brown recorded that the council meeting of the seventeenth of September was "a knock-down drag-out affair" and that "for the first time Molotov was critical of the U.S." Nor did the atmosphere improve that evening at a dinner party held at St. James's Palace. Pierson Dixon described the dinner as a "solemn masque." After the dinner, Byrnes "concluded that he had to talk to Stalin and have an understanding whether Russia was preparing for war or peace." Byrnes decided it would be best to finish the conference as soon as possible and arrange the next meeting in Moscow. Walter Brown stated that there "we can be close to Stalin and JFB could work on him."[26]

It was in this atmosphere that the secretary of state wrote a harshly worded preamble to the American amendment to the Russian draft treaties for Romania and Bulgaria. Byrnes was in a fiery temper and ignored Charles Bohlen's suggestion that the secretary write a "non-provocative" statement. Bohlen's view was supported by chief advisers Benjamin Cohen and John Foster Dulles. Dulles feared that a strongly worded protest against the two governments would "force a Soviet defense of Groza" and make the Soviet position even more rigid. Dulles personally doubted the "long-range efficacy of non-recognition."[27]

Byrnes rejected their advice and wrote a statement that reflected his determination to force the issue and his frustration at not being able to alter Molotov's positions. The preamble bluntly stated: "The United States will not negotiate a treaty of peace with Rumania until there has been established a government broadly representative of all democratic elements in the population and pledged to the earliest possible establishment through free elections of a government responsive to the will of the people, which can be recognized by the United States." Dulles commented that the wording

26. Walter Brown's Book, September 17, 1945, in Byrnes Papers; Dixon, *Double Diploma*, 184; Byrnes, *Speaking Frankly*, 106–107; Rose, *After Yalta*, 124–25.
27. "Reservations Regarding the Groza Government," undated, in Council of Foreign Ministers London Notebook, Vol. II, pt. I, in Dulles Papers.

directly attacked the Soviet Union and would only hinder relations between the Soviets and the Americans. Undeterred, the secretary of state prepared the statement for introduction at the next meeting of the council.[28]

Before the morning session of the September 19 meeting, Molotov visited the American delegation. He was worried that the United States would refuse to discuss the Eastern European treaties. Coldly, Byrnes assured him that he would discuss the treaties, although he repeated that the United States would not conclude the treaties until the Romanian and Bulgarian governments met American requirements. Irritated, Molotov told Byrnes that to the Soviet Union all of Hitler's allies looked the same and that if the United States "refused to sign the treaties with Rumania and Bulgaria the Soviet Union could not sign the treaty with Italy." Molotov also noted that "the present attitude of the U.S. Government was in distinction of that of President Roosevelt, who had been friendly to the Soviet Government." He left saying that if the secretary of state continued to believe "it necessary to express his views on the Government of Rumania," he would be forced to present the Soviet Union's views on United States policy toward Romania.[29]

Byrnes was not deterred by Molotov's tough talk. On September 19, Byrnes presented the American amendment and preamble to the Soviet draft treaties for Romania and Bulgaria. Molotov rose to the challenge: he "could not ignore" the position in the preamble and promised to respond later. Worried about Molotov's reply and hopeful of deflecting the Soviet counterattack, Byrnes visited the Soviet minister the next morning. He offered the Russians a twenty- or twenty-five year, four power treaty to demilitarize Germany. With Germany demilitarized and the United States willing to "rally to Russia in case of attack," the secretary of state argued, the Soviet Union would be better protected than if it relied on buffer states. Byrnes added that Truman's initial reaction to the plan was "favorable." Molotov grimly said that he could not speak for his

28. *FR, 1945,* II, 266; "Reservations Regarding the Groza Government," in Council of Foreign Ministers London Notebook, Vol. II, pt. I, in Dulles Papers.

29. *FR, 1945,* II, 243–47, 262, 266; Byrnes, *Speaking Frankly,* 98–100; "Reservations Regarding the Groza Government," in Council of Foreign Ministers London Notebook, Vol. II, pt. I, in Dulles Papers.

government but that personally he thought it was a very interesting idea. He promised to relay the proposal to officials in Moscow.[30]

The idea of a treaty to demilitarize Germany, however, did not reduce Molotov's anger about the United States statement on Romania and Bulgaria. He immediately returned to the subject. "He said he had the impression that the United States was seeking to oppose the Soviet Union in every way, and the note . . . was in effect a challenge directed against the Soviet Union, and to which he would be forced to reply." Byrnes argued it was not meant as "a challenge nor directed in any way against the Soviet Union" but only as a written record of what he had told Molotov in private. Molotov questioned whether it represented the same "spirit" as Byrnes's verbal statement and "asked why it had been necessary to put that statement in writing." He added that he must still defend the Romanian government and make a reply. Byrnes's Irish temper exploded: "Of course you can answer it and when you do, I will answer you. Do you understand that?" With that the secretary of state "picked up his hat and walked out." Later Byrnes spoke at length about the Soviet minister to his advisers: "M. was a semicolon figure, could not see the broad picture. . . . Unless M. was ousted he would lead Russia to the same fate that Hitler led Germany and Mussolini Italy."[31]

The Soviet reply to the American preamble on the Romanian and Bulgarian peace treaty came at the council meeting on September 21. A tension fell over the room. Molotov heatedly rejected the idea that the Romanian government was undemocratic. He suggested that the regime's friendly and close relations with the Soviet Union were the real reasons behind the American objections to the government. Molotov added that the Americans' failure to support Russia's request for a trusteeship further demonstrated their hostility toward the Soviet Union.[32]

Byrnes commented that the State Department's willingness to recognize the Hungarian government proved that the United States gladly accepted governments friendly to the Soviet Union—pro-

30. *FR, 1945,* II, 267–69, 276–77; Walter Brown's Book, September 20, 1945, in Byrnes Papers.

31. *FR, 1945,* II, 268–69; Byrnes, *Speaking Frankly,* 101; Walter Brown's Book, September 20, 1945, in Byrnes Papers.

32. Walter Brown's Book, September 20 and 21, 1945, in Byrnes Papers.

vided they were also representative. This had no effect on Molotov. The secretary again attempted to argue that the Soviets did not understand the nature of Stettinius' "pledge." According to Byrnes, the United States supported Russian eligibility for a trusteeship but not necessarily any specific requests. Reaching for an example, the secretary compared the Russian request to Britain's asking for a trusteeship over the sun and the moon. That, Byrnes boldly stated, the Americans would also oppose. Tongue in cheek, Bevin interjected that "British ambitions had never reached so high." Seeing the direction of the argument, Molotov pronounced he would "like to enjoy more sunshine." Byrnes retorted "that Mr. Molotov was responsible for most of the gloom at their meetings." The Soviet foreign minister shrugged and agreed to "share the blame fifty-fifty." He had no takers. After hearing the debate, Walter Brown grimly expressed the obvious: "A few short weeks after victory the two great powers of the world were clashing."[33] It did not augur well for a continuation of the Grand Alliance.

The afternoon meeting proved just as rancorous as the morning. Bevin began the diplomatic jabbing with contrasts between Greece and Romania and Bulgaria. He emphasized that, unlike the nations under Soviet control, the undemocratic nature of the Greek government was temporary and that free elections, open to inspection, would be held soon. Bevin continued by saying that there was freedom of press in Greece and that, unlike in Romania, reporters were free to go wherever they wanted.

Molotov expressed shock and dismay, and he informed Bevin that Western reporters were roaming freely throughout Romania reporting the facts. Having recently spoken with Burton Berry, who complained of restraints on the Western press, Byrnes questioned Molotov's assertion. Perhaps on cue, Bevin broke in to suggest a solution to the question of press freedom in Romania: the formation of "a Commission to examine the whole problem on the spot and make recommendations to the Council for decision." Byrnes rapidly seconded Bevin's proposal. Molotov would have none of it. He said there were enough commissions loose in Romania already. The ministers from France and China voiced their

33. *FR, 1945*, II, 290–98; Byrnes, *Speaking Frankly*, 101–102; Walter Brown's Book, September 21, 1945, in Byrnes Papers.

support for the commission of inquiry, but Stonebottom Molotov proved immovable. Bevin gave up—"agreement was apparently impossible."[34]

The next morning, September 22, the Soviets informed the American delegation by telephone that the Russian delegation would miss the morning session of the council. Minutes later, the Soviet embassy telephoned again and invited Byrnes to a private meeting with Molotov at half past eleven. The Americans immediately "went into a huddle," pondering the meaning of the Russian absence from the scheduled seventeenth meeting as well as the invitation to the secretary of state. Did it mean that Molotov was ready to modify his Eastern European policy? Or did it mean that the Russians were withdrawing from the meeting? The majority of advisers decided that Molotov "had decided to withdraw from the Conference."[35] They were wrong.

When the secretary of state arrived at his meeting with Molotov, he soon discovered that the Soviet Union was not going to withdraw from the conference. The opposite was true. Molotov insisted that the future of Japan be opened as a topic of debate. He said that it appeared to the Soviet Union that the United States was not punishing Japan severely enough to prevent a recrudescence of Japanese aggression. To correct the delinquency, he suggested a joint Soviet and American treaty similar to the one Byrnes proposed for Germany. Before the secretary could reply, James Dunn, who had accompanied Byrnes to the meeting, reminded both ministers that the Far Eastern Advisory Commission was the proper place for the Soviet Union and others to discuss Japan and the Far East. Molotov, not interested in going to the American-dominated advisory commission, asked the United States to support a Soviet request for the formation of an Allied Control Council for Japan. It was an "embarrassing situation" for the secretary of state, and he attempted to back away from the issue quietly by telling Molotov that the subject was not on the agenda and that he could not possibly discuss the question until he consulted with officials in Washington and Tokyo. Unimpressed, Molotov officially called for the creation

34. *FR, 1945*, II, 300–310.
35. Walter Brown's Book, September 22, 1945, in Byrnes Papers.

of the Allied Control Council for Japan during the September 24 meeting. He stated that the matter was "urgent."[36]

As Molotov may have known, Byrnes had not been totally honest with the Soviet foreign minister. Ten days earlier, without consultation with American and Japanese officials, Byrnes had started discussions on the Japanese issue with the British. Like Molotov, Bevin wanted to form an Allied Control Council. The Foreign Office had wanted to place the issue on the agenda but had been dissuaded by a cautious Bevin, who wanted to speak with Byrnes first. On September 12, Bevin forwarded a "personal and confidential" message to the secretary of state reminding him of Britain's proposal in August for an Allied Control Council. Bevin requested a "personal discussion" on the subject. Four days later, during an official reception at Chequers, Bevin got a short reply: "American plans for the control of Japan had been shaped not to give away to the claims of the Russians, who wished Japan to be divided into zones." J. C. Sterndale Bennett, the Foreign Office's director of far eastern affairs, considered the reply "a plausible enough answer." However, he warned that it was equally possible that Byrnes was telling the Soviets that American plans were designed "to avoid some difficulty with us."[37]

Molotov's request for discussion of Japanese affairs prompted Byrnes to open talks with Bevin on the issue. For four days, from September 24 to 28, Byrnes "put strong pressure" on the British "to agree forthwith" to the Far Eastern Advisory Commission and abandon the idea of an Allied Control Council. The secretary of state employed arguments ranging from the need for harmony between Britain and America in the face of Russian intentions to suggestions that the British loan might be affected by the Foreign Office's stand on the issue of control over Japan.[38]

36. Memorandum of Conversation Between Byrnes and Molotov, September 22, 1945, London Conference Notebook, Walter Brown's Book, September 22, 1945, both in Byrnes Papers; Feis, *Contest Over Japan*, 36–38; Byrnes, *Speaking Frankly*, 102; Dixon, *Double Diploma*, 185; FR, *1945*, II, 336–39.

37. J. C. Sterndale Bennett's Notes of September 12, 1945, Foreign Office Memorandum, September 29, 1945, F 6699/364/23, Memorandum of Conversation Between Bevin and Byrnes, September 16, 1945, F 7090/364/23, Comment by Sterndale Bennett, September 18, 1945, F 7090/364/23, all in FO 371, 1945, PRO.

38. Foreign Office Memorandum, September 29, 1945, F 6699/364/23, in FO 371, 1945, PRO.

On September 25, Bevin explained the issue to the cabinet at a special meeting. He informed the cabinet that "it would be most difficult to resist this pressure without serious reactions on various questions of high policy . . . weighing on Anglo-American relations." The foreign secretary suggested three alternatives: join the Far Eastern Advisory Commission but stipulate that it be transferred to Japan and given some executive functions; join the commission with an amendment referring any divergent views to the Council of Foreign Ministers; or join the commission but demand a strong, independent political representative in Japan with a large staff. The cabinet gave Bevin full discretion on the matter, although it recommended that he support Byrnes's rejection of the Soviet attempt to place the subject of Japan on the agenda.[39]

On the afternoon of September 25, Bevin followed the cabinet's suggestion and forcefully supported his American colleague in keeping the Russian proposal off the agenda. By the following afternoon, Sterndale Bennett was fashioning an agreement with the Americans. The United States was willing to move the headquarters of the Far Eastern Advisory Commission to Japan and increase its executive function. In turn, the British agreed to join the commission. But when the British asked Byrnes to put the agreement in writing, the secretary of state balked. Concerned about the Russian reaction if word of the agreement leaked, Byrnes asked Britain to "trust" the United States to keep its part of the bargain. Reluctantly the British agreed.[40]

Even as the British were joining the commission, Byrnes was working to keep the Soviets from leaving it. He blamed the inactivity of the commission on the British refusal to participate. He sought to buy Soviet membership on the commission by implying that once it was operating, he would personally favor the formation of an Allied Control Council. Molotov remained stubborn. The Soviet minister repeated that the question of the council "was very urgent and essential" to his government and that it should immediately be added to the agenda.[41] Molotov wanted to institute an

39. *FR, 1945,* II, 360–70; Foreign Office Memorandum, September 29, 1945, F 6699/364/23, in FO 371, 1945, PRO.
40. Bevin to Byrnes, September 28, 1945, F 7613/364/23, Foreign Office Memorandum, September 29, 1945, F 6699/364/23, both in FO 371, 1945, PRO.
41. *FR, 1945,* II, 418–21.

Allied Control Council for Japan; Byrnes wanted to exclude the question of Japan altogether from the meeting. Neither was to have his way. For the rest of the conference, the issue of Allied control over Japan remained a stumbling block hindering the successful conclusion of the meeting.

However, Japan was not the issue that destroyed the effectiveness of the conference. Nor was it the only subject Molotov had on his mind when he called Byrnes to the private meeting on September 22. To the secretary of state's surprise, Bevin arrived at the Soviet embassy at noon. Bevin, too, had been invited. With Bevin present, Molotov announced that his government would refuse to participate further in the foreign ministers' sessions unless France and China were excluded from debating the peace treaties for Romania, Bulgaria, and Hungary. Molotov's action reversed Byrnes's opening day maneuver and threatened the existence of the council.[42]

Bevin's and Byrnes's initial reactions reflected their personalities. More direct and blunt, Bevin heatedly told Molotov that he could not accept the Soviet position on the exclusion of France from the discussions about the European treaties. Facing Stonebottom, Bevin thundered that the real problem confronting the conference was "the philosophy and attitude of the Soviet Government." More diplomatic and loquacious, Byrnes lectured Molotov that the spirit of the Potsdam agreement allowed those interested in the matter to be present. If they were present, Byrnes continued, it logically followed that they be allowed to speak. "Some headway had already been made" on the treaties with France and China participating. He saw no reason why they should alter the present arrangement.[43]

Molotov remained steadfast. Bevin, seeing that neither anger nor logic was going to change the Russian's mind, offered a compromise. He asked whether a special committee of the five deputies, composed of representatives of those nations that were signatory to the armistice and directed to write the treaties, would be acceptable to the Soviet Union. Such a compromise, Bevin said, would meet Soviet demands that the drafting be done by those nations

42. Foreign Office Memorandum of Conversation Among Bevin, Byrnes, and Molotov, September 22, 1945, U 7384/5559/70, in FO 371, 1945, PRO; Dixon, *Double Diploma*, 185; Dilks, *The Diaries of Cadogan*, 785.

43. *FR, 1945*, II, 313–15; Foreign Office Memorandum, September 22, 1945, U 7384/5559/70, in FO 371, 1945, PRO; Byrnes, *Speaking Frankly*, 102–103.

specified by the Berlin Protocol and allow the deputies of all five powers the opportunity to provide guidance. He offered a compromise, the British foreign minister explained, only "in the hope of making for unity and avoiding a division in European affairs." Molotov replied that he was just as anxious to promote European unity but that he still must reject the plan. Bevin exploded. His Majesty's government held that the unanimous decision of September 11 allowed the French and Chinese to participate in discussing all the peace treaties and that the decision was binding on all parties until all five council members agreed to change it. Unshaken, Molotov offered a different view of the council's unanimity: "the Council could only proceed by agreement between all members." He further stated that until the Soviet government received "satisfaction," the Soviet delegation would be absent from all council meetings. At an impasse, the three ministers agreed to break for lunch and return in two hours.[44]

During the break, Byrnes met with Benjamin Cohen and Walter Brown. He expressed his concerns over Molotov's actions. He noted that the Russians were correct in their interpretation of the Potsdam agreement on writing the peace treaties. France and China had no right to participate in discussions of the treaties for Eastern Europe. Because the Russians were correct about the procedural point, blaming them for the breakup of the conference would be nearly impossible.

Of equal importance, Byrnes believed, was the possibility of France's reaction. If France, a major power, were to remain aloof from the United States camp, a wedge would be driven between the Western European Allies. Also, if France and China were not treated as equals on the council, the same treatment might be accorded them on the Security Council of the United Nations. Molotov's position was well-prepared and fraught with disastrous consequences for the United States.[45]

Cohen, fearing Soviet obstructionism more than French reactions, suggested that Byrnes concede the exclusion of France and China. To soothe French and Chinese feelings, Cohen thought the

44. *FR, 1945,* II, 313–14.
45. *Ibid.,* 329; Walter Brown's Book, September 22, 1945, in Byrnes Papers; Byrnes, *Speaking Frankly,* 102; Harry S Truman, *Years of Decision* (Garden City, N.Y., 1955), 567–69.

secretary might stress that all peace treaties would eventually face final approval by all members of the United Nations. Byrnes rejected Cohen's suggestion and contacted the White House to ask Truman to intercede with Stalin to reverse Molotov's position. Truman was absent from Washington, but Admiral William Leahy agreed to forward the request to the president.[46]

Meanwhile, the afternoon session of September 22 proved no more productive. Bevin again offered his compromise. This time he received Byrnes's full and immediate support. Molotov continued to demand French and Chinese exclusion and to hold to the literal interpretation of the Berlin Protocol. Seeing that the discussion was getting nowhere, Byrnes suggested that the ministers consult with their heads of state to find a solution to the impasse. All agreed. Molotov, however, warned that he was acting under Stalin's direct instructions to bar France and China. Until the matter was resolved, the ministers agreed to discuss issues other than the peace treaties.[47]

Within the British and American delegations almost everyone had an explanation as to why Molotov had reversed his earlier position. Few officials, if any, believed that the role of France and China in discussing the treaties was the real problem. Most thought that the Soviet minister's actions were merely another example of the Soviet method of negotiation whereby point after contested point was added until the opponents willingly conceded in order to resume meaningful discussions.

The real point of debate in both the American and British delegations was deciding what concessions the Soviets were seeking. Byrnes and most of the United States delegation believed that the Russians wanted American approval of the regimes in Romania and Bulgaria. Ambassador Harriman informed the secretary of state that "Molotov's objective is now clear." According to Harriman, the Soviets' chief objective at the conference was to obtain British and American recognition of the governments of Romania and Bulgaria. But when the Soviet minister found France, Britain, China, and the United States working together on the issue of East-

46. Truman, *Years of Decision*, 567–70; *FR, 1945*, II, 329.

47. Foreign Office Memorandum of Conversation Among Bevin, Byrnes, and Molotov, September 22, 1945, U 7384/5559/70, in FO 371, 1945, PRO; *FR, 1945*, II, 313–15; Dixon, *Double Diploma*, 185; Byrnes, *Speaking Frankly*, 102–103.

ern Europe, he had to do something to break up the bloc. By refusing to allow French and Chinese participation, Harriman concluded, Molotov was attempting to get the negotiations "transferred to Moscow." He added that Molotov's position regarding an Allied Control Council for Japan was designed "to divert attention from his unilateral action in the Balkans to our unilateral action in the Pacific." Most of the American delegation accepted Harriman's explanation, and no one in the delegation believed that the Russians really wanted to break off discussions with their Western Allies.[48]

Byrnes's reaction was to play Molotov at his own game. "He is waiting him out," noted Walter Brown. Waiting Molotov out meant offering no solutions until Truman and Stalin exchanged notes and evaluated responses. If Stalin was supporting his foreign minister, Byrnes intended to suggest an alternative he believed more distasteful to the Soviets than a five-member council. Byrnes instructed Cohen and Dulles to write a proposal calling for a general peace conference that would include representatives from all states interested in the peace treaties. "We offered them five and they would not take it," he exclaimed, "now we will give them 50." The secretary privately informed the Soviets that the State Department now had full control over the disposition of the Soviet Union's request for postwar credits. Byrnes believed that firmness, pressure, and patience were the best ways to deal with Molotov and make the Soviets more reasonable.[49]

In Washington, Truman was dismayed by the London deadlock. In a wire to the Foreign Office, Lord Halifax stated that during a meeting with Truman, "The President was frankly fogged as to what had apparently so soon and so darkly clouded the atmosphere of Potsdam." Truman gave the British envoy his views on Soviet reactions to the British and American objections to the governments in Romania and Bulgaria. "The Russians who did not

48. Byrnes, *Speaking Frankly*, 105; Dixon, *Double Diploma*, 189; John Foster Dulles, *War or Peace* (New York, 1950), 25–26; Memorandum for Secretary of State, September 28, 1945, in Council of Foreign Ministers London Notebook, Vol. II, pt. 2, in Dulles Papers.

49. Walter Brown's Book, September 24 and 28, 1945, in Byrnes Papers; *FR, 1945*, II, 331, 334; Foreign Office Memorandum, September 26, 1945, N 12728/20/38, in FO 371, 1945, PRO.

understand much about elections anyway, were inclined to suspect some sinister purpose in our minds when we appeared to favor a substitution of the Governments in Roumania and Bulgaria, admitted authentic to Soviet, by something . . . less friendly; and presumably not understanding the way our minds worked in this field, they cast about for some explanation of interest thus inconveniently exhibited by us in a sphere of direct influence to them and sought to offset it by themselves showing interests in spheres of more direct interest to us."[50]

Like the Americans, the British were evaluating Molotov's actions. Orme Sargent linked the Russian's behavior to recent attacks in the Soviet press on the possible formation of a Western bloc. Sargent concluded that the procedural point was designed less to gain British and American acceptance of the governments of Romania and Bulgaria than to divide the Western allies over France's postwar position. Such a maneuver, if successful, he told his colleagues, would reduce France to a second-class power, destroy any chance of a Western bloc, and possibly isolate Britain from the United States. Sargent believed that Great Britain should continue to support France's right to participate in European affairs even if American support soon faded.

Pierson Dixon agreed with Sargent that the Russians had "skillfully chosen" the procedural question "to drive a wedge between us and the French," but he believed that the "main objective" was to gain access to the Mediterranean by forcing the Western Allies to accept a Russian trusteeship in Africa. Alexander Cadogan, permanent undersecretary of state, reviewed Dixon's views and decided that Russia's claim as a trustee for Tripolitania was merely a "retort to Anglo-American claims to interfere in Russian interests nearer at home." Thus there was divergent opinion on Soviet goals among the British, but no divergence as to what they must do. Britain must support France, as Britain was "not in a position to lose more friends."[51]

On September 25, Bevin told the cabinet that the Soviets' proce-

50. Lord Halifax to Foreign Office, September 25, 1945, U 7478/5559/70, in FO 371, 1945, PRO.
51. Memorandum by Sir Orme Sargent, September 22, 1945, N 13100/20/38, Pierson Dixon, "Possible Soviet Tactics at London," September 24, 1945, N 13101/20/38, both in FO 371, 1945, PRO; Dixon, Double Diploma, 189–90.

dural point was not the cause of the impasse. Rather, it was only part of a Soviet plan to "oppose any proposals which might affect the territories within what they regard as their zone of influence." Faced with "increasing hostility and distrust between the United States and the Soviet Delegations, each of whom sought to strengthen its own position without regard to our point of view," Bevin recommended ending the London conference.

The British cabinet accepted the foreign minister's evaluation of Soviet actions and his recommendation to end the meeting. As for relations between Britain and the United States, the cabinet instructed Bevin to tell the Americans that "it was impossible . . . to work with them if they constantly took action in the international sphere, affecting our interests, without prior consultations."[52] The British delegation was tired of American unilateralism as well as Soviet obstructionism.

Diplomatic swordplay over the procedural question continued until the conference ended on October 2. On September 26, Byrnes informally presented the proposal drafted by Dulles and Cohen. It specified that the peace treaties would be written as mandated by the Berlin Protocol but strongly recommended that a general peace conference be called to discuss the proposed peace treaties. While both Bevin and Molotov agreed to consider the plan, Molotov privately told Bevin that he believed the scheme unsuitable. The Soviet minister added he believed the dispute "was 'an artificial pretext' to set the French against the Russians."[53]

Over the next three days, Byrnes and Molotov sparred, offering several proposals and modified proposals. This accomplished little except increased aggravation. By September 30, the procedural point impinged on the writing of the protocol and final communiqué. Having agreed to end the conference, the ministers could not agree on the words to announce its termination. Molotov flatly refused to accept any statements that included what he called the "error" of September 11. Bevin was equally stubborn in demanding that the decision of the eleventh that allowed France and China to discuss the peace treaties remain part of the record. At one point he

52. Extract of Cabinet Conclusions, 34 (45), September 25, 1945, U 7479/5559/70, in FO 371, 1945, PRO.
53. Record of Conversation Between Bevin and Molotov, October 1, 1945, N 13613/13/38, in FO 371, 1945, PRO.

lashed out at Molotov, calling the Russian's actions "the nearest thing to the Hitler theory I have ever heard." According to Walter Brown, "Molotov went pale and blotchy and got up and walked to the door, saying that he had been insulted." Regaining self-control, Bevin diplomatically called out that if he had "said anything offensive" he withdrew it and apologized. Molotov, who was walking slowly, returned to his seat and continued his speech in his usual cool and precise manner.[54]

Later, Bevin suggested a course of action for Molotov to follow: "As Secretary of State for Foreign Affairs of Great Britain, if I entered into that agreement on September 11 with other Foreign Ministers, and then sought to go back on it in any way, there is only one course open to me in this country, and that is for me to resign." Molotov had no intention of resigning and ignored the verbal blast. Instead, he accused Bevin of engaging in a conspiracy designed to invalidate the Berlin Protocol by enlarging the responsibilities of some of the council's members.[55]

While Bevin and Molotov argued, Byrnes searched for suitable language for the protocol that would permit its publication and retain the September 11 agreement. Byrnes reasoned with Molotov that the protocol was only a statement of events; the decision of September 11 was an event, and, therefore, it was only correct to include it in the protocol. At one point he mentioned that Molotov had not made a motion to invalidate the decision but had only protested it. He asked Molotov to say exactly when the Soviet Union officially asked the Council of Foreign Ministers to reject or revoke the disputed decision. Molotov seemed flustered but continued to state that an error had been made and that it would have to be corrected before he could sign anything.[56]

Those watching the spectacle agreed that lawyer Byrnes was getting the best of Stonebottom Molotov. Pierson Dixon wrote that "Byrnes, in his element in these legalistic points, grows steadier and steadier." Still, Molotov seemed unmovable. Finally, the chairman of the council, Shih-chieh Wang, broke in to ask that the closing date for the conference be set for October 2. He added that he

54. FR, 1945, II, 417–27, 440–47, 482–85; Dixon, Double Diploma, 191–92.
55. FR, 1945, II, 496–505.
56. Ibid.; Walter Brown's Book, September 30, 1945, in Byrnes Papers.

hoped the conferees would try very hard to resolve the procedural issue before that date.[57]

Bevin took Wang's request to heart. Meeting with his advisers during the night of September 30, he devised a ten-point program that he hoped would mollify Molotov into admitting France as a full council member. This meant giving the Soviets what they wanted in Eastern Europe. As members of the Foreign Office saw it, the major obstacle would be the United States. If the Americans "could be brought into line about the Roumanian and Bulgarian Governments," a compromise with Molotov was possible.[58]

Bevin met with Byrnes at two o'clock in the afternoon of October 1. He tried to have the secretary of state withdraw the American reservation to the Romanian and Bulgarian peace treaties, agree to a "guarantee of elections to be held on the same line as Finland," and pledge immediate United States recognition of the two governments after the elections. Byrnes asked, "Who was to say whether in fact the elections . . . would be on the lines of Finland?" Bevin, knowing that there was only the remotest chance that elections in either Romania or Bulgaria would be free or fair, smiled and told Byrnes that they must "be prepared to exchange one set of crooks for another."[59]

Byrnes was unwilling to accept any elections in Romania that would deny Iuliu Maniu and Constantin Bratianu cabinet posts. He demanded, as the price of his support, that Bevin amend the British proposal to include a provision that "an independent enquiry" verify the conduct and results of the elections. He also categorically refused to withdraw the American reservation from the Bulgarian and Romanian peace treaties. As Bevin left, Byrnes noted the obvious: he saw "little chance" of a compromise being accepted by the Soviets.[60]

Byrnes destroyed Bevin's compromise because of three interrelated considerations. First, he still hoped the Russians would accept the proposal he made on September 26. Second, he believed reports from United States officials in Romania and Bulgaria that

57. FR, 1945, II, 506–507; Dixon, Double Diploma, 191.
58. Foreign Office Memorandum, October 1, 1945, U 7669/5559/70, in FO 371, 1945, PRO.
59. Ibid.
60. Ibid.

the Communist regimes were near collapse and would soon be forced to broaden their governments and ask the United States for economic and political assistance. Third, John Foster Dulles threatened to play partisan politics if the secretary dared to alter his position on Eastern Europe. On the morning of September 30, Byrnes told Dulles that he might adopt a recommendation made by Benjamin Cohen and accept Molotov's procedural point without waiting for a positive Soviet reply to his request for a general peace conference. Dulles very forcefully argued against Cohen's idea. He said that "if Byrnes attempted such a move he would telephone Vandenberg and have the secretary denounced on the Senate floor."[61] Dulles' threat effectively killed Cohen's and Bevin's compromises.

Bevin's meeting with Molotov achieved nothing. After reading the proposal, complete with Byrnes's amendments, the Soviet minister dismissed it. France could not be an equal partner, as France had no army and must be given time to recover and to get stronger. As for Romania and Bulgaria, the Soviet Union recognized the democratic and representative regimes in both nations. The Soviet Union was quite willing to wait for the moment when the United States and Britain recognized them as well.

Molotov then turned the discussion to Italy's African colonies and the Soviet request for a trusteeship. He offered a diplomatic and territorial deal: all of Cyrenaica as a British trusteeship in exchange for only "a corner" of Tripolitania. "After all," he said, "a Russian trusteeship for ten years would do no harm." Bevin disagreed, ending the discussion. Bevin returned to the Foreign Office determined to conclude the conference as soon as possible.[62]

Before the London conference ended, however, there was one more significant diplomatic riposte. The occasion was an official party held at the Soviet embassy. During the party, Molotov seemed to take special pleasure in baiting Bevin on events in Greece, British predominance in the Mediterranean, and a possible Soviet trusteeship over the Belgian Congo. The climax came late in the evening, just as Bevin was leaving. "You know we have the atomic bomb," Molotov blurted out.

61. Dulles, *War or Peace*, 29–30; Transcript of Theodore Achilles Interview, John Foster Dulles Oral History Project, in Dulles Papers.
62. Record of Conversation between Bevin and Molotov, October 1, 1945, N 13613/18/38, in FO 371, 1945, PRO; Dixon, *Double Diploma*, 193–94.

In stunned silence, the former merrymakers watched as Soviet Ambassador Fedor Gousev placed his hand on Molotov's shoulder and hurried the minister from the room. As the British and American guests left the embassy they could only guess as to the reason for Molotov's unexpected and uncharacteristic behavior. Bevin did not think it was possible for the Soviets to possess an atomic bomb, but when the boast was added to the Soviets' earlier interest in the Belgian Congo, the source of uranium for the United States and Britain, he grew more worried.[63]

Byrnes told Ambassador John Winant that "whether this incident was all prearranged, or just a slip of the tongue was not known, but it is more likely just another attempt upon the part of the Russians to instill the impression upon the rest of the peoples of the world that they too have the bomb." Still, the secretary of state was concerned. Later he expressed his fears to the State-War-Navy Coordinating Committee.[64]

At 7:25 P.M., on October 2, 1945, the London Conference of the Council of Foreign Ministers quietly ended. After a full day of attempting to find suitable and acceptable language for the protocol and final communiqué, Chairman Wang finally asked if anyone wanted a meeting the following day. When no one responded, he formally closed the conference.[65] The foreign ministers, tired of bickering and looking for agreements that left sacrosanct their principles and interests, simply quit trying and marched down the hall to Bevin's office to toast the end of the meeting with champagne.

The London conference was to have started a new era of postwar international harmony and peace. By October 3, it appeared that the achievement of a continuation of the Grand Alliance was far, far away. Instead, the beginnings of a divided world could be seen. The Grand Alliance was breaking apart, and all three partners were to

63. Colonel H. K. Calvert to General L. Groves, November 13, 1945, in Folder 20, Manhattan Project Files, 1942–46, in Manhattan Engineer District Files, NA. Hugh Dalton heard Molotov differently: "Here's to the Atom Bomb! . . . We've got it." Dalton Diary, October 17, 1945, in Dalton Papers.

64. Dalton Diary, October 17, 1945, in Dalton papers; Colonel H. K. Calvert to General L. Groves, November 13, 1945, in Folder 20, Manhattan Project Files, 1942–46, in Manhattan Engineer District Files, NA; Rose, After Yalta, 131; Walter Millis and E. S. Duffield (eds.), The Forrestal Diaries (New York, 1951), 101–103.

65. FR, 1945, II, 544–55.

blame. Representing the world's strongest nation, the American secretary of state from the beginning attempted to dominate the meeting. Using the Soviet Union as a bogeyman, Byrnes successfully convinced Bevin to accept the United States' plans for Italy's colonies and Japan and not to oppose the American stance toward the governments of Romania and Bulgaria. In return, Britain received little except the assurance that its request for a loan was not prejudiced.

Molotov, however, refused to be intimidated by the United States, by the American monopoly over atomic energy and postwar credits, or by Byrnes's firm position against recognizing Romania and Bulgaria. Characteristically, Molotov had counterattacked, noting the obvious double standard the United States applied in formulating policies in Japan and Eastern Europe. Finally, the Soviet minister deadlocked the conference on a procedural point that had grave consequences.

Between Byrnes and Molotov there was not the slightest hint of compromise. Bevin had learned that on October 1, when Byrnes demanded changes in Bevin's ten-point proposal. Members of the Foreign Office blamed the American for Molotov's rejection of the proposal and the demise of the conference, and British statesmen worried that Bevin's support of American programs served to undermine Britain's credibility as an independent power. As Bevin told Pierson Dixon shortly after the London conference, "If we are not careful our victory in war may lead to us being plucked by our Allies." [66]

66. Foreign Office Memorandum, October 1, 1945, U 7669/5559/70, Foreign Office Minute, October 22, 1945, N 15653/13/38, both in FO 371, 1945, PRO.

V

Repairing the Grand Alliance

T HE LONDON CONFERENCE was a diplomatic setback for the
major powers, threatening the unity and operation of the Grand
Alliance and the possibility of a stable postwar settlement. Each
foreign minister left London anxious to evaluate the others' behavior and to confer with advisers and heads of state. Serious questions needed to be considered. Did the breach in the Grand Alliance mean the United Nations would be stillborn? Would the
United States and the Soviet Union revert back to prewar isolationism? Would Britain be alone in contesting the power of the Soviet Union? Would further pressure be placed on the Soviet Union
to reduce its influence in Eastern Europe?

Secretary of State James F. Byrnes returned to Washington embar-
rassed and fearful. He was "'almost ashamed' for having taken
what he did from Molotov." He was worried that the failure to win
concessions in London might weaken his control over foreign policy. Herbert L. Matthews reported in the New York *Times* that some
members of the American delegation worried that the failure in
London would encourage isolationists. Upon his return, however,
Byrnes found little pressure for a return to isolationism. Instead, he
found himself caught between statesmen like Senator Arthur Vandenberg, Admiral William Leahy, and Secretary of the Navy James

Forrestal, who wanted a tougher policy toward Russia, and those like Secretary of Commerce Henry Wallace, Rexford Tugwell, and Joseph Davies, who blamed Byrnes for the failure of the conference. Davies thought Byrnes was too insensitive to the fears and needs of the Soviets. Tugwell wrote in his diary that "Byrnes seems to have made a failure of the conference. . . . Evidently the Russians are scared by our possession of the bomb and exaggerated demands, etc."[1]

Byrnes weathered the storm of criticism and maintained control of foreign policy. A Gallup Poll found that only 14 percent of the nation believed Republicans could conduct better foreign policy. 88 percent of the editorial comment in American newspapers applauded Byrnes's actions in London and his conduct of foreign policy. The Senate Foreign Relations Committee and the cabinet gave him a vote of confidence. Truman continued to refer questions of foreign policy to Byrnes and to accept his views.[2]

More worrisome than domestic reaction to the events in London were possible changes in Soviet foreign policy. The London debacle provided the Soviets an excellent opportunity to change the focus of their foreign policy away from international cooperation and toward more dangerous options. From Moscow, George Kennan wired on October 4 that a return to Leninist "isolationism" was possible. He believed that Russian adherence to such a policy would force the return of an unflexible system of power blocs. In a world divided into such blocs, the effectiveness of the United Nations would be destroyed and the chances of another global war increased.[3]

Other State Department officials doubted that the Soviet Union

---

1. Gaddis, *The US and the Origins of the Cold War,* 266–67; Acheson, *Present at the Creation,* 125; New York *Times,* October 2, 1945, Sec. 1, p. 6; Balfour to Foreign Office, October 12, 1945, AN 3111/35/45, in FO 371, 1945, PRO; Rexford Tugwell Diary, October 11, 1945, in Rexford Tugwell Papers, Franklin D. Roosevelt Library, Hyde Park.

2. Byrnes, *All in One Lifetime,* 357–60; Harold J. Sylwester, "American Public Reaction to Communist Expansion From Yalta to NATO" (Ph.D. dissertation, University of Kansas, 1970), 125; *Twohey Analysis of American Editorial Opinion,* October 6 and 13, 1945; George H. Gallup, *The Gallup Poll: Public Opinion, 1935–1971* (New York, 1972), I, 513.

3. Kennan to State Department, October 4, 1945, in File 740.00119 (Council)/10–445, DSR-NA; *FR, 1945,* V, 881–91; New York *Times,* October 7, 1945, Sec. 1, p. 8.

would return to isolationism. Rather, they feared that the Soviets would withdraw from international diplomacy and cooperation and embark upon a unilateral policy designed to increase Soviet influence where it already existed and extend it into areas where it did not. Europe and Asia provided excellent opportunities for the expansion of Soviet and Communist influence. A November State-War-Navy Coordinating Committee report expressed doubts as to whether the United States could counter "Russian methods of political infiltration" in Asia. It stressed the United States' basic disadvantage:

> Because of their different political traditions, methods and ideological sympathies, the United States and the USSR are almost automatically inclined to sympathize and deal with different native factions . . . even where objectives are much the same. The United States leans toward propertied classes who place a premium on order and trade. This element constitutes a small fraction of native peoples, which although in the forefront of movements for national independence and economic expansion, usually oppose popular democracy and social reform. The Soviet Union favors non-propertied disenfranchised elements—the satisfaction of whose reasonable demands is the only source of long-range stability and progress in the Far East.

Other evaluations indicated the possibility of Communist gains in Western Europe during the winter and a tightening of Soviet control in Eastern Europe.[4]

Byrnes feared the possibility of both isolationism and expansionism on the part of the Soviets. He favored tactics designed to assure the Russian, British, and American people of the United States' willingness to continue with international cooperation while, at the same time, demonstrating its strength and commitment to principles. The effort would take place on a variety of public and private levels, utilizing a full range of diplomatic means. Time, however, was of the essence. A solution to the diplomatic stalemate had to be found before the United Nations met in January, 1946. Boosting Byrnes's confidence that such an approach

4. Meeting of Secretaries of War, State, Navy, October 10, 1945, in File 740.00119 EW/10–1045, DSR-NA; SWNCC Memorandum, PR-33, "Political and Military Problems in the Far East," November 29, 1945, in Byrnes Papers; *FR, 1945,* V, 337, 620–24; Winant to State Department, October 18, 1945, in File 761.00/10–1845, DSR-NA.

would work were reports from Moscow during the second week of October indicating that Stalin was still interested in the Grand Alliance.

As the London conference broke up, harsh statements emanated from the Soviets. An editorial in *Izvestia* on October 4 stated that if the Western Allies continued in their attitude toward the Soviet Union, they would "shake the very basis of collaboration among the Three Powers." The "seriousness" of the London setback should not be "underestimated," the editorial warned. The Soviet press further fixed the blame for the conference's failure squarely on the two pawns of Western reactionary forces, Byrnes and Bevin. But on October 6, *Pravda* reversed the Soviet line and stressed the positive results of the conference. Kennan noted the sharp contradictions. "Most striking differences between editorials is their conclusions. Pessimistic and threatening note of *Izvestya's* last two paragraphs . . . is replaced in *Pravda* by evocation of successful collaboration of Foreign Ministers at . . . Conference." Kennan suggested that *Pravda's* position left the "door open for possible future settlement of disputed issues." He noted that this was the first time "in which editorials . . . have differed so substantially."[5]

Western observers offered two explanations about the contradiction in the Soviet press. Most believed that Molotov, in his attempt to drive a wedge between the Western powers, had miscalculated and "committed himself so far . . . he was unable to withdraw without losing face." In Moscow, however, the breakup of the London conference came as a "disagreeable surprise," but Soviet leaders decided that "such ups and downs were inevitable in international negotiations." It was believed that as a result, Stalin had overruled Molotov's position. Supporting this thesis was Molotov's November 7 speech that emphasized Russia's commitment to international diplomacy and acknowledged the ups and downs of diplomacy.[6]

5. Jonathan Knight, "Russia's Search for Peace: The London Conference of Foreign Ministers, 1945," *Journal of Contemporary History*, XIII (1978), 155–56; Kennan to State Department, October 4, 1945, in File 740.00119 (Council)/10–445, DSR-NA; Kennan to State Department, October 8, 1945, in File 500, Moscow Post Files, DSR-Suitland, Md.; New York *Times*, October 6, 1945, Sec. 1, p. 2.

6. Foreign Office Minute, October 6, 1945, N 13432/18/32, Foreign Office to Lord Halifax, October 6, 1945, U 7856/5559/70, Roberts to Foreign Office, October 24, 1945, N 14705/18/38, all in FO 371, 1945, PRO.

Kennan offered another opinion. He believed that the Soviet leadership was so "dangerously ingrown and remote" from the Russian people that it could not survive a sudden and unexpected break with its wartime allies. He suggested that such a break would be a "direct source of deep disappointment" for the Russian people and shake the Soviet political structure to "its foundation."[7] Either explanation gave Byrnes confidence that his tactics would bring the Soviets back to the negotiating table before the end of the year. Foremost among the problems needing to be resolved were those of Eastern Europe and the Far East. On both issues, the secretary of state decided on a little private, direct diplomacy.

Believing that the irascible Molotov was responsible for many of the problems in relations between the United States and the Soviet Union, Byrnes sought to isolate the foreign minister and deal directly with Stalin. Ambassador Harriman agreed with Byrnes's view and, during the last dismal week of the conference, had asked permission to arrange a meeting with Stalin. He had even drafted a possible message for the Soviet leader. After the conference, officials in Washington, seeing the conflicting signals coming from Moscow, decided that a meeting with Stalin would be beneficial. Director of European Affairs Herbert Matthews urged all possible speed in sending the message before the Russians "crystallized their position." By October 12, Truman gave his approval for Harriman to seek a private meeting with Stalin.[8]

Not everyone was pleased with Harriman's effort. The British in particular were opposed and attempted to prevent the meeting. Bevin and Foreign Office officials reacted to the failure of the London conference with anger and apprehension. More than the Americans, the British were offended by Molotov's actions. They became almost bitter when it seemed the Soviet press was launching a full-scale attack on the Labour government and British foreign policy in the weeks following the conference. There was little willingness to make overtures to Moscow.[9]

7. *FR, 1945*, V, 888–91.

8. Winant to State Department, October 4, 1945, in File 740.00119 (Council)/10–445, Memorandum for Secretary Byrnes, October 8, 1945, in File 811.001/10–845, Memorandum for Secretary Byrnes, October 9, 1945, in File 811.001/10–945, DSR-NA; *FR, 1945*, II, 562–63.

9. Foreign Office Minute, October 6, 1945, N 13432/18/32, Foreign Office to Lord Halifax, October 6, 1945, U 7856/5559/70, both in FO 371, 1945, PRO.

Members of the Foreign Office did notice the wavering editorials in *Pravda* and *Izvestia* and drew the conclusion that the Russians were interested in renewing discussions. But, unlike Byrnes, Bevin was opposed to any approach by the West, especially a unilateral United States effort. Bevin was apprehensive about the Americans' commitment to Britain and their willingness to confront the Russians. Byrnes's actions at the London meeting, the Truman administration's delays in considering Britain's request for sharing postwar atomic energy information, and American actions in the Middle and Far East convinced some within the Foreign Office that the United States might easily sacrifice British interests to gain agreements with the Soviet Union.[10]

To Bevin, even more was at stake than the United States' readiness to ignore British interests. The British foreign minister believed that two of the few diplomatic levers the Soviets understood were strength and resolve. He felt that if the Soviets wanted to renew discussions, they should make the first move. Bevin was convinced that any American or British overture to repair the damage done in London would only be seen in Moscow as a sign of Western weakness. What was needed was a strong, unified stand against Soviet actions by the United States and Britain.[11]

Therefore, when Bevin learned of Harriman's proposed visit to Stalin, he quickly instructed Lord Halifax to tell the secretary of state that "it would be a mistake to be in any hurry to decide on, and still more to make, any move" to reopen discussions with the Soviets. He hoped that Byrnes would agree about "the undesirability of taking any early initiatives vis-à-vis the Soviet Government." The American response was extremely disappointing: Harriman would go ahead with his meeting, and the United States was not going to follow through on the promise made in London to enhance Britain's role in the Far Eastern Advisory Commission. Sterndale Bennett characterized the Americans' actions as "pure 'jungle diplomacy.'"[12]

Harriman arranged to meet Stalin at the Black Sea resort of Gagra on October 24 and 25. State Department officials told the ambas-

10. Foreign Office Minute, October 6, 1945, N 13432/18/32, in FO 371, 1945, PRO.
11. *Ibid.*; Gowing, *Policy Making*, 66–68.
12. Foreign Office to Lord Halifax, October 6, 1945, U 7856/5559/70, Foreign Office Note, October 14, 1945, F 10102/3641/23, both in FO 371, 1945, PRO.

sador that discussions should center on finding a formula to draft
the peace treaties, thereby getting the Council of Foreign Ministers
restarted and resolving Russian objections to American control
in Japan. American officials were aware of the double standard
they followed regarding Russia's position in Eastern Europe and
the United States' position in Japan. Admiral Richard Gates commented to the Committee of Three in early October: "I can picture
Mr. Byrnes being in a pretty tough spot when he is sitting in London, discussing Four Power arrangements for certain countries in
Europe, and then they turn around and say that they want the
same arrangement in Japan and he says, 'No, you can't have it in
Japan.'" Harriman was told that the United States could accept the
creation of an Allied Control Council for Japan only if General
Douglas MacArthur maintained total executive authority within
the area of his command.[13]

Harriman's diplomacy was designed to resolve problems between
the United States and the Soviet Union, but it was not intended to
be the only effort undertaken by the United States. Harriman's visit
took place within the context of other efforts to demonstrate American strength and willingness to consider Soviet needs. Prominent
in these other demonstrations were Truman's Navy Day speech on
October 27 and a fact-finding trip by Mark Ethridge, publisher of
the Louisville *Courier-Journal*, to Bulgaria and Romania.

Byrnes's policy toward Eastern Europe was at best devious and
was designed to deal with several issues. During the London conference, Dulles and Cohen had recommended not taking an ada-
mant position toward the regimes in Romania and Bulgaria. After
the conference, others within and outside of the State Department
said that Byrnes and other officials needed to reevaluate their policy
toward Eastern Europe to better take into account Soviet needs.
Cloyce Huston, the chief of the Southern European Department,
wrote a lengthy memorandum to John Hickerson and H. F. Matthews that criticized the policy toward Eastern Europe.

Huston characterized American policy as unproductive and
injurious to relations between the Soviet Union and the United

13. *FR, 1945*, VI, 751–56, 765–67; Feis, *Contest Over Japan*, 56–57; Minutes of Top
Policy Group, Department of the Navy, 35th Meeting, October 8, 1945, in Secretary
of Navy Papers, NA.

States. He recommended that officials in Washington issue a "fresh statement of American policy . . . which, in addition to affirming the principles . . . in the Atlantic Charter and the Crimea Declaration, would proclaim as an active tenet of . . . policy the support of Soviet aims to establish free and mutually advantageous relations between Soviet Russia and her Western neighbors." Huston's point of view found little favor among other State Department officials, particularly Bohlen, Matthews, and Hickerson, who feared total Soviet control over all of Eastern Europe. Nevertheless, Huston's opinion matched that of many public critics of American policy and needed to be answered. Huston's memorandum might have accounted for his transfer, two weeks later, to Oslo, Norway, as the first secretary to the United States ambassador.[14]

Rather than change United States policy, as Huston recommended, Byrnes intended to adopt a new tactic that had enough appearance of change to hush domestic critics and show the Soviets that the United States was willing to reexamine its position. Mark Ethridge's trip served both needs. On October 10, the secretary of state announced that Ethridge would go on a fact-finding mission to Romania and Bulgaria. He placed special emphasis on Ethridge's status as an independent publisher not connected to the Washington bureaucracy or the Department of State. Turner Catledge of the New York *Times* expressed a widely held view when he stated that the mission signaled "a new approach" to the Balkan problems, as well as possible mistrust of the State Department's personnel.[15]

Ethridge, of course, had his biases. His paper, the Louisville *Courier-Journal,* had assailed the American monopoly on the atomic bomb and various "Red-baiters" as contributing to Soviet fears that the United States sought anti-Soviet governments in Eastern Europe. But, in true liberal fashion, the *Courier-Journal* held that the

14. Cloyce Huston, "Suggested Extension of American Policy in Eastern Europe," October 24, 1945, in File 711.61/10–2445, DSR-NA; Eduard M. Mark, "Charles E. Bohlen and the Acceptable Limits of Soviet Hegemony in Eastern Europe: A Memorandum of 18 October 1945," *Diplomatic History,* III (1979), 201–13; U.S. Department of State, *Biographic Register of the Department of State, 1946* (Washington, 1947), 549; Davis, *The Cold War Begins,* 321.

15. Mark Ethridge and C. E. Black, "Negotiating on the Balkans, 1945–1947," in Philip E. Mosely (ed.), *The Kremlin and World Politics,* 190–202; Rose, *After Yalta,* 151.

United States was "undeniably right on the subject of political freedom in the Balkans" and should "claim a right and duty to oversee
the organization of peace in Bulgaria, Rumania, and Yugoslavia."[16]

Accompanying Ethridge as adviser and translator was Cyril E.
Black of Princeton University. Black's mother was Bulgarian and his
father was the former president of the American University in
Sofia. At the time of the mission, Black's father was being denied
admission to Bulgaria by the Bulgarian government. Black, no
doubt, was moved in his opinions by these circumstances.[17]

Byrnes's reason for picking Ethridge was to obtain an "outsider's
unbiased" evaluation of the undemocratic and unrepresentative
politics of Romania and Bulgaria. The evaluation would surely
support State Department findings and might be used effectively
against Molotov. Byrnes vividly remembered that in London the
Russian claimed that American sources of information in Eastern
Europe were inaccurate. Ethridge would prove them right and
Molotov wrong. After speaking to various members of the State Department, Lord Halifax assured officials in London that the Ethridge mission represented "no change in [United States] policy."[18]

Once in Eastern Europe, Ethridge lost no time in living up to
State Department expectations. In Bulgaria he found the Bulgarian
government "totalitarian," with a small "clique running the whole
country doing what it believes is best for the whole, using force to
impose its decisions." In Romania he "found Groza a singularly
stupid, incoherent, and brutal looking man" and the influence "of
the Western Democracies . . . disintegrating fast." He concluded
that the domestic and foreign policies of both nations were dictated
by the Soviets.[19]

Ethridge recommended that the United States maintain its public

16. Lord Halifax to Foreign Office, March 5, 1945, AN 885/245/45, in FO 371,
1945, PRO; Louisville *Courier-Journal*, October 19, 1945, Sec. 1, p. 12.

17. Lord Halifax to Foreign Office, October 17, 1945, R 17708/5063/67, in FO 371,
1945, PRO.

18. Dominion Office to Dominions, DO 181, October 14, 1945, R 17305/5063/67,
Lord Halifax to Foreign Office, October 24, 1945, R 18146/231/7, both in FO 371,
1945, PRO.

19. Houstoun-Boswell to Foreign Office, October 23, 1945, R 18018/21/7, La Rougetel to Foreign Office, November 21, 1945, R 19799/5063/67, La Rougetel to Foreign
Office, November 22, 1945, R 19859/2796/47, all in FO 371, 1945, PRO; *FR, 1945*, IV,
357–60; Black, "The Start of the Cold War," 185–91; *FR, 1945*, V, 627–31, 633–37.

insistence on representative government in Eastern Europe and continue the pressure of nonrecognition. Both actions, he believed, would "strengthen the hands of the moderates, including some of the older and more seasoned Communists" who sought an end to the internal political struggle and desired recognition by the United States and Britain. He also suggested that the United States try to influence the peasants by buying "their specialised products like tobacco and attar of roses" and telling them that the United States was "ready to pay altogether higher prices than the Russians." This last idea, however, was omitted from Ethridge's official report to the secretary of state. The official report was a lengthy memorandum that outlined the undemocratic and unrepresentative nature of the Romanian and Bulgarian governments and expressed hopes that a solution to differences between the Americans and Soviets would be found by examining the precedents of Austria and Hungary.[20]

While Byrnes used the prospect of a more lenient Eastern European policy to encourage a Soviet belief in compromise, the British were adopting a softer policy. In the Foreign Office's opinion there were two Eastern European problems: the Russian attempt to exclude Western influence, and the United States' insistence that Britain follow its lead in opposing the regimes in Romania and Bulgaria. D. L. Stewart, the Foreign Office desk officer for Eastern Europe, noted that to "a large extent at American instigation, we have put direct diplomatic and public pressure upon the Soviet Government to agree to the reorganisation of the present puppet Governments . . . and to the institution of a truly democratic system of government on Western European lines on free elections" with negative results. Stewart urged a policy that traded British and American recognition and approval of the peace treaties for the removal of Soviet troops. With the Red Army gone, Britain would rely on time, trade, and traditional pro-British sentiments to pry Eastern Europe from Russia's influence.[21]

By the end of October, members of the Foreign Office had ac-

20. Black, "The Start of the Cold War," 185–91; Record of Conversation between Wright and Ethridge, November 30, 1945, R 20247/21/7, in FO 371, 1945, PRO.

21. Foreign Office Memorandum, October 25, 1945, N 15085/18/38, Foreign Office Memorandum, November 9, 1945, R 18970/5063/67, Foreign Office Memorandum, November 26, 1945, R 18981/5063/67, all in FO 371, 1945, PRO.

cepted Stewart's recommendations and informed the State Department of the new policy. They knew it would not be easy to convince Byrnes to alter his former position. "Our main objective must be on the one hand," Lord Halifax was told, "to reconcile the U.S. Government to the idea of concluding peace treaties with unrepresentative Governments, and on the other hand, to secure some concession as we can from the Soviet Government . . . to help us bring the U.S. Government into line and give us a more satisfactory line of retreat from the position we have hitherto taken." [22]

When Lord Halifax attempted to persuade the State Department of the wisdom of the Foreign Office's "change of tactics," the State Department rejected his arguments out of hand. American officials believed the British effort would certainly undermine, if not repudiate, British and American policies of the past and further weaken Western influence in Eastern Europe. Faced with the Americans' refusal to budge from their hard-line position, Bevin decided not to press the issue and to wait for a more opportune time to present the new approach. [23]

While the British were discovering that the United States intended to hold firm on its policy in Eastern Europe, Harriman was discovering that Stalin intended to hold firm to his demand for an increased role for the Soviet Union in the Far East. Harriman's primary goal at his meetings with Stalin at Gagra was to restart the process to draft the peace treaties. He planned to deal with the Japanese issue only if pressured by Stalin. The pressure began almost at once as Stalin, after reading Truman's message concerning the procedure to draft treaties, noted that the communiqué said nothing about Japan. [24]

A Soviet role in controlling Japan became the primary issue as Stalin stressed to Harriman that the Soviet Union considered the control of Japan an issue of vital importance. It was an issue that reflected Russian national honor and international prestige. Stalin

22. Foreign Office to Lord Halifax, November 9, 1945, R 18970/5063/67, in FO 371, 1945, PRO.

23. Foreign Office Memorandum, November 26, 1945, R 18981/5063/67, Foreign Office Minute, December 12, 1945, R 21263/5063/67, both in FO 371, 1945, PRO; *FR, 1945*, V, 633–37.

24. *FR, 1945*, VI, 783–85, 787–93; Feis, *Contest Over Japan*, 58–66; Harriman and Abel, *Special Envoy*, 512–13.

bluntly told Harriman that without a solution to the Japanese question no other disputes could be resolved.

Harriman replied that American policies in Asia were not intended to antagonize the Soviet Union and that the United States wanted to avoid any "misunderstandings" on the issue of an Allied Control Council for Japan. He promised that the secretary of state was ready to begin bilateral talks with the Soviet representatives in the Far Eastern Advisory Commission who were already in Washington, and to make "every effort to come to an agreement" on the subject. Unofficially, he confided that the Americans favored inviting other nations to supply occupation forces and was considering the formation of a special council to advise MacArthur on military, or perhaps even political, affairs. Harriman stressed, however, that it was the State Department's position that in all cases MacArthur must maintain final and complete authority.[25]

Stalin countered that he did not mind if MacArthur kept final authority but that he did mind that the Americans never bothered to consult the Soviet Union on Japanese issues and that MacArthur allowed the Japanese press to vilify the Soviet Union. The Soviet Union wanted, Stalin complained, a role in the formation of policy for Japan, and for a control vehicle to be established for that purpose. Until that occurred, Stalin said, the Soviet Union would not participate in the activities of the Far Eastern Advisory Commission, and he suggested that the Soviet Union might follow a policy of isolationism and unilateralism. Harriman's final meetings with Stalin on October 25 provided no solution, and Harriman left the Black Sea resort having accomplished nothing beneficial. In Moscow he would open discussions with Molotov on restarting treaty negotiations and listen again to Russian protests about United States policy in Japan. Before leaving for Moscow, he wired the State Department. "I am satisfied that nothing will move Stalin from his position."[26]

Stalin's interest in the Japanese problem worried Harriman. He did not believe that the Soviets lay "awake nights worrying about recrudescence of Jap imperialism and aggression." But Harriman did believe that security-minded Soviet leaders could see "Japan

25. *FR, 1945*, VI, 783–860 *passim*; Harriman and Abel, *Special Envoy*, 512–13.
26. Harriman and Abel, *Special Envoy*, 512–13; *FR, 1945*, VI, 783–860 *passim*.

like Germany" being used as a "springboard" for attacking the Soviet Union. He recommended, in the interest of reducing tensions between the two nations, that the United States make some concessions to the Soviet Union regarding the role of the Far Eastern Advisory Commission.[27]

Harriman's reports on the meeting with Stalin, along with disquieting reports from China and Korea, heightened fears within the Truman administration about Soviet policy in Asia and forced some hard thinking on the American commitment to eastern Asia. On November 1, Secretary of War Patterson asked the State Department to name "minimum interests from which the United States will not retreat in the event of a clash of interests [with the Soviet Union] in the Far East." He was particularly concerned with Manchuria, Inner Mongolia, northern China, and Korea.[28]

Patterson's reply came on November 29 in a report by the State-War-Navy Coordinating Committee. The report pictured the Far East as being divided into Soviet and American spheres of influence. The American zone included the Pacific, Japan, and China. The Soviet zone included Sinkiang, Mongolia, Manchuria, Korea, and the Kuril Islands. The zones overlapped and existed in an unstable equilibrium beset with stresses caused by differences between the Soviets and Americans in other areas, the Soviet emphasis on security needs, and the policies of Asian leaders who were trying "to play one country off against the other." The report bluntly stated that in the region the United States was ill-equipped to oppose Soviet overt or covert operations and should protect its interests only in the Pacific, Japan, and China.[29]

Korea was listed as an especially worrisome problem because the Soviet Union and the United States occupied the nation: "The existing situation in Korea may well endanger friendly relations between the United States and the USSR." To deal with the problem of Korea, the committee's report recommended ending military occupation as quickly as possible "through [a] cooperative process" with the Russians. Korea might be neutralized between the two spheres of influence. Specifically, the committee favored the formation of an international trusteeship to run Korea until the Koreans

27. *FR, 1945,* VI, 815–20; Feis, *Contest Over Japan,* 74.
28. SWNCC PC-33, November 29, 1945, in Byrnes Papers.
29. *Ibid.*

were ready for independence. The report stated that the Soviets might "seek to exploit the machinery of the trusteeship," but the committee still favored trusteeship over immediate independence or occupation by the two powers.[30]

This view differed significantly from the view held by the American commander in chief in Korea, General John Hodge, Secretary of the Navy Forrestal, General MacArthur, and Admiral Leahy. They favored immediate independence under the political leadership of Dr. Kim Koo and Syngman Rhee. Under these two pro-American leaders, Sovietization of northern Korea would be halted and the growth of radical and Communist political parties in the south would be prevented. Byrnes heard both views and leaned toward that offered by the State-War-Navy Coordinating Committee, although, like Hodge, he was concerned about Korea falling under Soviet control. In early November, the secretary of state told Prime Minister Attlee that it "was essential to reach an early decision regarding the future administration of Korea" or else face sure Soviet control.[31]

The desire to keep Soviet influence out of Korea paled next to the need to keep China in the American sphere of influence. In China there was the prospect of full-scale civil war between the forces of Chiang Kai-shek and the Communists. The Soviet Union had pledged to support Chiang's government, but everyone believed that the pledge depended upon Chiang's ability to control China. T. V. Soong, the Chinese foreign minister, told Bevin that the Soviets "abhorred a vacuum" and would always try to fill it. By the autumn of 1945, a vacuum appeared to be forming in northern China, where Nationalist forces were unable to occupy the region because of resistance from the Chinese Communist Eighth Route Army.[32]

30. *Ibid.*

31. U. Gene Lee, "American Policy Toward Korea, 1942–1947" (Ph.D. dissertation, Georgetown University, 1974), 12–96; Leahy Diary, September 29, 1945, in Leahy Papers; Millis and Duffield (eds.), *The Forrestal Diaries*, 97–98, 115; Foreign Office Memorandum, September 14, 1945, F 7143/186/10, Lord Halifax to Foreign Office, November 15, 1945, F 10156/1394/23, both in FO 371, 1945, PRO; "Memorandum on Korea," December 19, 1945, in James V. Forrestal Papers, Firestone Library, Princeton University, Princeton, N.J.

32. Iriye, *The Cold War in Asia*, 109–119; Foreign Office Memorandum, September 14, 1945, F 7143/186/10, in FO 371, 1945, PRO; Memorandum for Record, War

Forrestal and Patterson, fearful of Soviet domination of China, recommended increasing American military aid to the Nationalists and using American Marines in China to help Chiang gain control over northern China. John Carter Vincent, director of the Office of Far Eastern Affairs and Byrnes's primary adviser on Asian matters, rejected the idea of increased American military aid to Chiang. Instead, he recommended that the United States work to negotiate a political settlement between the Nationalist and Communist elements in China.[33]

In early December, the opposing views of the State Department and the Departments of the Navy and War were settled. The use of American forces to aid Chiang in gaining control over northern China was approved due to fears of Soviet domination. The State Department's view, however, was not totally ignored. While American transports and Marines would be used to disarm and repatriate Japanese troops in northern China, General George Marshall would go to China and attempt a political settlement between Chiang and the Communists. In Vincent's estimation, Marshall's mission was flawed from the start, since the United States had no real intention of decreasing any support to the Nationalists. Only the reality of decreased support, Vincent believed, would pressure Chiang to make concessions to the Chinese Communists.[34] For Byrnes, the decision to use American troops and transports to help the Nationalists gain control over northern China could only complicate relations with the Soviets. It would underline further the American double standard toward events in Asia and Eastern Europe.

By late November, 1945, a stalled peace process, tensions be-

---

Department General Staff Operations Division, December 10, 1945, OPD 366 (TS), in Plans and Operations Division of the Army General Staff Records, NA, hereinafter cited as PODR-NA.

33. Leahy Diary, December 11 and 12, 1945, in Leahy Papers; Memorandum for Record, War Department General Staff Operations Division, December 10, 1945, OPD 366 (TS), in PODR-NA; Gary May, *China Scapegoat: The Diplomatic Ordeal of John Carter Vincent* (Washington, 1979), 132–39.

34. *FR, 1945*, VII, 639–43; May, *China Scapegoat*, 132–39; Memorandum for Record, War Department General Staff Operations Division, December 10, 1945, OPD 366 (TS), in PODR-NA.

tween the United States and the Soviet Union over Eastern Europe and Asia, heightened anti-Soviet sentiment in the United States, and increasing Soviet press attacks on the United States threatened to collapse the Grand Alliance and to end attempts to fashion a durable postwar settlement. A grand gesture was needed to bridge the gaps in the Grand Alliance and to permit the peace process to continue. By Thanksgiving Day, Byrnes concluded that a quick trip to Moscow to meet with Stalin before the end of the year was necessary. Timing was critical, for the first meeting of the United Nations was scheduled for early January. If that meeting was a disaster caused by tensions between the Americans and the Soviets, the United Nations would be stillborn. But the trip to Moscow by itself would not be a grand enough gesture to solicit a positive Soviet response. Harriman's private diplomacy with Stalin had accomplished little. Byrnes intended to impress the Soviets with his willingness to include them in joint British, American, and Canadian efforts to regulate atomic energy and weapons. The offer of nuclear partnership was to be the grand gesture.

There was no question that the Russians were concerned with the atomic bomb and the American monopoly over nuclear "secrets." A Soviet atomic spy ring existed. The Russians had played down the importance of the bombings of Hiroshima and Nagasaki in ending the war with Japan. At the London conference, Molotov went to unusual lengths to dismiss the American atomic bomb and to suggest that Russia had its own. Just recently the Soviet press had denounced American atomic diplomacy and attacked the agreements reached by the American, British, and Canadian heads of state on international control of atomic energy at a conference held in Washington.[35]

Byrnes had unsuccessfully resisted the Washington conference. He had been opposed to the sharing of American atomic information with any nation, even Britain. The British, along with American critics of Truman's atomic policy, had forced the November meeting in Washington. Byrnes had played only a small role in the discussions during the meeting, but by the end of November he

35. Herken, *The Winning Weapon*, 43–61; Rose, *After Yalta*, 129–35; Hewlitt and Anderson, *The New World*, 455–59; Nogee, *Soviet Policy*, 14–15.

was ready to take the lead in offering Moscow a partner's role in shaping a system of international control.

The British had pushed for a meeting to discuss postwar atomic policy for two reasons. They feared that the United States meant to deny them any access to peaceful as well as military uses of atomic energy, and they believed that Soviet fears and suspicions arising from American control of atomic energy contributed to disharmony among the Allies. The British chargé d'affaires in Moscow, Frank Roberts, reported that many Russians attributed the breakup of the London conference to American "atomic diplomacy." He wrote that "many Soviet citizens were quick to realize the political importance of the bomb and to consider as a definite possibility its being used against them." Bevin told the cabinet that "many of the difficulties encountered" during the London meeting arose from "Russian resentment at exclusion from . . . the new development [atomic energy]."[36] These British views were echoed in the United States by politicians, scholars, and concerned citizens who called upon the Truman administration to take the lead in establishing international controls over atomic energy and the atomic bomb. Within the administration, many agreed with Undersecretary of State Dean Acheson, who believed that there could be no "long-range understanding" with the Soviet Union unless there was international control over atomic energy.[37]

Even before the London conference ended, Attlee was convinced that it was necessary to push the United States into dealing with the issue of postwar controls for atomic energy. On September 23, Attlee wrote Truman asking for discussions on the problem of atomic control. "I think it may be essential that you and I should discuss this momentous problem together so that we may agree what the next step should be and be in a position to take it before the fears

36. Roberts to Foreign Office, October 9, 1945, U 8093/6550/70, Memorandum by the Prime Minister, "International Control of Atomic Energy," Cabinet Paper (45) 272, November 5, 1945, U 9660/6550/70, both in FO 371, 1945, PRO; Gowing, *Policy Making*, 63–70.

37. Public Affairs Branch, "Special Memorandum on American Opinion on Control of Atomic Energy," October 15, 1945, in File 811.2423/10–1545, DSR-NA; *Twohey Analysis*, October 6, October 13, and December 4, 1945; Hewlitt and Anderson, *The New World*, 418–21; *FR, 1945*, II, 49–50.

and suspicions which may be developing elsewhere have got such a firm hold as to make even more difficult any solution we may decide to aim at." Attlee favored including the Russians in any discussions and sharing atomic information with other nations.[38]

Truman took three weeks to reply. When it came, the response was disappointing. Truman only hinted at a meeting to be held some time in the future. Undaunted, Attlee continued to ask Truman for a conference. His second request repeated the need for consultation among atomic partners but rejected any role for the Soviet Union until its international behavior improved. Bending under British as well as domestic pressure, Truman agreed to a meeting with Attlee and Prime Minister William Lyon Mackenzie King of Canada. The meeting to discuss international controls for atomic energy was scheduled to begin on November 11.[39]

The Truman administration's hesitancy to participate in atomic discussions delayed preparations for the meeting until just a week before Attlee and King were to arrive. Even then the initiative came not from the White House or the State Department but from the secretary of war, Robert Patterson. Patterson convinced Dr. Vannevar Bush to draft a policy for the United States on international control of atomic weapons. Completed on November 3, it was approved by President Truman on the eighth. The conference started three days later.

Bush's plan provided for continued United States atomic research and control of atomic information while allowing a slow increase in international atomic collaboration. He proposed a three-step formula that would, over a period of years, provide for the diffusion of nuclear information and materials, on-site inspections of "any laboratory or plant . . . where atomic fission" was possible, and eventual banning of all atomic weapons. In explaining the proposal to Byrnes, Bush was careful to stress that "years would be necessary to carry out all three steps" and that the United States did not

38. Gowing, *Policy Making*, 70–72; Cabinet Paper (45) 272, November 5, 1945, U 9660/6550/70, in FO 371, 1945, PRO; Report by Joint Chiefs of Staff, C.O.S. (45) 601 (o), October 6, 1945, in File 80/97, Cabinet Papers, PRO.

39. Harry S Truman to Clement Attlee, October 5, 1945, President's Secretary's File, Box 170, in Truman Papers; Gowing, *Policy Making*, 71–72; Hewlitt and Anderson, *The New World*, 455–59.

have to worry about losing its nuclear advantage. He also emphasized that it was vital to "make it clear to the world that this is the way in which we would like to proceed."[40]

The Washington conference lasted five days and left Attlee and the British delegation exasperated. Attlee arrived with a proposal on atomic energy control significantly different from that drafted by Bush. Attlee's approach was simple, based on an assumption that nuclear scientific knowledge could not be restricted and that the most important goal was to prevent international antagonism over control of the bomb. The British plan asked only that all nations pledge "not to use atomic weapons except . . . against any country making use of the atomic bomb in violation of the pledge" and that all countries "enter into full exchange of the basic scientific information relating to the use of atomic energy." The British plan rejected the concept of inspections and other forms of physical control as "highly dangerous sham[s]" that produced "endless suspicions and friction."[41]

Truman quickly dismissed the British proposal and insisted that Attlee and King accept the American plan. Late in the morning of November 15, Truman, Attlee, and King gathered in the Oval Office to sign their "Allied Declaration" calling for the establishment of a United Nations commission on atomic energy and the institution of Bush's three-step program for the sharing of information and arms control. Truman read aloud: "We are not convinced that the spreading of specialized information regarding the practical application of atomic energy, before it is possible to devise effective, reciprocal

40. Vannevar Bush, *Pieces of the Action* (New York, 1970), 296–97; Hewlitt and Anderson, *The New World*, 459–61; Barton J. Bernstein, "The Quest for Security: American Foreign Policy and International Control of Atomic Energy, 1942–1946," *Journal of American History*, LX (1974), 1023–25; Vannevar Bush, Memorandum for Secretary of State, November 9, 1945, in Folder 10, Manhattan Project Files, 1942–46, Interim Committee Log, November 2, 1945, Folder 98, both in Manhattan Engineer District Files, NA; "Negotiating with the British," November 1–16, 1945, War Department Notes, Box 809, Lot 57 D 688 4.11.6 (1945), in State Department Files, U.S. Department of State.

41. Wheeler-Bennett, *John Anderson, Viscount Waverley*, 333–35; Notes of U.K. Delegation, "Washington Discussions on Atomic Energy," November 11, 1945, U 9660/6550/70, in FO 371, 1945, PRO; "Negotiating with the British," War Department Notes; Sir E. I. C. Jacob, "Diary of Archer Conference" (MS in possession of Sir Jacob); Hewlitt and Anderson, *The New World*, 462–64.

and enforceable safeguards . . . would contribute to a constructive solution of the problem of the atomic bomb."[42]

The declaration left unanswered the central problem facing international control—the role of the Soviet Union. Few observers believed that the Soviets would accept on-site inspection of their plants or territory. This belief gained greater credence as the Soviets' reactions to the Washington conference and the declaration became known. The Soviet press denounced both as attempts by the Western powers to apply "atomic diplomacy" against the Soviet Union. Ambassador Harriman's evaluation was that the Russians were returning to the "tactics of obtaining . . . objectives through aggressiveness and intrigue" while making every effort to appear fearless in the face of the United States' nuclear capacity.[43]

Byrnes decided to gamble. To remove Soviet fears of American nuclear power and resolve other outstanding issues between the United States and the Soviet Union, the secretary of state believed it necessary to go to Moscow and offer Stalin a nuclear partnership, at least in the effort to establish international atomic controls. Without informing Bevin, Byrnes recommended a Moscow conference to Molotov on November 23. Molotov was pleased. Former Foreign Minister Maxim Litvinov told Harriman that the proposed meeting "put a new complexion on the whole situation" and that relations between the two countries were "emerging from a long dark tunnel."[44]

Byrnes told Bevin about the meeting on the twenty-fifth. Bevin, who already knew about the American overture to the Soviets, was furious. Ambassador Winant summarized Bevin's reaction: "Situation serious. Unilateral action deeply resented by both Bevin and Cabinet. Bevin refuses to talk . . . [or] attend the conference." The British knew, however, that their refusal was pointless if Molotov accepted the American offer. If the United States and the Soviet Union agreed to meet, Britain would have to attend to save its rank

42. Truman, *Years of Decision*, 542–44; Jacob, "Diary of Archer Conference"; Notes of U.K. Delegation, November 11, 1945, U 9660/6550/70, in FO 371, 1945, PRO.

43. Harriman to State Department, November 27, 1945, in File 761.00/11-2745, DSR-NA; M. Tolchenov, "The Atomic Bomb Discussion in the Foreign Press," *New Times*, November 1, 1945, pp. 14–22; New York *Times*, November 25, 1945, Sec. 2. pp. 4–5.

44. *FR, 1945*, II, 578–85.

as a first-class power and to protect its interests. After trying to dissuade the secretary of state from the conference, Lord Halifax told Byrnes: "You've got us in a bit of a hole." On November 29, Molotov accepted the idea of a Moscow Conference. The die was cast. On December 7, the British agreed to send a delegation to Moscow.[45]

As Byrnes approached Molotov and Bevin, he set into motion work on his grand gesture. A special working group composed of State Department, War Department, and Manhattan Project personnel worked feverishly to draft proposals to gain Russian support for a United Nations atomic energy commission. Speaking as the expert on the Soviet Union, Charles Bohlen reminded the group that "Russia [was] interested in substance and that the bait approach" was wrong. "Stalin," he explained, was "100% practical—interested in specific and concrete proposals."[46]

On December 10, the working group presented the secretary with three possible courses of action. All three sought to gain Russian cosponsorship of the American proposal for a United Nations atomic energy commission. But the working group's recommendations varied as to the types of information and materials to be offered Russia, and when such information should be made available, as encouragements for Soviet cooperation. Two of the proposals offered the release of fundamental nuclear knowledge, useful isotopes, and "a limited number of controlled nuclear reactors . . . for scientific research" to the Soviets. The third draft proposal was substantially less specific, making no mention of the types of materials Russia might receive in return for its cosponsorship of the atomic commission and offering only a carefully phrased promise of atomic partnership: "It is the belief of this Government that successful international action with respect to any phase of the problem of atomic control is not a necessary prerequisite for undertaking affirmative action with respect to other phases. Affirmative action should be taken whenever it is likely to be fruitful."[47]

45. Foreign Office to Lord Halifax, November 25, 1945, U 9442/6550/70, in FO 371, 1945, PRO; Memorandum of Conversation between Lord Halifax and Byrnes, November 29, 1945, in Folder 596 (2), Byrnes Papers; Dixon, *Double Diploma*, 199.

46. State Department Memorandum (Draft), "U.S. Position Toward UNO Commission," November 29, 1945, Box 816, Lot 57 D 688, 17a, in State Department Files, U.S. Department of State; Working Group Committee, December 5–10, 1945, in Folder 63, Harrison-Bundy Files, Manhattan Engineer District Files, NA.

47. "Proposals on Atomic Energy for Submission to U.S.S.R." (Draft), December 10, 1945, in Folder 63, Harrison-Bundy Files, Manhattan Engineer District Files, NA.

Secretary Byrnes picked the third, less precise draft. But he had the information about isotopes, nuclear reactors, and other forms of atomic information placed in a one-hundred-page briefing book. In case the Russians needed someone to explain the briefing book, he invited Dr. James B. Conant to Moscow. Conant was a respected educator and nuclear scientist, formerly of the Manhattan Project. With Truman's approval of the atomic energy proposal, Byrnes was ready to meet the Russians more than halfway. His hope was to restart the peace process and to reaffirm the unity of the Grand Alliance.[48]

48. James B. Conant, *My Several Lives: Memoirs of a Special Inventor* (New York, 1970), 477–78; "Proposals on Atomic Energy for Submission to U.S.S.R." (Draft), December 10, 1945, in Folder 63, Harrison-Bundy Files, Manhattan Engineer District Files, NA.

VI

The Moscow Conference

SECRETARY OF STATE James F. Byrnes carried to Moscow a nineteen-page exposition on the nature of Soviet foreign policy, the relationship between American actions and Russian policy, and three possible courses of United States policy vis-à-vis the Soviet Union. In analyzing Soviet policy, the State Department memorandum listed three factors influencing Soviet behavior: "The comparative capabilities of the U.S.S.R., and the ideology and desires of the Soviet leaders"; the "relative strength . . . of competing domestic forces in the chief problem areas of the world"; and "the foreign policy and intentions of the United States (and Great Britain), as they appear to the Soviet leadership."[1]

Elaborating on the first factor, the memorandum held that while it could be argued that Soviet leaders believed "in the inevitability of conflict between the U.S.S.R. and non-Soviet powers," it was unlikely that ideology would be a prime factor in determining Soviet foreign policy after World War II. In support of this conclusion, the memorandum pointed out that ideology had not been of primary

1. State Department Memorandum, "Capabilities and Intentions of the Soviet Union as Affected by American Policy," December 10, 1945, in File 711.61/12–1045, DSR-NA.

importance in the formation of Russia's policy since the late 1930s, either because "of a basic change of outlook" by the Russian hierarchy or because "of the lack of adequate capabilities 'at home and appropriate revolutionary situations' abroad." The lack of such capabilities and conditions, the memorandum optimistically concluded, would continue well into the immediate post-war period.[2]

Turning specifically to the issue of Russian capabilities to confront the United States, the memorandum established three time frames ranging from a period of overwhelming American superiority, 1945–1955, to a period of near-balance of power, 1965–1970. The key to the difference was atomic strength. America's control of the atomic bomb gave the United States "decisive military superiority." Therefore, during the period from 1945 to 1955, the United States did not need to be "acutely concerned about the current intentions of the Soviet Union" and had "considerable latitude in determining its policy toward the U.S.S.R."[3]

Having made the point that the United States enjoyed diplomatic flexibility, the memorandum recommended three separate policies that the secretary of state could follow. The first policy involved promoting increased trust and cooperation between Russia and the United States. It called upon the United States to share atomic information, avoid "unilateral statements of principle," and seek "substantially less" diplomatically than American "capabilities could secure." At the same time, the United States should continue to take the initiative in offering specific solutions to international problems and in promoting "economic recovery." Economic recovery would deter the creation of conditions favorable to revolutionary activities, thereby restricting Soviet capabilities and pushing the Soviet leadership toward open diplomacy. If successful, the memorandum summarized, the policy would not sacrifice any of the "superior capabilities" of the United States and would convince Russian leaders to continue to deemphasize ideology and work to solve external problems through diplomacy and the United Nations.[4]

The second policy offered was the opposite of the first. It sought to develop the "maximum alignment of power against the Soviet Union." It ignored considerations of Soviet sensitivities and needs

2. *Ibid.*
3. *Ibid.*
4. *Ibid.*

and attempted to construct a global *cordon sanitaire* around the Soviet Union strong enough to contain and restrain the Soviets from
any thoughts of aggression. The memorandum suggested that the
policy be adopted only if "the Soviet leadership were known to be
irrevocably committed to a policy of expansion facilitated by revolution," because by adopting such a policy, the United States would
force the Soviet Union into an aggressive, expansionistic anti-
capitalist policy.[5]

The memorandum's third policy offered a middle course designed
to keep relations between the two countries "somewhat indetermi-
nate and fluid." With this policy, the United States would appear to
be understanding of Russian needs and fears, even to the point of
offering concessions, while at the same time working quietly to construct an anti-Soviet bloc and to limit the spread of Soviet influence.
The memorandum warned that, in time, the third policy would
produce the same results as the second—Soviet expansionism.[6]

In traveling to Moscow, Byrnes adopted the first suggested policy. But it was a qualified adoption, a test to determine Soviet intentions. Byrnes told Walter Brown that he needed to go to Moscow to
see if Stalin was preparing for peace or war. If, as a result of the
meetings in Moscow, the Soviets appeared to be interested in world
cooperation, then the first policy could be implemented. If the Soviets seemed intractable and hostile, then the second or third policies could be implemented.[7]

The American delegation arrived in Moscow on December 14,
after a harrowing flight through a blizzard. They arrived at the
wrong airport and were welcomed by a small group of Russian officials sent to the airport as a precaution against such an eventuality.
Byrnes sprang from the plane wearing his light overcoat and usual
grey fedora, as if to show that this was all business as usual. Soon
Ambassador Harriman and Andrei Vyshinsky arrived to greet
Byrnes, and within a few moments the cold and exhausted delegation departed for the American embassy.[8]

5. *Ibid.*

6. *Ibid.;* Robert L. Messer, "Paths Not Taken," *Diplomatic History,* I (1977),
297–320.

7. Walter Brown's Book, September 28, 1945, in Byrnes Papers; Department of
State, "Union of Soviet Socialist Republics," *Policy Manual, 1945,* December 15, 1945,
in File 711.00/12–1545, DSR-NA.

8. Byrnes, *Speaking Frankly,* 110–11; Harriman and Abel, *Special Envoy,* 523;

Bevin and the small British delegation arrived the following day. They waited out the storm in Berlin. As General E. I. C. Jacob recalled, their first decision was "[w]hether to put on . . . the whole armour of God, furry boots, fur-lined coats, jerseys, fur caps, and gauntlets, or whether to take a chance and wear a reasonable coat and hat." In the subfreezing temperatures, most of the British delegation opted for the whole armor of God. "Bevin had a rather tapering astraken" and a woolly fur coat. He had to turn sideways to get through the airplane door. Waiting to greet the British foreign minister were Vyshinsky, Harriman, and Clark Kerr. After a round of platitudinous greetings, Bevin, Cadogan, and Pierson Dixon left for the British embassy. The rest of the delegation, "the lesser lights," headed for the National Hotel.[9]

The members of the British delegation familiar with Moscow found some significant changes. The war camouflage was gone and the streets were filled with people. Lenin was back in his tomb, and British officials and officers were no longer treated as honored guests. Not only did the National Hotel fail to offer the large private dining room, but more important, the drinks were no longer free. Vodka cost nearly three shillings a bottle. Careful drinking would be called for. Caviar cost eighteen pounds a kilo, thus completely off the menu.

One Russian custom, however, remained: electronic and personal surveillance. The British, as well as the Americans, assumed that all their rooms were equipped with listening devices and soon developed the habit of taking walks for serious conversations. One official recorded a comic picture of a group of American officials huddled in the center of a room discussing the pros and cons of an issue in low voices to avoid the sharp ears of the assumed Soviet listeners. The surveillance did have one advantage. It was possible, just by wishing aloud, to have the Russians provide hot drinks and biscuits without having to ask directly for them.[10]

The Moscow conference began promptly at five in the afternoon

---

Bohlen, *Witness to History*, 247–48; Conant, *My Several Lives*, 477–78; New York *Times*, December 15, 1945, Sec. 1, p. 1, December 16, 1945, Sec. 1, p. 1; Supply Inventory, December, 1945, Moscow Post Files, Suitland, Md.

9. Dixon, *Double Diploma*, 200; London *Times*, December 13, 1945, Sec. 1, p. 1; Sir E. I. C. Jacob, "To Moscow with Bevin" (MS in possession of Sir Jacob), 1–6.

10. Jacob, "To Moscow," 6–7.

of December 16 at Spiridonvka Palace. A villa maintained by the Soviet government for international conferences, Spiridonvka was anything but proletarian in decor and style. It contained towering white marble walls and rich red carpets on the floors. Two large green marble dragons guarded the stairway, and in the conference room the large oval table was bathed in sunlight. Surrounding the table were enough chairs for the ministers, their translators, and one or two advisers. Other advisers had to wait outside in a small alcove under the watchful eyes of Russian guards carrying machine guns and claiming to understand no English.[11]

As the first session started, Secretary Byrnes, as the initiator of the conference, presented an eight-topic agenda:

1. Creation of a United Nations atomic energy commission.
2. Drafting of peace treaties for Italy, Hungary, Bulgaria, Romania, and Finland.
3. Establishment of a unified and independent Korea.
4. Terms of reference for the Far Eastern Advisory Commission and Allied Control Council for Japan.
5. Disarmament and evacuation of Japanese forces in northern China.
6. Transfer of control over Manchuria from Soviet forces to the Nationalist Chinese.
7. Withdrawal of Allied forces from Iran.
8. Establishment of governments in Romania and Bulgaria that the United States and Great Britain could recognize.

Molotov objected. He wanted the first topic, the atomic energy commission, placed last on the agenda. He also wanted to discuss the complete removal of American forces from China and British forces from Greece as well as "developments in Indonesia." General Jacob, a veteran of many conferences with the Soviets, complained privately: "When either we or the Americans suggest anything for the agenda the Russians don't like, or don't want to discuss, the Russians make a counter-suggestion by putting forward some item they know will annoy us."[12]

The ministers debated the agenda for an hour and a half. The result was acceptance of Molotov's recommendations and an agreement to hold two types of meetings, formal and informal. The for-

11. *Ibid.; Time,* December 17, 1945, p. 20.
12. *FR, 1945,* II, 610–29; Jacob, "To Moscow," 7–8.

mal meetings would be for public record and include the eight topics offered by Byrnes except those dealing with the presence of troops in foreign territories. The presence of troops in Manchuria, Greece, Iran, China, and Indonesia, plus other private negotiations, were to be subjects of the informal sessions and not for public record.[13]

For the American delegation, the changes in the format of the conference and on the agenda produced a revision of their proposal on atomic energy. Some historians believe that the placement of the atomic issue last on the agenda instead of first was a diplomatic defeat for Byrnes because it undermined his plan to use the sharing of atomic information and control as a weapon to solicit Russian compromises on other issues. Actually, the record indicates that the placement of an issue on the agenda made little difference, because all issues on the agenda were open to discussion at any time. As for Byrnes's intention to offer nuclear materials and an atomic partnership to Russia in exchange for Soviet concessions, it had vanished by the afternoon of December 16.[14]

Immediately after the council meeting, Benjamin Cohen and James Conant scrapped the proposal submitted by the State Department's special working group. In its place, they prepared one that offered only paragraphs four, five, and six of the Washington Declaration of November 15, 1945—a declaration that the Soviet Union already had denounced. The paragraphs of the declaration that were incorporated into the new American proposal simply stated that the United States, Great Britain, and Canada were willing "to proceed with the exchange of fundamental scientific information for peaceful ends with any nation that will fully reciprocate"; that the United States, Great Britain, and Canada believed in the free exchange of scientific information; and that the three countries were "not convinced that the spreading of the specialized information regarding the practical application of atomic energy, before it is possible to devise effective, reciprocal, and enforceable safeguards acceptable to all nations, would contribute to a constructive solution of the problem of the atomic bomb." Dropped from the proposal were any hints that the United States might

13. *FR, 1945*, II, 611–29.
14. Bernstein, "The Quest for Security," 1028–29; Feis, *Contest Over Japan*, 87; Herken, *The Winning Weapon*, 69–81.

make specialized information available to the Soviet Union before agreements on safeguards were reached or that the step-by-step procedure established at the Washington conference could be circumvented.[15]

The changes were made by the morning of the seventeenth, and a copy of the revised proposal was delivered to the British for information only. Although not asked to comment or to make suggestions, the British quickly asked for meetings—one to be held between Bevin and Byrnes and one between the delegations' atomic experts. The Americans consented and within hours Conant and Cohen were meeting with Jacob and Cadogan.

The British feared that the Soviets might ask for full and immediate partnership, and they asked that the Americans restore paragraph eight of the Washington Declaration to the proposal. This paragraph specified that the "work of the Commission should proceed by separate stages, the successful completion of each one of which will develop the necessary confidence of the world before the next step is undertaken." In addition, Jacob and Cadogan asked that the proposal not be introduced until the British cabinet's opinion was known and that the atomic energy commission be placed under the control of the United Nations Security Council rather than the General Assembly. Cohen and Conant made no commitments. Jacob thought the American attitude was "doubtful . . . and uncooperative." He hoped that Bevin would have better luck with Byrnes.[16]

Bevin's meeting appeared to produce more favorable agreements. Byrnes agreed to withhold the proposal for two days, until December 19, or until the British cabinet's reply was received. He also said he would consider adding paragraph eight of the Washington Declaration to the proposal. On the issue of having the United Nations General Assembly control the atomic energy commission, he refused to budge.[17]

15. *FR, 1945*, II, 663–64; "Draft Proposals on Atomic Energy for Submission to the U.S.S.R.," December 10, 1945, in Harrison-Bundy Files, Manhattan Engineer District Files, NA.

16. Jacob, "To Moscow," 10–12; Bevin to Foreign Office, December 17, 1945, U 10134/6550/70, in FO 371, 1945, PRO.

17. Bevin to Foreign Office, December 17, 1945, U 10134/6550/70, in FO 371, 1945, PRO; *FR, 1945*, II, 629–31; Herken, *The Winning Weapon*, 81–82.

Having exhausted the subject of atomic energy, Bevin next in-
quired about Byrnes's views on Soviet policy and intentions toward
Iran. Bevin offered the view that the Russians were trying to undermine British influence in the Middle East and that the revolt in
northern Iran was engineered and directed by the Soviets, whose
goal was to obtain Iranian oil and turn Azerbaijan into a "subser-
vient area."[18]

Byrnes disagreed and played down the Soviet role in the rebellion.
He stated that Russia had oil enough and did not need to physically
control northern Iran to exert great influence in the region. Further,
he pointed out, the natives of northern Iran had a "real grievance"
against the Iranian government on matters of local control, and
"provincial autonomy" was guaranteed in the Iranian constitution.
Byrnes suggested that the best course for Britain and the United
States to follow was to recommend to the Tehran government that it
grant some local autonomy to the Azerbaijanis, if only "to cut the
ground from under the Soviet Government, who were posing as
the defenders of democracy in Persia." The Russian posture as de-
fender of democracy, Byrnes explained, was untrue and offended
"American sensibilities." Bevin agreed it would be prudent to suggest governmental reforms to the Iranian government but thought
it more important to have a "frank" talk with Molotov to determine
exactly what the Soviets wanted in Iran. Byrnes also believed a
frank talk with the Soviet foreign minister would help.[19]

The formal session on December 17 proved to be brief. Molotov
stubbornly reaffirmed his position, given at the London conference, on who should participate in writing the peace treaties for
Germany's European allies. Only those nations, the Soviet minister
repeated, that signed the armistice should draft and approve the
treaty. Thus, France, Britain, Russia, and the United States would
draft and approve the Italian treaty; Britain, Russia, and the United
States would work on the Eastern European treaties; and only
Russia and Britain would deal with the Finnish treaty. Bevin and
Byrnes rejected the Russian position as too narrow and suggested
that the next topic, Japan, be considered. Molotov said that he was

18. Bevin to Foreign Office, December 17, 1945, U 10134/6550/70, in FO 371, 1945,
PRO; *FR, 1945*, II, 630.
19. Bevin to Foreign Office, December 17, 1945, U 10134/6550/70, in FO 371, 1945,
PRO; *FR, 1945*, 629–31.

not ready to discuss Japan, Korea, or China. With only the atomic issue left on the formal agenda, and having promised the British not to introduce it, Byrnes recommended that, in the face of Molotov's inability to discuss the issues, they adjourn.[20]

The morning of December 18 was cold and cloudy, matching the feelings of the American delegation. With two sessions over and three full days gone, nothing had been accomplished. Harriman feared the conference would end like the London meeting. He blamed Byrnes's impetuous manner and unwillingness to ask for and take his advice. The British, who never wanted to go to Moscow, also blamed Byrnes for inadequate time for preparation. They took offense at the secretary of state's imperial attitude and the manner in which he ignored their opinions and presumed to speak for Britain as well as the United States. Nor were Byrnes's spirits buoyant as he left the embassy for a morning session with Molotov to discuss the governments of Romania and Bulgaria. He expected a thorny session. He was not disappointed.[21]

The first thing Byrnes did upon meeting with Molotov was to present the Soviet minister with a Russian translation of Mark Ethridge's report on conditions in Romania and Bulgaria. In giving Molotov the report, Byrnes assured the Russian that Ethridge was "absolutely independent" of the State Department and held "liberal political views and [a] sympathetic attitude towards the Soviet Union." The report, Byrnes continued, confirmed the position taken by the United States government that the regimes were neither representative nor democratic. He asked the Soviet minister to study the report and search his mind for a way to end the differences over Romania and Bulgaria. Molotov quickly dismissed Byrnes's contention that Ethridge, or any American observer, could impartially evaluate Eastern-style democracy and said that he could get a totally different report, one favorable to the two governments, by sending an equally independent Russian correspondent. Nevertheless, Molotov agreed to read the report.[22]

Having turned aside Byrnes's attempt to convince him to abandon support for the pro-Soviet governments in Romania and Bul-

20. FR, 1945, II, 632–40.
21. Harriman and Abel, Special Envoy, 523–24; Byrnes, Speaking Frankly, 112–13; Dixon, Double Diploma, 201.
22. FR, 1945, II, 643–47; Byrnes, Speaking Frankly, 115–16.

garia, Molotov discussed the writing and ratification of the peace treaties. The writers, he announced, should be those who signed the armistice; the ratifiers, those who were actually attacked.[23] Replying to Molotov, Byrnes suggested that the Soviet minister did not fully understand the critical differences between judges and witnesses. Judges, Byrnes continued, were those countries responsible, as defined by the Berlin Protocol, for drafting and approving the treaties; witnesses were those nations permitted to present their opinions on the treaties. The judges had all the power, the witnesses none, the secretary concluded. He "added that Mr. Vishinsky as a lawyer would appreciate . . . [the] point." Vyshinsky "said he did and that it reminded him of a lawyer's proverb that Turkish judges listened to what the witnesses had to say and then always did the exact opposite."[24]

Molotov had just finished talking with Byrnes when Bevin arrived for his meeting with the Soviet minister. Bevin said he came to discuss spheres of influence. The British foreign minister began with a stirring defense of Britain's role in Greece. The Greek government, facing political chaos, had requested British aid in restoring order. Bevin added that free elections would be held in March, 1946. Good-humoredly but pointedly, Molotov interjected that "the Greeks were not masters in Greece . . . the British were." He added that elections had already been held in Bulgaria and that "many people had no faith in Greek elections." Not missing his opportunity, Bevin retorted that "there was wide spread distrust of elections in all the Balkan countries." Grinning, the Soviet minister admitted that Soviet influence "was 'not weak' in Bulgaria."[25]

Dropping comparisons between Greece and Eastern Europe, Bevin next discussed Iran. He reminded his Soviet colleague that in Iran "Soviet . . . and British interests touched" and that it was important to understand the other's intentions. Bevin remarked that "The last thing he wanted to see was conflict with the Soviet Union over Iran or anywhere else." Forcefully, he asked Molotov to "tell

23. FR, 1945, II, 644, 647; Bevin to Foreign Office, December 19, 1945, U 10223/6550/70, in FO 371, 1945, PRO.

24. FR, 1945, II, 644–48.

25. Record of Meeting Between Bevin and Molotov, December 18, 1945, in File 740.00119 (Council)/12–1845, DSR-NA; Bevin to Foreign Office, December 19, 1945, U 10223/6550/70, in FO 371, 1945, PRO; Dixon, Double Diploma, 200–201.

him what the Soviet Government was up to" in Iran. Cooly, Molotov repeated the standard Soviet reply: the Soviet Union regarded the terms of the Tripartite Treaty of Alliance binding; the revolt in northern Iran was purely local in character and origins; Soviet occupation troops did not interfere with "local national" movements; and Russia had no designs on Iranian territory. Molotov candidly agreed that the foreign ministers should be honest with one another and avoid clashes. However, he observed that "at least in certain places . . . Britain did not seem to take Soviet interests into consideration." Without further elaboration, Molotov ended the meeting. Bevin left impressed with Molotov's admission that Soviet influence was not weak in Bulgaria and that the Russian's attitude toward Iran was "singularly unhelpful, if not . . . sinister."[26]

As a result of their meetings with Molotov, neither Bevin nor Byrnes was successful in fathoming Soviet motives or altering Soviet policies. Stonebottom had not moved from the original positions he took at London, and as the third formal meeting began fears increased that the London stalemate would be repeated. The third formal session provided little cheer for the disillusioned. For the British, Byrnes provided a major surprise when he introduced the proposal on atomic energy a day ahead of schedule. The early part of the meeting was given over to who should and should not be invited to the peace conference. Byrnes and Bevin sought a general peace conference attended by any nation with a direct interest, but Molotov maintained that at most only those nations actually attacked by the Axis powers should participate. The Soviet minister emphasized that the question was not one of "compromise" but one of "compliance" with the Berlin Protocol. The biggest commotion occurred at the end of the meeting, however, when Byrnes flabbergasted his British colleagues by introducing his proposal on atomic energy control. The British, who were preparing to leave, sat back in their seats shocked, hoping the Russians would postpone discussing the subject. To their relief, Molotov did. After the meeting, Bevin "strongly protested to Byrnes" the American action, only to have the secretary of state "plead a misunderstanding." General Jacob despaired at "the American way of doing business." He wrote: "When taken to task they look pained and plead a

26. Bevin to Foreign Office, December 19, 1945, U 10223/6550/70, in FO 371, 1945, PRO.

misunderstanding! . . . Common courtesy . . . demanded that they should tell us before hand that they were going to circulate a paper which had been subject of discussion and amendment between us."[27]

Wednesday's meetings, one formal and one informal, proved no more productive. In the informal meeting, Byrnes pressed the United States' justification for the presence of American forces in China: they were needed to disarm and evacuate remaining Japanese troops. Molotov thought "it very abnormal . . . that there were still fully armed [Japanese] troops in China" and changed the subject to India's right to participate in the proposed peace conference. He informed Byrnes that the Soviet Union could not accept India's participation unless the Baltic states—Estonia, Latvia, and Lithuania—were also invited. Byrnes immediately offered that it might be possible to exclude India. Bevin rejected totally such a course and suggested that Britain was willing to let the Baltic states participate. Molotov no doubt enjoyed the sight of the two Western Allies debating each other on Baltic and Indian participation. The meeting ended without any issues being resolved. Angrily, Bevin wired the Foreign Office: "Byrnes has once again let us down and played the Russian game. But he has been much shaken by my readiness to entertain Molotov's suggestion for a deal between India and the Baltic Republics." The formal afternoon meeting continued the discussions with no solutions. Evaluating the conference and the fourth formal session on December 19, Byrnes concluded that the meetings were "pretty abortive," and he worried over an emerging pattern of stalemate.[28]

DIPLOMATIC BREAKTHROUGH

Byrnes hoped to break the pattern of stalemate that evening when he met with Stalin in the Kremlin. Accompanied by Harriman and Bohlen, he presented the premier with a personal message from Truman. The message expressed Truman's belief that differences be-

27. *FR, 1945*, II, 647–60; Dixon, *Double Diploma*, 201; Jacob, "To Moscow," 13–14; Bevin to Foreign Office, December 19, 1945, U 10219/6550/70, in FO 371, 1945, PRO.

28. *FR, 1945*, II, 665–71, 672–80; Bevin to Foreign Office, December 19, 1945, U 10190/10235/7714, in FO 371, 1945, PRO; Byrnes to State Department, December 20, 1945, in File 740.00119 (Council)/12–2045, DSR-NA.

tween the United States and the Soviet Union were only procedural
and that both nations wanted "to live in peace . . . and help . . .
restore the damages of war." Stalin accepted the message and expected the secretary of state to follow it up with some information
about the pending Soviet request for a loan.[29] Instead, Byrnes
launched into a discussion about Indian and Baltic participation in
a peace conference. If they were invited, he complained, the United
States would be faced with its two allies each having six votes.
Having heard similar statements before, Stalin magnanimously
offered the United States five additional votes. He added that "soon
the United States would have to recognize" the Baltic states anyway.
Byrnes replied that including the Baltic republics at the peace conference "created certain difficulties" for the United States, and he
asked if Stalin could "see some other way . . . out of the difficulty."
Byrnes then turned to discuss Iran and the governments of Eastern
Europe.[30]

In raising the Iranian matter, Byrnes told Stalin that he did so
only as a friend and because the Iranians were going to complain to
the United Nations about Soviet intervention in Iranian internal affairs. The secretary expressed hope that all British, United States,
and Soviet troops would be removed soon, allowing the Iranians to
settle their own affairs and making the United Nations referral
unnecessary.

Stalin's reply was blunt. The United States did not understand the
facts: the government of Iran was "hostile" to the Soviet Union; Soviet oil fields in Baku needed protection from reactionaries in Iran;
and "the Soviet Government was unable and did not wish to withdraw their troops until the date set by the treaty." His spirits sink-
ing, Byrnes heard that the Soviet Union, under the provisions of a
1921 treaty with Iran, did not have to remove its troops at all.[31]

Disheartened, the secretary of state could only remind Stalin that
"Great Powers should always be in a position to show that they were
behaving correctly and in accordance with agreement in regard to
small nations." Smiling, promising to see him again, Stalin ushered
Byrnes from the meeting. He reassured his departing guest that

---

29. *FR, 1945*, II, 680–88; Byrnes, *Speaking Frankly*, 113–14; Harriman and Abel,
Special Envoy, 532.
30. *FR, 1945*, II, 684–87.
31. *Ibid.*

Russia "had no designs territorial or otherwise against Iran." Byrnes left knowing that his first meeting with Stalin had accomplished nothing and that the pattern of deadlock still remained.[32]

As Byrnes left the Kremlin, Bevin arrived. The British foreign minister was primarily interested in reaching an understanding with the Russian leader on spheres of influence. He was concerned about Soviet interest in the Middle East, and spoke of this concern to Stalin. Stalin responded that the Soviet Union "had no intention of incorporating any part of Persia into the Soviet Union" and that all Soviet actions in Iran were made to protect Baku oil.[33]

Realizing that Stalin would offer no further explanation of Soviet intentions in the Middle and Near East, Bevin asked Stalin about a formal extension of the treaty of friendship between Britain and the Soviet Union, and to the formation of an anti-German, British-led, Western bloc. Stalin gave no direct answer on the extension of the treaty of friendship, merely commenting that if "the three Governments could keep the spirit of their treaties it would be a long time before another war occurred." Almost as an afterthought, the Soviet leader noted that the Soviet Union did not have a treaty of friendship with the United States. On the question of a Western bloc, Stalin said he had no objections. Bevin left the meeting in "high fettle," satisfied with Stalin's acceptance of the Western bloc. He quickly wired the Foreign Office the good news.[34]

The following morning, the British and Americans met to discuss their differences over atomic energy and Eastern European questions. General Jacob and Alexander Cadogan repeated the British desire to place the atomic energy commission under the jurisdiction of the Security Council and to have paragraph eight of the Washington Declaration added to the American proposal. Cohen and Conant replied that paragraph eight was being added, having been left off by mistake. Also, the United States delegation was waiting for the Russians to request that the commission be placed under the Security Council before making the change. It would be a good concession to throw to the Soviets.

Cadogan presented a memorandum on British policy in Eastern

---

32. *Ibid.*

33. *Ibid.*

34. *Ibid.*, 688–91; Bevin to Foreign Office, December 20, 1945, U 10270/6550/70, in FO 371, 1945, PRO; Dixon, *Double Diploma*, 202.

Europe that called for a token enlargement of the Romanian and Bulgarian regimes by one or two opposition leaders and immediate British and American recognition. H. F. Matthews replied curtly: "Too weak!" He then presented a proposal that stipulated that the Bulgarian government be reorganized to include all opposition groups and that American guidelines be accepted for holding free elections and protecting civil liberties. Matthews' formula for Romania was similar. The Groza government, in order to be recognized by the United States, had to include members from the National Peasant and Liberal parties, guarantee free elections, institute the secret ballot, grant a general amnesty for all "political acts and offenses committed since August 23, 1944," and protect civil and political freedoms.[35]

Jacob and Cadogan made no comments and said only that they would give a copy of the American proposal to Bevin. Privately, they did not believe the Russians would give the proposal a second reading. After listening to Jacob's and Cadogan's report, Bevin said he would support the American plan. It would make a good initial bargaining point, he said. Jacob was thoroughly disgusted: "Unfortunately, it is always we or the Americans who have to make concessions . . . there are frequent signs that Byrnes is quite prepared to sell us out if by doing so he can get something out of Molotov. It is awful to think that the foreign policy of a great country like the U.S.A. should be in the hands of a shanty Irishman from Carolina, advised by a rather vague visionary like Cohen."[36]

For the Irishman, the following day, December 21, was the turning point of the conference. He initiated a move toward compromise by announcing that with a few minor changes the United States could accept the Soviet position on Korea. On December 22, the Korean issue was settled, and Molotov removed his objections to the terms of reference for the Far Eastern Advisory Commission and the Allied Control Council for Japan. He also accepted the secretary's distinction between judges and witnesses at the peace conference and surprised his colleagues by supplying a list of invited states that included India and excluded the Baltic states and Al-

35. Jacob, "To Moscow," 17–19; Bevin to Foreign Office, December 21, 1945, U 10272/6550/70, Bevin to Foreign Office, December 21, 1945, U 21284/5063/67, both in FO 371, 1945, PRO.
36. Jacob, "To Moscow," 19.

bania. Three of the six issues on the formal agenda were now resolved. Byrnes left the conference table in an expectant mood,
hoping to be home for Christmas. In a less cheery mood, Bevin
grumbled that Byrnes was "prepared to yield to the Russian point
of view in order to get quick agreement." [37]

The spirit of compromise, however, barely carried over to the
issue of the regimes in Romania and Bulgaria. Molotov remained
determined that the Bulgarian national election made any Allied
intervention unnecessary, and he would hear of no suggestions
about either formal or informal prompting of Bulgaria to alter the
composition of the government. On Romania there was a small
glimmer of hope. Molotov admitted that the Groza government
might accept "a suggestion" by the Big Three to broaden itself by
including "one or two ministers without portfolio . . . from non-
party statesmen, on the condition that the Three Governments
would agree not to delay the conclusion of a treaty of peace with
Rumania." [38] Molotov's position satisfied the British but still fell
short of the American position.

Fearing that Bevin might accept the Russian proposal, Byrnes
immediately demanded that the National Liberal and Peasant parties be designated as the parties from which the two ministers must
come. He also asked that the Romanian government make specific
assurances that it would respect civil and political rights and grant
a general amnesty. Angered, Molotov pointed out to Byrnes that
members of the National Liberal and Peasant parties were already
functioning within the Groza government and that, therefore,
there was no need to mention the two parties by name.

Rebuffed, the secretary of state replied that he understood that
those already participating in the government "were not the real
representatives" of the two parties but added that he would verify
the point with his advisers. Byrnes was clearly distraught upon
leaving the session. Outside of the conference room, Byrnes wrung
his hands and moaned to Bevin: "What are we going to do now?
What are we going to do now?" Exasperated with Byrnes, Bevin
turned and replied: "Chuck the bomb at 'em!" [39]

37. *FR, 1945*, II, 815–20, 716–19; Bevin to Foreign Office, December 22, 1945, U
10281/6550/70, in FO 371, 1945, PRO.
38. *FR, 1945*, II, 727–34.
39. *Ibid.*; Jacob, "To Moscow," 24.

The next day found Byrnes recovered and anxious to meet with Stalin. He discovered that Stalin was ready to offer concessions. The premier offered to give the Bulgarians the Soviet Union's "advice" that they should enlarge the government, although he wanted it understood that there must not be a hint of Russian pressure on the government in Sofia. Regarding Romania, Stalin speculated that "in a pinch it might be possible to suggest to the Rumanian Government that two statesmen representing the National Peasant Party and the National Liberal Party be included in the Government." Stalin asked for only one small condition, that the leaders of the two dissident parties (Iuliu Maniu, Dinu Bratianu, and Niculae Lupu) be excluded from participating in the enlarged government.

Stalin's concessions did not stop with Romania and Bulgaria. He went on to approve the American military presence in China. He said he did not care if they stayed or left; he only wanted to be kept informed. He also accepted, in principle, the American proposal on the atomic energy commission. He asked only that the commission be placed under the control of the United Nations Security Council. Byrnes left his meeting with Stalin overjoyed and ready to see a special performance of the ballet *Cinderella*.[40]

The Bolshoi Theater was filled with Moscow's foreign officials and many high- and mid-ranking Communist officials. Bevin, Molotov, and Byrnes entered together to the ringing applause of the audience. Watching the spectacle, Jacob recorded: "Byrnes radiated false bonhomie, putting his arm around Molotov's shoulders," waving to the audience, and flashing the "V" for victory sign. Not wanting to be outdone, "Bevin wiped Byrnes's eye by giving the clenched fist salute, which brought the house down!" Jacob stated that this was "all in very doubtful taste, I fear, but perhaps understandable."[41]

In the morning following the ballet, December 24, Byrnes wired a summary of his meeting with Stalin to the State Department and the president. He concluded: "The situation is encouraging and I hope that today we can reach final agreement on the questions and wind up our work tomorrow."[42]

40. Byrnes, *Speaking Frankly*, 116–17; FR, 1945, II, 750–58.
41. Jacob, "To Moscow," 28; Byrnes, *Speaking Frankly*, 117–20; Dixon, *Double Diploma*, 202.
42. *FR, 1945*, II, 760.

Molotov dampened Byrnes's optimism that same afternoon. After accepting the American proposal on the atomic energy commission, amended to put jurisdiction under the Security Council, Molotov introduced two resolutions on Romania and Bulgaria that seemed to run counter to the understanding Byrnes reached with Stalin. Molotov wanted to ensure that those included in the governments were members of the "loyal opposition," and he asked that Maniu, Bratianu, and Lupu be excluded, in writing, as part of the formal agreement.[43]

Byrnes objected that the term "loyal opposition" could be misconstrued and should not be used. As for naming those not qualified to be in the government, he was opposed. Bevin rose to support Byrnes: "It would be awkward publicly to ostracize men in their own country." Unable to agree on the language of the two Molotov resolutions, the three ministers considered Byrnes's request for the release of a public statement announcing their agreement on a procedure to draft the peace treaties and to call a general peace conference. After some discussion, all agreed to release an interim communiqué on Christmas Eve. Byrnes called it a Christmas present to the world. Molotov and Bevin only nodded.[44]

Whereas the Americans chafed over Molotov's stand on the broadening of the Romanian and Bulgarian governments, the British attempted to resolve the Iranian question by meeting with Stalin. Bevin had a plan that he believed would defuse the crisis in northern Iran. On the evening of December 24, the British foreign minister presented his proposal to Stalin. The first section called for a commission composed of representatives from the United Kingdom, Soviet Union, and United States to oversee the establishment of provincial Iranian assemblies that would officially answer to the central government but in reality be autonomous. The second part of the plan created a three power liaison group to coordinate the mutual evacuation of their forces from Iran. The proposal called for the removal of Allied troops on schedule, the maintenance of *de jure* control by the Tehran government, and the establishment of local self-rule. The proposal left intact Soviet influence in north-

43. *Ibid.*, 767–68; Bevin to Foreign Office, December 26, 1945, U 10377/6550/70, in FO 371, 1945, PRO.

44. *FR, 1945*, II, 761–76; Bevin to Foreign Office, December 26, 1945, U 10377/6550/70, in FO 371, 1945, PRO; Jacob, "To Moscow," 30–31.

ern Iran and British influence in southern Iran. After examining the plan, Stalin said that he thought it "might serve as a basis for some agreement," and he told Bevin that minor amendments, reflecting Soviet wishes, would be delivered in the morning.[45]

Stalin did not let Bevin relax too long. Perhaps hoping to trade concessions, the Soviet leader asked why Great Britain opposed the Soviet request for a trusteeship over Tripolitania. "Could not the interests of the Soviet Union be taken into account?" Britain, Stalin complained, "would have lost nothing . . . she already had plenty of bases all over the world, even more than the United States." Recognizing the drift of Stalin's argument, Bevin chose to raise the level of conversation above the realities of power politics and spheres of influence. He heaped praise upon Byrnes's concept of international trusteeships. Stalin returned the discussion to the level of power politics. He suggested that "the British were not prepared to trust the Soviet Union in Tripolitania" and lamented that "Britain had India and her possessions in the Indian Ocean and her sphere of influence; the United States had China and Japan . . . but the Soviet Union had nothing." Incredulous, Bevin "pointed out that the Russian sphere extended from Lubeck to Port Arthur."[46] The debate over spheres of influence could have easily continued for the rest of the evening, but both Stalin and Bevin agreed that the time had come for them to attend a Christmas Eve dinner being held below in the salon of the Order of St. Catherine.

Most of the guests had arrived when Stalin and Bevin made their entrance. Stalin appeared fresh and rested. General Jacob had not seen Stalin since 1943 and noted: "Stalin looked well, but aged. His hair is greyer and thin, and his expression is less alert and animated. His smile is no longer so genial, if crafty, but is more the leer of an old man." Bevin looked tired and dejected.[47]

The dinner was the customary Russian feast with many and varied courses. Each course was preceded and followed by toasts. Many of the toasts were friendly, but a few were fraught with diplomatic implications. One particularly noteworthy exchange took place halfway through the dinner. Benjamin Cohen rose to toast

45. *FR, 1945,* II, 774–76; Bevin to Foreign Office, December 26, 1945, U 10377/6550/70, in FO 371, 1945, PRO.

46. Bevin to Foreign Office, December 26, 1945, U 10377/6550/70, in FO 371, 1945, PRO; Dixon, *Double Diploma,* 202–204; Jacob, "To Moscow," 31.

47. Dixon, *Double Diploma,* 204; Jacob, "To Moscow," 31–32.

James Conant, whose "work was too secret to mention." Molotov responded that they all had enough "drink to explore secrets" and that he "could now drink a toast to Dr. Conant, who, perhaps, had a bit of the atomic bomb in his pocket."[48]

As the rest of the guests raised their glasses to drink to Molotov's awkward humor, Stalin interrupted. "This is too serious a matter to joke about. I raise my glass to the American scientists and what they have accomplished. We must now work together to see that this great invention is used for peaceful ends." Relieved, the guests drained their glasses.[49]

After dinner, Stalin spoke directly to Conant about his "admiration for the great work of Anglo-American scientists in producing the atomic bomb." He added that "Soviet scientists were not very good although he hoped they would improve." Both the British and Americans left the dinner considering the effect the atomic bomb was having on Soviet policy, aware that the Russians were pressing to close the nuclear gap.[50]

Christmas Day found the ministers busy trying to resolve the few remaining questions. During an informal afternoon session, Byrnes and Molotov battled over whether the new members of the Romanian and Bulgarian governments should be termed "loyal opposition" or "truly representative" of the opposition parties and whether Lupu, Maniu, and Bratianu should be listed as persona non grata. Hoping to find common ground, Byrnes asked if the names could be deleted from the official communiqué and letter to the Groza government but included in the private instructions to the tripartite commission that was to be formed to oversee the broadening of the Romanian government. Molotov agreed, but in return he asked that Bevin and Byrnes accept the wording "two representatives loyal to the present Government—truly representative of those groups of the National Peasant and Liberal parties not at the present participating in the present Government." If they could not, Molotov stated, then he could not accept the deletion of the names from the communiqué.[51]

48. Conant, *My Several Lives*, 482–83.

49. Conant, *My Several Lives*, 482–83; Clark Kerr to Foreign Office, December 25, 1945, U 10330/6550/70, in FO 371, 1945, PRO; Byrnes, *Speaking Frankly*, 268.

50. Byrnes, *Speaking Frankly*, 268.

51. *FR, 1945*, II, 781–92.

Faced with a decision, Byrnes and Bevin asked for a definition of "loyal" and "truly representative." Angered, Molotov icily noted that without consultation or Soviet approval the Americans had altered part of the proposal already agreed upon by affirming the Americans' right to decide unilaterally whether the Romanians had fulfilled the conditions of the proposal. He observed that the new United States reservation undermined not only the proposal but the tripartite commission, whose duty it was to implement the decisions made in Moscow.[52]

Byrnes rose to the attack and asked if Molotov intended for the commission to have authority over a sovereign nation. In a solemn voice, Byrnes announced that the United States held the right to determine whether or not it would recognize Romania or any other state based on its own evaluations and not those of a commission. For once outmaneuvered, Molotov conceded that the secretary of state was correct, but only after he extracted from Byrnes a statement that the United States had a "moral" obligation to recognize Romania if the commission recommended it.[53]

After more debate the ministers found a sentence that met all of their requirements: the additional statesmen were to be "truly representative of the groups of the parties not represented in the Government" and willing "to work loyally with the Government." However, the three ministers were unable to find any acceptable language to frame the instructions to the Bulgarian government and, after another full day of discussions on Bulgaria on December 26, decided to delete the subject of Bulgaria from the formal agenda and communiqué.[54]

Christmas Day also found the ministers occupied with negotiating the Iranian problem. In the morning, Byrnes visited Bevin and found the British foreign minister hard at work incorporating Stalin's changes into the British proposal on Iran. Looking over Bevin's shoulder, Byrnes commented that the Soviets were removing all references to the specific withdrawal date and referring only to the terms of the 1942 treaty. He interjected that it should be stipulated that all Allied forces would be removed from Iran no later than March 2, 1946. He further argued that the proposal should be ap-

52. *Ibid.*, 783–92.
53. *Ibid.*, 785–92.
54. *FR, 1945,* II, 781–95, 805–806, 813.

proved by the Iranian government before being implemented. Using forceful language and implying that the United States might not support the proposal unless his ideas were followed, Byrnes convinced Bevin to ignore Stalin's minor amendments and to incorporate Byrnes's.[55]

Byrnes next visited Molotov. Molotov wanted to discuss Iran, and he referred to the British proposal. He asked for Byrnes's opinion. The secretary of state confided that he "did not especially like the proposal" but said that he would accept it to solve the matter.[56]

The effect of Byrnes's qualified acceptance of the British proposal on Molotov or Soviet policy is unknown. But, when the ministers met that afternoon, Molotov's position had changed. He read Bevin's revised paper and flatly rejected it. He said that the Soviet Union refused to consider the matter any further. Shocked and dismayed, Bevin refused to abandon his proposal. He reminded Molotov that Stalin had all but promised a solution to the Iranian question and had accepted the British plan as the basis for agreement. Molotov was unmovable. Equally shocking to Bevin was Byrnes's nonchalance and unwillingness to support the proposal. "There would never be a time when all questions could be settled," the secretary of state rationalized. Because "many questions had been disposed of and the conference could not remain in session indefinitely, he proposed that the delegates proceed to consider the communiqué and protocol." He quipped that "after all, the delegates would be together again in January." Watching the division between Bevin and Byrnes widen, Molotov added "that if Mr. Byrnes and Mr. Bevin did not wish to deal with [the] remaining questions, he could but concur."[57] The meeting thus ended for Bevin on a sour note, but he had not conceded defeat.

The British foreign minister sought another meeting with Stalin. Stalin was unavailable and Bevin was forced to settle for another meeting with Molotov. Holding his temper in check, Bevin listened as Molotov listed alleged Iranian abuses against the Soviet Union.

---

55. *Ibid.*, 799; Discussions of the Iranian Question—Moscow, December 16–26, 1945, January 3, 1946, in File 740.00119 (Council)/1–346, DSR-NA; Bevin to Foreign Office, December 27, 1945, E 10191/103/34, in FO 371, 1945, PRO; Dixon, *Double Diploma*, 205.

56. *FR, 1945*, II, 777–79; Discussions of Iranian Question, January 3, 1945, in File 740.00119 (Council)/1–346, DSR-NA.

57. *FR, 1945*, II, 795–97, 805–806.

Finally, his patience at an end, Bevin told Molotov that he could well understand the Tehran government's frustrations at being denied access to part of its territory. Leaving, he remarked: "I do not want to be faced with *faits accomplis*." Quietly, Molotov replied there would be none and that the Soviet government had "no claims on Persian territory."[58]

Disappointed and angry, Bevin returned to the British embassy. He told his colleagues that he faced two choices: he could either accept the Russian dismissal of the Iranian issue, or he could refuse to end the conference until the matter was resolved. To do the latter, he realized he would need Byrnes's support, and Bevin knew he did not have it. Reluctantly, he told his delegation that they had no choice but to end the conference without solving the Iranian question and to "continue the struggle over Persia through diplomatic channels after the Conference."[59] Dejected and beaten, Bevin returned to Spiridonvka Palace at eleven that night to sign the communiqué and protocol.

During the final hours of the Moscow conference (from 11:00 P.M. to 3:30 A.M.), Byrnes was the driving force to finish the conference before morning. Byrnes had told his staff to prepare for an early 7:30 A.M. takeoff. From the outset there was a lengthy delay because the Russian copy of the communiqué and protocol was still being typed. When it finally arrived, Molotov burst into laughter, explaining to his startled guests that the delay occurred because the Russian typist mistakenly included the Soviet proposal on Bulgaria. Good-naturedly, Bevin and Byrnes chuckled—until Molotov asked if the "mistake" could not, after all, be included in the final communiqué. Could not, after all, Molotov asked, Britain and the United States accept Stalin's offer to advise the Bulgarians to broaden their government? Bevin and Byrnes firmly answered no. In return, Byrnes asked if Molotov could accept the United States wording of the Bulgarian proposal. In a moment of unusually slapdash diplomacy, Molotov said he could. Quickly all three copies of the communiqué and protocol were turned over to the typists for alterations.[60]

The retyping took another hour and a half, but finally at "3:30,

58. Record of Conversation Between Byrnes and Molotov, December 26, 1945, in File 500, Moscow Post Files, Suitland, Md.

59. Jacob, "To Moscow," 34.

60. *FR, 1945*, II, 813–14; Byrnes, *Speaking Frankly*, 121; Dixon, *Double Diploma*, 205–206; Jacob, "To Moscow," 34–35.

amid the usual battery of pressmen" gathered for the event, the foreign ministers of the United States, United Kingdom, and the Soviet Union signed the Moscow conference protocol and final communiqué. Pierson Dixon observed: "As everyone was feeling cross and exhausted, headachy and grubby, cordiality is hardly likely to be the caption."[61]

The communiqué of the Moscow conference was released at 10:00 P.M. Washington time, on December 27, 1945. It revealed a carefully constructed series of compromises designed to protect specific interests in areas of special concern to the United States and the Soviet Union as well as to bridge the differences in each nation's views on the form of a postwar settlement. The communiqué addressed the preparation of the peace treaties for Italy, Romania, Bulgaria, Hungary, and Finland; the role and makeup of the Far Eastern Advisory Commission and the Allied Control Council for Japan; and specific policies regarding Korea, China, Romania, and Bulgaria. The communiqué also included recommendations for the establishment and functions of a United Nations commission on the control of atomic energy. (See Appendix.)

The conference left Stalin, Molotov, and Byrnes satisfied. Through pragmatic quid pro quo bargaining reminiscent of Yalta, the United States and the Soviet Union reached understandings on Eastern Europe, atomic energy, and the nature of future big-power negotiations. Bevin was less pleased, but his and other British concern was tempered by overall, favorable international support for the decisions made at Moscow. Reflecting international sentiment, a New York *Times* headline flashed: "New Start For Peace." Edward R. Murrow called the Moscow conference "one of the most important political events of the last twelve years . . . an end of an era of American methods, and the beginning of an era of world methods."[62]

Morrow was wrong. The spring would see the collapse of the Grand Alliance and the start of an era characterized by confrontation between American and Soviet ways.

61. Jacob, "To Moscow," 35; Dixon, *Double Diploma*, 206.
62. New York *Times*, December 28, 1945, Sec. 1, p. 1; Sylwester, "American Public Reaction," 146; *Twohey Analysis*, December 29, 1945, and January 5, 1946; Press Summaries, White House Files, December 30, 1945, in Truman Papers; Kennan to State Department, December 28, 1945, in File 500, Moscow Post Files, Suitland, Md.; Kennan to State Department, January 15, 1946, in File 740.00119 (Council)/1–1546, DSR-NA.

VII

The Grand Alliance Collapses

THE DEADLOCKED London conference demonstrated the ease with which the Big Three could disagree. The Moscow conference was an opportunity to repair the damage done to the Grand Alliance and to restart the process of building a lasting peace. In Moscow, the foreign ministers tried to break through the circle of suspicion and to fashion agreements that balanced national needs with the principles of international cooperation. The final communiqué and departing statements affirmed the unity of the Big Three and signaled a rekindling of the Grand Alliance.

But the Moscow accords were flawed and fragile. Suspicions and mistrust lingered. The British delegation left disappointed, angry, and suspicious. Britain's status as a major power seemed threatened, for the United States and the Soviet Union had disregarded British opinions and needs. Despite British concern over Iran, Bevin was unable to convince Byrnes and Molotov to lengthen the meeting and find a solution. Further, Ambassador Archibald Clark Kerr's report revealed that Stalin did not like Bevin or the way the British treated Russia. Clark Kerr reminded the Foreign Office that "there were those at the Kremlin who could not forget that . . . [Bevin was] a man of the 'old international' which had been against the Bolsheviks in 1917." For the departing British delegation there were no customary departing gifts, not even a smoked salmon.[1]

Assessing the Moscow conference, members of the Foreign Office admitted that some short-term benefits might have been gained but doubted that these would smooth out long-term relations between the Soviets and the West. Any accomplishments "were more than outweighed by the lack of any agreement on Persia and the continued stubbornness of the Soviet attitude on Turkey." It seemed that Britain was "left to face, with doubtful American backing, constantly increasing Soviet pressure in the whole zone vital to British security between India and the Dardanelles." A Foreign Office memorandum concluded that "the Russians are satisfied as well they may be."[2]

Less worrisome than Soviet behavior, but still of concern, was the attitude of the United States and its secretary of state. That "Irishman," Byrnes, had ignored the British during the Moscow conference, and John Balfour reported that in Washington there was a tendency to refer to the conference "solely in terms of an improvement in Big Two relations." It appeared that across the United States, the role of the United Kingdom was being discounted. Balfour added that many Americans seemed to blame the British for nearly all international tensions.[3]

On a positive note, the British chargé d'affaires said that there were some "sensible Americans" who realized that the "survival of Britain as a strong and prosperous country was an essential American interest." Officials in the Foreign Office agreed and sought ways to show Americans that England was still strong, vital, and capable of defending its own interests.[4]

If the British view of the Moscow conference was gloomy, the Soviet view was cheerful. Public statements by Russian officials and public lecturers expressed strong support for the conference and its agreements. *Red Fleet* and *Pravda* announced that the accords re-

1. Lord Inverchapel to Foreign Office, January 29, 1946, N 4977/140/38, in FO 371, 1946, PRO; Jacob, "To Moscow," 31–33.
2. Roberts to Foreign Office, March 14, 1946, N 4065/97/38; Foreign Office Memorandum, January 2, 1946, U 10435/6550/70, both in FO 371, 1946, PRO.
3. Balfour to Foreign Office, January 11, 1946, AN 205/5/45, in FO 371, 1946, PRO.
4. *Ibid.*

pudiated the "reactionary elements abroad." *Pravda* hailed the atomic energy decision as one "of great importance." Both newspapers reported that the "new year opens hopefully."[5]

The Russians also stressed the importance of the cooperation of the Big Three as an integral part of international relations. Affirming the Soviet Union's role as an international power, Soviet spokesmen announced that the Soviet Union "must play her part and be properly represented in the wider circle" of international affairs. Stalin admitted that he still liked "smaller meetings of the Big Three and the Big Two" but stated that he would support fully the United Nations and a general peace conference.[6]

However, caution was expressed that the spirit of the Moscow agreements might dissipate with implementation. *New Times* worried about Romania and Bulgaria. It stated that even though the agreements "put an end to outside attempts to impose abstract standards of western-democracy" on the two nations, the Soviet people would anxiously wait to see if Britain and the United States recognized the two governments. A Soviet lecturer told an overflowing Moscow audience that the Bulgarian agreement was a potential source of trouble and that the Soviet Union would not allow "America or Britain to drive the Bulgarian people back on 'the path of death.'"[7]

Of the three foreign ministers, James Byrnes was the most pleased with the Moscow meeting. Stonebottom Molotov, viewed as an obstacle to East-West cooperation, was overcome by direct meetings with Stalin. The premier had presented the secretary of state with an autographed picture as a parting gift. It appeared that Byrnes's Moscow gamble had paid off. The road to further international meetings and the establishment of an enduring peace was open.

When he arrived in Washington on December 28, Byrnes discovered that public support for the agreements was already slipping. The Christmas Eve communiqué had received over 74 percent editorial support in the nation's newspapers. That support stood at less than 66 percent on the day he arrived. Several well-known radio personalities and newspapers were criticizing the conference

    5. Roberts to Foreign Office, January 1, 1946, N 97/97/38, in FO 371, 1946, PRO.
    6. Roberts to Foreign Office, January 23, 1946, N 1026/605/38, in FO 371, 1946, PRO.
    7. Roberts to Foreign Office, January 14, 1946, N 977/650/38, in FO 371, 1946, PRO; *New Times*, January 1, 1946, pp. 1–4.

and the secretary of state. Walter Winchell announced over ABC radio that the Moscow agreements were "a terrific triumph for Molotov" and that Byrnes was traded out of "his striped pants" for nothing more than a handshake. The Chicago *Tribune* called Byrnes "a silly little man" who believed that the United States should trust the Russians.[8]

Dissent was also evident among politicians and presidential advisers. Senator Vandenberg denounced the atomic control agreement and demanded to see President Truman. Admiral Leahy, Judge Samuel Rosemann, and former Ambassador to the Soviet Union William Bullett considered the final communiqué from Moscow "an appeasement document" and the conference another "Munich." All informed Truman of their opinions. The president was unsure of how to react to the Moscow meeting, but he knew he disliked learning of the agreements through the press. When Byrnes landed in Washington, Acheson strongly recommended that the secretary see Truman as soon as possible.[9]

Truman and many of Byrnes's detractors were on board the presidential yacht *Williamsburg*, sailing up and down the Potomac. Byrnes arranged to see the president and asked Acheson to line up the major radio stations for an address on the Moscow agreements. At 5:15 P.M., less than three hours after arriving, the secretary of state faced Truman. Immediately, Truman asked why the President of the United States "did not know of the adjournment of the conference until he heard it over the radio while in Kansas City." Drawing a deep breath, Byrnes explained that the final meeting lasted nearly nonstop from seven in the evening until three in the morning and that "the long report could not be put into code . . . as quickly as a broadcasting company could announce the adjournment and the substance of the agreements." Truman nodded, saying "he could understand the situation."[10]

8. Sylwester, "American Public Reaction," 145–46; *Twohey Analysis*, December 29, 1945, and January 5, 1946; Gaddis, *The Origins of the Cold War*, 282–90; Press Summaries, White House Files, December 29, 1945, and January 3, 1946, in Truman Papers.

9. Vandenberg (ed.), *The Private Papers of Vandenberg*, 232–33; Rose, *After Yalta*, 158–59; Gaddis, *The Origins of the Cold War*, 286–96; Acheson, *Present at the Creation*, 135–36; Curry, *James F. Byrnes*, 183–85; Leahy Diary, December 28, 1945, and January 8, 1946, in Leahy Papers; Transcript of Jonathan Daniels' interview with Clark Clifford and Admiral William Leahy, in Box 88, Daniels Papers.

10. Unused notes for *Speaking Frankly*, in Byrnes Papers.

Next Byrnes went over the agreements point by point. The Japanese agreement was "the same as that presented by the U.S. except for the insertion of the mission of the Allied Council." The power and the prerogatives of the Supreme Allied Commander remained intact and General MacArthur would be allowed to change policy "by issuing interim directives and by changing Japanese officials." [11]

The Romanian agreement was a "victory," Byrnes boasted. The Soviets accepted the applicability of the Yalta Declaration and recognized opposition parties as legitimate forms of expression and political activity. He admitted that the Bulgarian decision was unacceptable because it did not guarantee the broadening of the government or the protection of civil and political rights. [12]

The atomic energy agreement was the same as the one written by the State Department committee. As for Soviet requests for information and atomic materials, Byrnes said that it was his "general impression . . . that the Russians didn't expect the U.S. to give away any secrets . . . [and] would consider it foolish if the United States did." He added that although Soviet propaganda agencies might ask for atomic information, Soviet officials "would never strain the credulity of American diplomats by making such a suggestion." [13]

Stalin also agreed to work with the Nationalist Chinese and to support the unification of Korea after a limited trusteeship. Only Iran, Byrnes said, remained an unresolved issue. It was his view that the Soviets did "not want anything to do with the present Iranian government." [14]

The briefing lasted a little more than an hour. When the two emerged for drinks and dinner, Leahy noted that Truman seemed fully satisfied with the secretary of state's account of the meeting and the agreements. Truman told his secretary, Charles Ross, to line up CBS radio for Byrnes's message on Sunday. [15]

The national speech followed the pattern of Byrnes's briefing of Truman. Byrnes expressed the belief that, taken as a whole, the

11. Memorandum of Conversation Between Charles Bohlen and General G. A. Lincoln, December 29, 1945, OPD 334.8 (TS), in PODR-NA.

12. Ibid.

13. Ibid.

14. Ibid.

15. Leahy Diary, December 29, 1945, in Leahy Papers; Daniels' interview with Clifford and Leahy; Charles Ross to Eben Ayers, December 29, 1945, in William Rigdon Papers, Truman Library.

Moscow conference was a major step toward peace and inter-national cooperation. He concluded: "We must not slacken in our efforts. With patience, good will, and toleration we must strive to build and maintain a just and enduring peace." Privately, Byrnes confided that the United States "had done all we could to try and produce a good feeling" and to "bring about peace and Four-Power amity." [16]

The speech convinced a majority of Americans of the accom-plishments of the Moscow agreements. Truman wrote to Henry Stimson on January 2, 1946: "The international situation I think is very much improved—the domestic one is still a very bad head-ache." Nevertheless, the furor over the agreements and the criti-cisms by important individuals convinced Byrnes that in 1946 the United States must appear to gain more than it conceded. Senator Vandenberg made that clear when he announced that he was going to the London meeting of the United Nations "to insure there would be no more 'give aways' to the Russians." Commenting on the climate of opinion, Donald Russell, close friend of Byrnes and the assistant secretary of state for administration, wrote: "I must confess . . . that there is apparently more anti-Russian spirit than I thought possible." [17]

By the time Byrnes left for the United Nations meeting, that anti-Soviet spirit appeared to be rising as it was becoming clear that implementation of some of the Moscow agreements was proving difficult. Big Three amity and cooperation seemed threatened over disagreements on Korea and Bulgaria, as Russia questioned Ameri-can sincerity and the United States suspected Soviet intentions.

Although Korean events were far from the public's attention, offi-cials in the Navy and War Departments were increasingly con-cerned about Soviet actions. Byrnes believed that the Far Eastern issues were solved in the United States' favor and that Stalin indi-

16. James F. Byrnes, "Report by the Secretary of State on the Meeting of Foreign Ministers," *DSB*, XIV (December 30, 1945), 1033–36, 1047; Memorandum of Conver-sation Between Bevin and Byrnes, September 25, 1946, N 12449/5169/38, in FO 371, 1946, PRO.

17. Leahy Diary, January 1, 1946, in Leahy Papers; Vandenberg to John W. Blodgett, December 24, 1945, Vandenberg to Brien McMahon, January 2, 1946, both in Arthur Vandenberg Papers, University of Michigan Library, University of Michi-gan, Ann Arbor; Donald Russell to Cassandra Conner, January 14, 1946, in Folder 569 (1), Byrnes Papers.

cated little interest in Korea, China, or Japan. In Byrnes's view, the agreements on Korea provided for the immediate creation of a provisional government under the direction of pro-American political groups.[18]

Koreans saw the agreement differently. They wanted immediate independence and denounced the idea of a provisional government and continued occupation. General John Hodge, commander in chief of the American occupation zone, encouraged the Koreans to think that the United States supported immediate independence and that the Soviets were responsible for the provisional government and trusteeship. He gleefully informed the War Department that never had American influence and prestige been so high and the Soviets' so low.[19]

Hodge's pleasure was matched by the Russians' anger and suspicion. On January 23, Stalin told Harriman that he "had little good news from Korea, and that it appeared that American representatives . . . were now backing away" from the Moscow agreement. He reminded the ambassador that Russia did not need the trusteeship and that it could be "abandoned." Harriman replied that there was some mistake. He knew that Byrnes looked upon Korea as "a splendid chance to demonstrate how the United States and the Soviet Government could work together." Stalin remained skeptical, and Tass printed a full account of the Moscow discussions on Korea. It showed that the United States proposed the trusteeship and provisional government.[20]

The Tass story turned Korean public opinion against the United States. Hodge frantically wired the State Department for proof that the account was false. He was dismayed to learn that the Russian version was correct. He was determined to halt any anti-American sentiments and to prevent Korea from becoming a Soviet puppet.

18. Memorandum of Conversation Between Bohlen and Lincoln, December 29, 1945, OPD 344.8 (TS), in PODR-NA; Iriye, *The Cold War in Asia*, 127; Bruce Cummings, "American Policy and Korean Liberation," in Frank Baldwin (ed.), *Without Parallel: The American-Korean Relationship Since 1945* (New York, 1974), 65–108.

19. Cummings, "American Policy and Korean Liberation," 65–108; Lee, "American Policy Toward Korea," 191–92, 225–31, 240–52.

20. Harriman and Abel, *Special Envoy*, 532–33; Lee, "American Policy Toward Korea," 189–91, 240–52; *FR, 1946*, VIII, 607–11, 617–22; Harriman to State Department, January 25, 1946, in File 740.00119 (Control) Korea/1–2546, DSR-NA.

He told his staff: "There is not a question but the Soviets want to have Korea become a Soviet state. There are many men here in South Korea who are right now taking orders from Moscow. Right now Communism is in the ascendency in the United States, in the Army, and right here in Korea. Believe me, Korea is just one pawn in their great ambition." [21]

Hodge's views were held by other American officials in Korea and in Washington. H. Merrell Benninghoff, the State Department's political representative in Korea, warned that the Koreans would soon "be at the mercy of the Soviets' highly organized steam-roller techniques should they reach the conclusion that the US talks big but acts little." Harriman visited Korea en route to Washington and also saw a serious Soviet threat. Once in Washington, he warned that the Russians intended to dominate Korea just as they did Eastern Europe. [22]

The Truman administration's reaction was to back away from the agreement made in Moscow. In late January, State Department officials informed Hodge he could limit participation in the government to non-totalitarian groups. Communists were considered totalitarian. Within the week, he was told that the United States was no longer committed to a trusteeship or any system that delayed Korean independence. By the end of February, Hodge was instructed to make "clear in a strong public statement" that the United States was "looking toward a free and independent Korea." Byrnes asked the navy to keep troops nearby "to reinforce Korea in case of a major emergency." His splendid chance to work with the Soviets no longer existed. [23]

While the United States reacted to fears of Soviet influence in Korea, the Russians watched closely the events taking place in Bulgaria. There, it seemed, American actions were preventing the implementation of the Moscow agreement regarding that nation. On

21. Quoted in Lee, "American Policy Toward Korea," 196; Forrestal Diaries, Vol. IV, January–April, 1946 (Korea), in Forrestal Papers; Millis and Duffield (eds.), *Forrestal Diaries*, 134–35; FR, *1946*, VIII, 628–30.

22. Leahy Diary, February 21, 1946, in Leahy Papers; Harriman and Abel, *Special Envoy*, 533–34; FR, *1946*, VIII, 619–20, 630–32.

23. SWNCC 176/18, January 22, 1946, in SWNCC Files; War Department to General Hodge, February 28, 1946, OPD 337 (TS), in PODR-NA; FR, *1946*, VIII, 623–27, 657–58, 685–89; Lee, "American Policy Toward Korea," 281–90.

January 8, Andrei Vyshinsky arrived in London for the United Nations meeting. He immediately complained that the Soviet Union was unhappy with the implementation of the Moscow accord on Bulgaria. It was a small case, he told Bevin, but one that "was poisoning relations between the powers."[24]

The Moscow agreement provided for the Soviets to give their recommendation to the Bulgarian government to enlarge its membership by adding two members from the political opposition. Both Russian and American leaders were skeptical that the accord would be faithfully executed. Western officials feared that the Soviets' suggestion would be ignored by the government in Sofia or that the Fatherland front regime would not pick meaningful opposition leaders. The Russians questioned whether the British and Americans would accept a truly pro-Soviet regime. The fear that the Fatherland front would violate the agreement soon proved unfounded. Even before the official Soviet suggestion, the Bulgarian government announced its willingness to broaden its membership by including two members from the opposition parties. Russian fears were not so unfounded.

Supported by Maynard Barnes, the American political representative, the opposition leaders announced that they would not join the government unless the Ministries of Justice and the Interior were removed from communist control. The Bulgarian government refused to consider the demand. Vyshinsky openly blamed Barnes and the United States for the opposition's demands.[25]

The impasse in Sofia presented Bevin, and to a lesser extent Byrnes, with a difficult decision. If they exerted pressure on the opposition to drop the conditions and join the government, they ran the risk of being refused and of losing influence. If they supported the opposition's demands, they risked the Soviets' anger. Weeks before, the Romanian opposition had suggested similar conditions before joining the Groza government but had dropped them when British and American representatives rejected any attempt to alter the Moscow agreement. British representative La Rougetel had warned King Michael that he "would get no sympa-

24. Memorandum of Conversation Between Bevin and Vyshinsky, January 27, 1946, N 1471/140/38, in FO 371, 1946, PRO.
25. *Ibid.*; Barnes to State Department, January 4, 9, 12, 13, and 21, 1946, in File 874.00/46, DSR-NA.

thy from British or United States representatives if he attempted to replace the present Minister of Interior, or display any independent action." In Romania, the Groza government was enlarged and recognized by the United States and Great Britain. Vyshinsky expected the same course in Bulgaria.[26]

But Bulgaria was not Romania. Byrnes and Bevin adopted "a neutral" position. They told Vyshinsky that they expected the Bulgarians to solve their own problems but held the Soviet Union responsible for enlarging the government. This position placed pressure on the Soviets to produce concessions from the Fatherland front that would benefit the pro-Western opposition parties. The Soviet representative to the United Nations argued that the opposition's stance was the direct consequence of Barnes's actions and that the United States and Great Britain should apply pressure on the opposition to join the government. Bevin and Byrnes refused, maintaining their "neutral" position. In Moscow, official news accounts leveled strong warnings at the Bulgarian opposition and blamed the United States and Britain for the inability to implement the Moscow accord on Bulgaria.[27]

The disputes over Korea and Bulgaria took place on a diplomatic level out of the view of the general American and British public. For the public, it was the confrontation at the United Nations over Iran that indicated the collapse of the Grand Alliance. The initial face-off between Vyshinsky and Bevin over Soviet troops in Iran was unexpected. During the Moscow conference, Stalin, who had been warned that Iran might present a complaint against the Soviet Union at the United Nations, said he was not worried and would not object. After the meeting, the British had worked to prevent the complaint. However, when Iran presented the complaint on January 19, the Soviets strenuously objected and Bevin rushed to support Iran.

Officials in the Foreign Office decided to give their full diplomatic support to Iran. It was hoped that such support would dem-

26. Foreign Office to Houstoun-Boswell, January 2, 1946, R 21519/5063/67, in FO 371, 1946, PRO; *FR, 1946,* VI, 46–47.

27. *FR, 1946,* VI, 57–59, 66–68, 78; La Rougetel to Foreign Office, December 30, 1945, R 21632/28/37, in FO 371, 1945, PRO; Barnes to State Department, January 21, 1946, February 11, 1946; Cohen to State Department, February 9, 1946, all in File 874.00/46, DSR-NA; Lundestad, *The American Non-Policy,* 275–78.

onstrate to the United States that Britain was willing to face the Russians. Intelligence reports from Moscow indicated that the Russians were seeking to expand their influence in the Middle East. Frank Roberts thought that the Soviets wanted to protect the autonomy of Azerbaijan and force a change of government in Tehran. Thomas Brimelow, of the Northern Department, believed that the Russians saw their southern border as the czars had in the early twentieth century. "We seem to be entering on a similar phase in contemporary history," he wrote; "and, if this hypothesis is true, we may be able to avoid a major clash, but we can hardly look forward to good relations." The Foreign Office concluded that support of Iran at the United Nations would awaken international public opinion to the threat of Soviet influence in the Middle East.[28]

American opinions were paramount among those to be awakened. The Foreign Office believed that Americans were unsure about their role as world leaders and on most international issues. John Balfour wrote that the United States was "ruefully aware that she is inadequately equipped with gifts of leadership." There was "an opportunity for Britain to set an example." British resolution in the face of Soviet intransigence would cast aside thoughts of British weakness and demonstrate to the "unstable Mr. Byrnes" how to deal with the Soviets.[29]

The Iranian motion drew unexpectedly bitter responses from the Soviet delegation and client states. Behind the scenes, Vyshinsky worked to have the complaint dropped. He claimed that bilateral Iranian-Soviet negotiations were the proper solution and that the United Nations should be used only as a last resort. Bevin and Byrnes exerted equally strong pressure to keep the motion before the world organization. On January 24, Vyshinsky and Bevin confronted each other publicly. Bevin objected to the Soviet "war of nerves" aimed at Iran. Vyshinsky retorted that the British were "hotheads." An open breach was once more apparent in the Grand

28. *FR, 1946*, VII, 1–6, 289–94; Roberts to Foreign Office, January 14, 1946, N 977/650/38, Foreign Office Minute, February 14, 1946, N 1965/140/38, Balfour to Foreign Office, January 22, 1946, AN 205/5/45, all in FO 371, 1946, PRO; Bevin to Foreign Office, December 28, 1945, E 10184/103/34, in FO 371, 1945, PRO.

29. Anderson, "Britain, the US, and the Cold War," 167–71; Boyce, "The British Foreign Office View," 308–309; Balfour to Foreign Office, January 22, 1946, AN 205/5/45, in FO 371, 1946, PRO.

Alliance. As for the Iranian complaint, it was set aside pending negotiations between the new Iranian prime minister, Qavam, and
the Soviet Union.[30]

Dissatisfaction with the Moscow conference, combined with the
events at the United Nations meeting, generated deep concern
about the direction of Soviet foreign policy within the Foreign
Office. Prospects seemed gloomy for cordial British-Soviet relations.
The Russians were intent upon producing "an atmosphere of tension . . . and deliberately stoking up an anti-British campaign."
Soviet election speeches analyzed by Roberts and the Northern Department implied "a return to [the] pure doctrine of Marx-Leninism-
Stalinism." Known hardliners Malenkov and Kaganovich were
openly advocating that "the Soviet Union should go her own way."
Even moderates placed extreme importance upon "building up industrial and military power." The "bogey of external danger" was
once again a popular part of Soviet speeches and announcements.[31]

Admitting that much of the reported election language was
rhetoric designed "to overcome postwar lethargy," members of the
Foreign Office still thought the statements important. "We should
have been wise to take *Mein Kampf* at its face value," Frank Roberts
stated.[32]

Two possible reasons were offered for the anti-British thrust of
Soviet actions. The first explanation acknowledged that the Soviet
Union acted to fill political and diplomatic vacuums caused by the
contraction of British power. This seemed particularly true in the
Middle and Near East. The second explanation diagnosed the cur-
rent ideological situation. British political observers, like many
Americans, saw a leftward shift in world politics. On the Left, the
battle for political preeminence was taking place between com-

30. Campbell and Herring (eds.), *The Diaries of Stettinius*, 446–48; Hess, "The Iranian Crisis," 132–40; Stettinius to State Department, January 28, 1946, in File
501.BC/1–2846, DSR-NA; *FR, 1946,* VII, 289–300, 306–11, 317; *FR, 1946,* VII,
335–49; Kuniholm, *The Origins of the Cold War in the Near East,* 304–308; Paterson,
Soviet-American Confrontation, 178–80; Anderson, "Britain, the US, and the Cold
War," 168–71.

31. Roberts to Foreign Office, February 23, 1946, N 2466/140/38, February 12,
1946, N 1965/140/38, C. F. A. Warner, "Soviet Campaign Against This Country," Foreign Office Minute, April 2, 1946, N 6344/605/38, all in FO 371, 1946, PRO.

32. Warner, "Soviet Campaign," April 2, 1946, N 6344/605/38, Roberts to Foreign
Office, February 12, 1946, N 1965/140/38, both in FO 371, 1946, PRO.

munism and social democracy. The Soviet Union was the heart of communism. Labor-controlled Britain was the champion of social democracy. Soviet attempts to link the Labour government to capitalism and old-fashioned imperialism were part of a campaign to discredit social democracy and Britain. Roberts wrote: "The rulers of Russia already realised when Labour returned to power . . . that there was now a progressive force in the world with an equal and possibly greater attraction than their own Communist system."[33]

Roberts' evaluation was that the "Soviet push" was designed to take advantage of the "fluid state of post-war Europe" before world opinion reacted against "high-handed Soviet actions." The newly formed Russia Committee concluded that "Russian aggressiveness" was a real threat to Britain's global interests. It suggested that the Foreign Office and Attlee government needed to produce means to counteract the efforts of the Russians fairly quickly. To those within the Foreign Office, the Grand Alliance was extinct. The Soviet Union was a dangerous threat to Britain, and a new international system was needed to deal with that threat.[34]

Like the British, officials in the Truman administration were also watching Russian behavior. They too were reaching conclusions much like those in the Foreign Office. Reports from Romania and Bulgaria showed no change in Soviet efforts to dominate those nations and to squeeze out Western and dissident influence. Events in East Asia were disturbing, and a crisis appeared to be developing in Iran. Kennan's reports from Moscow indicated a dangerous turn in Soviet attitudes toward the West and the United States in particular. It seemed to him that the Soviet government was trying to convince the Russian people that the West was an enemy. To maintain its strength and influence, the Soviet government needed to exploit "differences among the Great Powers." Like Roberts, the American chargé d'affaires noted the frequent references to "capitalistic encirclement" in Soviet election speeches.[35]

33. Warner, "Soviet Campaign," April 2, 1946, N 6344/605/38, Roberts to Foreign Office, March 14, 1946, N 4065/97/38, March 17, 1946, N 4157/140/38, Foreign Office Minute, May 6, 1946, N 6344/605/38, all in FO 371, 1946, PRO.

34. Warner, "Soviet Campaign," April 2, 1946, N 6344/605/38, Roberts to Foreign Office, March 14, 1946, N 4065/97/38, both in FO 371, 1946, PRO.

35. Kennan to State Department, January 30, 1946, in File 761.00/1–3046, DSR-NA; FR, 1946, VI, 694–96; Gaddis, The Origins of the Cold War, 300–301; New York Times, February 13, 1946, Sec. 1, pp. 11, 13; Time, February 18, 1946, p. 14.

One speech that gained great attention was Stalin's February 9 election speech. Aimed at the domestic audience, Stalin's address recounted party activities and stressed the Soviet economic program that would triple industrial production. However, Western observers reacted to those parts of the speech that seemed to indicate that the Soviets were moving away from international cooperation and toward an ideologically based world view. They focused on the beginning of the speech, where Stalin blamed World War II on still-existing forces of monopolistic capitalism, and on a later point in the talk, where he mentioned "capitalistic encirclement" and told the Russian people that they must be prepared for "all contingencies."

Although Kennan did not attach great emphasis to Stalin's election speech, Kremlin watchers in the United States were almost obsessed with it. Lord Halifax commented: "Stalin's speech is the event of the week." Supreme Court Justice William O. Douglas saw it as a "Declaration of World War III," and H. Freeman Matthews believed the speech reflected Soviet hostility toward the West and complemented Vyshinsky's "antics" at the United Nations. Even Walter Lippmann found the speech threatening. Lippmann publicly called for the United States to rebuild and strengthen Western Europe and Asia against the Communist world system. In London, American expert J. C. Donnelly joked that the speech was causing a major uproar because it attacked the thing closest to an American national religion—capitalism.[36]

Fearful that the Soviets were marching away from international cooperation and that the United Nations would not be strong enough to guarantee peace, American policy makers sought to verify the nature of Soviet foreign policy and to project the United States' increased concern into international relations. Kennan was instructed to write an in-depth analysis of the Soviet Union's foreign policy. Within the State Department, Charles Bohlen and Dr. Gerold Robinson considered not only the nature of Soviet policy but alternative American reactions.

The Bohlen and Robinson report was finished by Valentine's Day.

36. Lord Halifax to Foreign Office, February 17, 1946, AN 423/1/45, in FO 371, 1946, PRO; Elbridge Dubrow, "Memorandum on Stalin's Election Speech," February 12, 1946, in File 861.00/2–1246, DSR-NA; H. F. Matthews, State Department Memorandum, February 11, 1946, in Matthews File, DSR-NA.

It stated that Soviet foreign policy stemmed from "internal situations and conditions" and would remain unchanged until Russia's internal affairs changed. Their report offered three alternatives for American policy toward Moscow; only one projected long-term harmony between the two nations. However, to adopt that alternative, the United States might again have to appear to be making concessions. "A careful overhauling of United States policy" would be required to avoid nearly all bilateral and unilateral actions. Full support would have to be given to the United Nations; opposition to Soviet nationalistic policies would have to be made through that agency. Over time, the report speculated, the Soviets would either be forced to accept the moral and international principles of the United Nations or "retreat into isolation."[37]

The remaining alternatives promised even less opportunity for peace and moderating Soviet actions. Rather, they carried the strong possibility of leading to an armed clash or the permanent division of the world into hostile spheres of influence. According to Robinson and Bohlen, the worst policy for the United States to follow was to accept the Russian view of international affairs—that is, close cooperation among the three powers and the division of the world into three spheres of influence with each power having a free hand in its sphere. Adoption of this approach, they contended, would destroy the usefulness of the United Nations, deny real international cooperation, and only delay "an eventual clash . . . under conditions infinitely worse for the United States."[38]

The third approach combined support for international principles and the United Nations with the protection of national interests and unilateral actions. It recommended that the United States should confront "Soviet nationalism and expansionism" with policies based on American interests and power. At the same time, officials in Washington would give "lip service" to the principles of international morality and world government. Following this alternative, Bohlen and Robinson saw the United States as embarking on an active and global foreign policy designed to deny military, economic, political, and diplomatic advantages to the Soviets by matching Russian actions with American counteractions. The policy

37. Charles Bohlen, "What to Do with the U.S.S.R.," Draft Memorandum, February 14, 1946, in File 711.61/2–1446, DSR-NA.
38. Ibid.

also meant referring some issues to the United Nations. Considering the lack of immediate United States power and leverage in the dispute between the Soviets and the Iranians, Bohlen recommended that the United Nations was the best vehicle to pressure the Soviets into a solution that favored the Tehran government.[39]

Prior to the London conference, the United States had identified two paths to peace—deterrence and multilateralism. However, by the middle of February the two paths were merging into one. Contributing to the merger was not only Soviet behavior but also Kennan's analysis of that policy. His long telegram of February 22 confirmed the administration's belief that Soviet policy was unchangeable because it was derived from the internal needs of a totalitarian system. More than Bohlen, Kennan emphasized the totalitarian, internal pressures that forced Soviet leaders away from cooperation with the outside world. Soviet leaders were "committed fanatically to the belief that with the U.S. there can be no permanent *modus vivendi*" and that Western principles and values needed to be destroyed "if Soviet power is to be secured." Kennan recommended that the United States assume a warlike posture toward Moscow and stated that only constantly exposed strength and counterpressure could maintain peace. He added thoughtfully that Stalin and the Soviet leadership were "highly sensitive to [the] logic of force," and when faced with resolute opposition, they would retreat.[40]

Kennan's telegram, combined with similar evaluations, and Soviet actions convinced American policy makers that the idea of cooperation and compromise with the Soviets would be less effective than matching Soviet demands with firm opposition. Byrnes admitted that he had tried to meet the Soviets more than halfway but that his efforts resulted in only a Russian "war of nerves all over the world." Truman simply stated that he was going to "stop babying the Russians." He told Byrnes to "stiffen up and try for the next three months not to make any compromises." The secretary needed no convincing.[41]

39. *Ibid.*
40. *FR, 1946*, VI, 696–709.
41. Memorandum of Conversation Between Bevin and Byrnes, September 25, 1946, N 12449/5169/38, in FO 371, 1946, PRO; Ayers Diary, February 28, 1946, in Ayers Papers; Cabinet Meeting Minutes, December 22, 1950, in Matthew Connelly Papers, Truman Library.

Along with the administration's decision to stiffen up came the need to educate the public about America's new role as world leader. Public opinion polls showed dissatisfaction with Soviet actions but little support for an active American role in world affairs. Many well-known politicians and personalities spoke favorably about American foreign policy apart from the affairs and intrigues of Europe and Asia. Other public figures favored giving full support to the United Nations and working to promote harmony with the Russians.[42]

Republican spokesmen like Robert Taft and Arthur Capper opposed any policy that seemed to pull European irons out of anticolonial fires. News personalities like Walter Lippmann and Raymond Swing spoke in favor of the United Nations and worldwide cooperation. Secretary of Agriculture Wallace and Senator Claude Pepper suggested that State Department officials misjudged Soviet actions and intentions. Wallace told Truman that Stalin's election speech was not a challenge to the United States but a predictable response to American construction of bases in Greenland, Iceland, Alaska, and Okinawa.[43]

The educational effort began on February 28, when Senator Vandenberg addressed the Senate calling for an end to compromises with the Soviet Union. He was received with hearty applause. Byrnes followed the next day with a speech to the Overseas Press Club. Truman read the speech and proclaimed that it was better than Vandenberg's. The speech spoke directly of American views on international affairs, listing those actions that no government should be allowed to practice: "We have no right to hold our troops in the territories of other sovereign states without their approval and consent freely given. . . . We must not unduly prolong the making of peace and continue to impose our troops upon small and impoverished states. . . . No power has a right to help itself to alleged enemy properties in liberated or ex-satellite countries before a reparation settlement has been agreed upon by the Allies. . . . We must not conduct a war of nerves to achieve strategic ends." Byrnes pledged that the United States was willing, if necessary, to use force

42. Richard J. Walton, *Henry Wallace, Harry Truman, and the Cold War* (New York, 1976), 75–76; Paterson, *On Every Front*, 119–20; Gaddis, *The Origins of the Cold War*, 309–15; *Twohey Analysis*, January 5, 12, 19, and February 5, 19, 26, 1946.

43. Walton, *Wallace*, 77; Gaddis, *The Origins of the Cold War*, 309–15; Thomas G. Paterson (ed.), *Cold War Critics* (Chicago, 1971), 27–39, 79–94, 116–34, 172–81.

to prevent such actions. Vandenberg's and Byrnes's speeches drew national attention and widespread public support.[44]

Byrnes soon got an opportunity to prove the American willingness to hold others accountable to the proper forms of international conduct. The Iranian problem became a crisis in early March. Throughout February, officials in Washington and London feared a confrontation between the Tehran government and the Soviet occupation authorities.

As the March 2 deadline for the removal of Soviet troops neared, there was no indication that Russian forces were preparing to leave. Rather, reports from northern Iran referred to the continued stockpiling of supplies and even troop buildups. In Moscow, Kennan feared that Prime Minister Qavam was conceding every negotiation point to the Soviets: Azerbaijani autonomy, oil concessions, and the continued Soviet presence in northern Iran.[45]

When the March 2 deadline passed and no Soviet troops left Iran, British and American statesmen acted quickly to bring the issue before the United Nations. Telegrams were sent to Moscow asking for an explanation; the government in Tehran was told of United States and British support. Openly and privately the possibility of war was expressed. The New York *Times* reported Soviet tanks heading toward Tehran. Byrnes considered Soviet actions a clear case of aggression, a military invasion, and resolved to "give it to them with both barrels."[46]

Backed by the United States and Britain, Iran brought its complaint before the Security Council on March 19. The Soviets tried to delay consideration. Byrnes, however, insisted "on full disposition now." Bevin seconded the motion. Soviet Ambassador Gromyko stalked out of the meeting. His action only seemed to prove the contentions that the Russians held nothing but contempt for the principles of the United Nations and did not respond to normal diplomacy.[47]

---

44. James F. Byrnes, "Speech to the Overseas Press Club, February 28, 1946," *DSB*, XIV (March 10, 1946), 355–58; Kuniholm, *The Origins of the Cold War in the Near East*, 311–12.

45. Kuniholm, *The Origins of the Cold War in the Near East*, 313–14.

46. *Ibid.*, 317–25; New York *Times*, March 13, 1946, Sec. 1, p. 1, and March 14, 1946, Sec. 1, p. 1; War Department Memorandum, "Azerbaijan—A Case History of Soviet Infiltration," April 13, 1946, OPD 350.50 FW, in PODR-NA.

47. Kuniholm, *The Origins of the Cold War in the Near East*, 326–31.

The crisis was soon over. An announcement that negotiations had resolved the issues and that Soviet troops would soon leave northern Iran reduced world fears of armed confrontation. There was little to indicate that the stand taken by British and American officials at the United Nations had solved the crisis, but the statesmen congratulated themselves on their role in removing the Russian forces. It was proof of the benefits derived from resolute firmness. The Russians had backed down. A State-War-Navy Coordinating Committee memorandum drew the conclusion that to achieve "peaceful coexistence," the United States must "demonstrate to the Soviet government, in the first instance by diplomatic means and in the last analysis by military force if necessary, that the present course of its foreign policy can only lead to disaster for the Soviet Union." A War Department officer equated United States policy toward Soviet Russia with that followed toward Japan in 1941.[48] Clearly, American officials viewed the Grand Alliance as dead; thoughts now turned to how to best construct new alliances to meet the Soviet threat.

The willingness of the United States and Britain to take parallel actions made the first months of 1946 a diplomatic disaster for the Soviet Union. To the Russian people, the Moscow conference was represented as a success that promised continued Big Three cooperation, peace, and an improved standard of living. In part, the confidence in the future rested upon perceived differences between Britain and the United States—a product, according to Marxist-Leninist doctrine, of capitalistic imperialism—and the ability of the Soviet Union to benefit from those differences. Russian propaganda reflected the supposed differences. Britain was vilified in the Soviet media and blamed for the international tensions, while little disparaging comment was made about the Truman administration and American foreign policy. As 1946 began, a sense of optimism and expectation was widespread throughout the Russian population.[49]

48. SWNCC Memorandum, April 1, 1946, in File 711.61/3–146, DSR-NA; War Department Memorandum, "Adequate Governmental Machinery to Handle Foreign Affairs," March 13, 1946, OPD 092 (TS), in PODR-NA.

49. Roberts to Foreign Office, March 4, 1946, N 4534/605/38, February 23, 1946, N 2466/140/38, March 14, 1946, N 4065/97/38, all in FO 371, 1946, PRO; Jacob, "To Moscow," 4–6; *FR, 1946*, VI, 638–85; William O. McCagg, *Stalin Embattled*, 149–59, 219–22.

By March and April that optimism was overwhelmed by a serious war scare. Whether artificial or not, the scare rested on the belief, generated by the Russian media, that Britain and America were joining forces to crush Soviet democracy. Frank Roberts observed that the Russians "seem genuinely alarmed by many recent signs of American rapproachment with Britain . . . and fear, however illogically, the establishment of an 'atomic Anglo-Saxon bloc.'"[50] Those signs of ganging up on Moscow started in January with disputes over Eastern Europe, Korea, Iran, and Manchuria, and they forced a reevaluation of the rift between the two capitalistic powers.

The February election speeches in the Soviet Union reflected the reexamination. In them, ideological differences between communism and capitalism were stressed and the specter of capitalistic encirclement raised. The speeches generated a widespread mistrust of the West. Paralleling the election speeches was an increased role for the Communist party apparatus in Russian life. By February, few praised the benefits of cooperation with Britain and the United States. Capitalism once more became the root cause of war, and the Soviet Union's role in winning the war against Germany and Japan was stressed. Molotov was the exception. He did continue to emphasize the unity of the Big Three but believed cooperation was possible only if Stalin and the Soviet Union were accorded the important world role they deserved. Prominent historian Evgeni Tarlé was, on the other hand, reproved for not following orthodox Marxist theory in his writings.[51]

On March 5, Winston Churchill became a symbol of hostile, reactionary forces in the United States and Great Britain advocating a Western bloc. The cause was Churchill's Fulton, Missouri, speech that spoke of an "iron curtain" and called for a British and American partnership to resist Soviet expansion.[52] Initial Soviet responses dismissed the speech as unimportant and referred to British and American critics of the speech. Roberts speculated that the Soviet

50. Roberts to Foreign Office, March 12, 1946, N 3333/140/38, in FO 371, 1946, PRO.

51. *FR, 1946*, VI, 690–91, 694–95, 709–10; McCagg, *Stalin Embattled*, 219–38; Roberts to Foreign Office, March 12, 1946, N 3333/140/38, in FO 371, 1946, PRO; Molotov, *Problems of Foreign Policy*, 28.

52. Jeremy Ward, "Winston Churchill and the 'Iron Curtain' Speech," *The History Teacher*, I (1968), 1–13; Anderson, "Britain, the US, and the Cold War," 175–79.

leadership sought to avoid items that could indicate to the Russian people the degree of Western concern about Soviet actions. He pointed out that Byrnes's February 28 speech had yet to be mentioned in the Russian press.[53]

That unconcern vanished on March 11, when *Pravda* attacked Churchill and the speech. The time—nearly a week—between the speech and the article suggested to Roberts that "careful consideration" was given to the response by the Soviet leadership. He thought that by attacking Churchill's call for an Anglo-Saxon bloc, by "frightening" the British and Americans "with the bogey of Soviet withdrawal from international cooperation," the Soviets hoped to prevent further cases of British-American "unity."[54]

The *Pravda* outburst was mild compared to an article written by Tarlé in *Izvestia* the following day. Tarlé continued the attack on Churchill and his views, mocking them. He also linked Churchill to the British government, calling him "a penname" for the Labour government. "He intends some of the mud flung at Mr. Churchill to stick on His Majesty's Government," wrote Thomas Brimelow of the Foreign Office. Roberts found Tarlé going to "great pains . . . to drive a wedge between us and the Americans" and to warn "Americans against being used as a catspaw by the British." Both attacks were given the widest possible coverage throughout the Soviet Union by the press and radio.[55]

As the State Department and the Foreign Office attempted to evaluate the articles, a truly unparalleled event took place: Stalin responded to Churchill's speech in an interview. In a bitter denouncement, Stalin equated Churchill with Hitler and stated that Churchill never had been a friend of the Soviet people. Stalin's interview was the culmination of the break with the idea of the Grand Alliance and added fuel to the growing fear of war in the Soviet Union. Russian housewives queued up to buy food supplies. On the streets of Moscow, talk of war with the West was common. Roberts termed it "hysterical reaction."[56]

53. Roberts to Foreign Office, March 7, 1946, N 3155/140/38, March 8, 1946, N 3172/140/38, March 12, 1946, N 3380/97/38, all in FO 371, 1946, PRO.

54. Roberts to Foreign Office, March 11, 1946, N 3315/140/38, in FO 371, 1946, PRO.

55. Brimelow's Minute, March 13, 1946, N 3335/140/38, Roberts to Foreign Office, March 12, 1946, N 3333/140/38, both in FO 371, 1946, PRO.

56. *FR, 1946*, VI, 716–17; Roberts to Foreign Office, March 14, 1946, N 3442/140/38, March 18, 1946, N 4388/140/38, March 21, 1946, N 3888/605/38, all in FO 371, 1946, PRO.

The Soviet leadership soon moved to reduce the fear of war and to reduce international tensions. Soviet spokesmen, including Stalin, assured the Russian people and a world audience that war was highly unlikely and that in no way was the Soviet Union threatened. Reducing international tensions, Russian troops were removed from Manchuria and Bornholm Island and an agreement was reached to remove Russian troops from northern Iran.[57]

Despite the attempts to lessen international tensions, the Russian media clearly indicated that the idea of the Grand Alliance was no longer valid. Britain and the United States were vilified as reactionary governments supporting worldwide imperialism and posing a threat to peace and stability throughout the world. Even liberal figures like Lippmann were pilloried in the Soviet press.[58]

For the Russians, as for the Americans and the British, the Grand Alliance was an idea of the past. All three governments realized that new relations would have to be worked out and made to fit into a new international system based not on the possibility of agreement and compromise but upon the possibility of war.

57. *FR, 1946,* VI, 725–26; Roberts to Foreign Office, March 21, 1946, N 3888/605/38, in FO 371, 1946, PRO.

58. Roberts to Foreign Office, May 17, 1946, N 6617/97/38, Minutes of Russian Committee Meeting, May 14, 1946, N 6733/140/38, Roberts to Foreign Office, June 14, 1946, N 7937/97/38, all in FO 371, 1946, PRO.

VIII

Instituting the Cold War

BY MARCH, 1946, the Grand Alliance had collapsed, but the cold war was not yet fully defined. None of the major powers appeared to want a breakdown in negotiations or a new war. Yet, none was willing to compromise and reach mutually acceptable solutions. Among the three powers, the shift from alliance to cold war was most abrupt for the United States. Byrnes announced in February that although the United States wanted friendship with the Soviet Union, it could not permit "aggression . . . by coercion or pressure or subterfuge." The New York *Times* noted two months later that officials in Washington seemed to be going to great lengths to stress a tougher policy toward Russia.[1]

Officially, American behavior toward the Soviets was "firm," but at the Paris Conference of the Council of Foreign Ministers, which took place in April, May, June, and July, it approached hostility. Privately, Byrnes told Georges Bidault that America's appeasement of

1. Memorandum for Secretary of Navy, March 17, 1946, in Miscellaneous Files, Box 24, Forrestal Papers; Balfour to Foreign Office, August 27, 1947, N 10052/1380/38, in FO 371, 1947, PRO; Daniel Yergin, *Shattered Peace: The Origins of the Cold War and the National Security State* (Boston, 1977), 178–92, 221–335; Melvyn P. Leffler, "From the Truman Doctrine to the Carter Doctrine: Lessons and Dilemmas of the Cold War," *Diplomatic History*, VII (1983), 245–67.

the Soviet Union was over. During the conference the change in attitude was noticeable. The British called Byrnes's posture "brusque." Soviet diplomat Kiril V. Novikov complained that the secretary of state sought a "diplomatic victory over the Soviet Union." Novikov's views paralleled those of Ambassador Walter Bedell Smith, who thought Byrnes wanted to either "force agreement" on his terms or show the world that Russia was responsible for "world turmoil." Firmness seemed to produce positive results. After Byrnes threatened to cancel further talks, the Soviets did an about-face and accepted proposals they had opposed for months. Vandenberg praised American actions as "Munich in reverse."[2]

The new toughness shown at Paris was not the only indication of the new American policy. The naval power of the United States was flexed in the Mediterranean, while tests in the Pacific reaffirmed the destructive power of the atomic bomb. American diplomatic commitments to Iran, Turkey, and Greece demonstrated what Balfour called an American "steady resistance" to Russian expansion.[3]

The resistance included a major economic dimension that sought to help friends and convince opponents to become friends. The American loan to Britain gained more and more support as American distrust of Russia increased. The Soviet loan request lagged, however, as several conditions were placed upon it, including a general improvement of American-Soviet relations and a reversal of Soviet economic policy in Eastern Europe. Kennan believed that such conditions would "shelve the question of the loan for some time."[4] Requirements designed to promote an integrated European economy were incorporated into the Marshall Plan. When the Russians rejected the plan and walked out of the Paris meetings, many blamed them for dividing Europe. The Soviets, of course, saw it in a

2. New York *Times*, April 17, 1946, Sec. 1, p. 1; Peterson to Foreign Office, June 14, 1946, N 7730/140/38, Foreign Office Minute, October 17, 1946, N 14167/140/38, both in FO 371, 1946, PRO; Yergin, *Shattered Peace*, 223; Smith to General Lincoln, May 11, 1946, OPD 092 (TS), in PODR-NA.

3. Yergin, *Shattered Peace*, 221–335; Herken, *The Winning Weapon*, 214–29; Leffler, "From the Truman Doctrine," 249–52; Balfour to Foreign Office, July 17, 1946, N 9816/140/38, in FO 371, 1946, PRO.

4. Paterson, *Soviet-American Confrontation*, 99–146, 159–207; FR, 1946, I, 1426, V, 422, 432, 443–45; Roberts to Foreign Office, September 19, 1946, N 12380/971/38, May 29, 1946, N 7138/971/38, both in FO 371, 1946, PRO; Yergin, *Shattered Peace*, 305–25.

different light. Responding to American dollar diplomacy, Anastas Mikoyan said: "At first sight the American proposals look like a tasty mushroom, but on examination they turned out to be a poisonous toadstool."[5]

The Truman administration's tougher policy was supported by efforts to develop firm popular support and to discredit those opposing it. By the middle of 1946, State Department and private opinion polls found that over 70 percent of those asked supported the firmer policy. Republicans and Democrats attacked those who recommended understanding the Soviets and their needs. Writings and statements critical of the policy were labeled part of a "typical communist smear" campaign. Truman wrote to his daughter Margaret that Davies, Pepper, Wallace, and "the actors and artists in immoral Greenwich Village" were all members of the "American Crackpot Association." Public revelations of Soviet atomic spies and the discovery of classified materials in the offices of the journal *Amerasia* further added to public and official fears of Communist subversion.[6] The success of anti-Communist efforts was almost too great. Lord Inverchapel reported in August that there was a near "hysteria" in the United States about the possibility of war with the Soviet Union and that the State Department was attempting to reduce the level of fear by providing examples of moderate Soviet behavior. He added that the efforts were mostly unproductive as American newspaper editors buried the stories on inside pages or rewrote them to feed "the tide of suspicion and hatred of the USSR."[7]

Despite the majority of Americans who favored the firmer policy

5. Roberts to Foreign Office, September 19, 1946, N 12380/971/38, in FO 371, 1946, PRO; Michael J. Hogan, "The Search for a Creative Peace: The United States, European Unity, and the Origins of the Marshall Plan," *Diplomatic History*, VI (1982), 267–86; Paterson, *Soviet-American Confrontation*, 208–34.

6. Ralph B. Levering, *The Cold War, 1945–1972* (Arlington Heights, Ill., 1982), 27–28; LaFeber, "American Policy-Makers," 45–47, 50–55; Balfour to Foreign Office, October 31, 1946, N 15252/971/38, in FO 371, 1946, PRO; Thomas G. Paterson (ed.), *Cold War Critics: Alternatives to American Foreign Policy in the Truman Years* (Chicago, 1971), 76–139; Margaret Truman, *Harry S Truman* (New York, 1973), 343.

7. Yergin, *Shattered Peace*, 247–58; Vandenberg Diary of First Paris Peace Conference, April 21, 1946, in Vandenberg Papers; Balfour to Foreign Office, October 31, 1946, N 15252/971/38, Lord Inverchapel to Foreign Office, September 10, 1946, N 11892/971/38, both in FO 371, 1946, PRO; Balfour to Foreign Office, August 29, 1947, N 10052/1380/38, in FO 371, 1947, PRO.

and worried about Russian intentions and future war, there was less support for an activist, global American foreign policy. Consistently, over 60 percent of those polled opposed any loan to Britain and any effort to pull British chestnuts out of the fire. 40 percent of those asked responded that they were against any American diplomactic or military commitments abroad. Like the new Republican-dominated Congress of 1946, the American people seemed to favor a tough policy, but not one that involved costly overseas commitments.[8]

Aware of the problem, foreign policy spokesmen emphasized that because Soviet policy was "emphatically aggressive and impervious to world opinion" more than American words would be needed to deter Soviet aggression. On a nationwide speaking tour, George Kennan harped on the theme of "setting will against will, force against force, idea against idea, down through the decades until Soviet expansion is finally worn down." The threat of Soviet expansion was clearly evident in Truman's request to Congress for aid to Greece and Turkey. He told his cabinet that the $250 million request was "only the beginning" of American involvement in "European politics," and that it would take "the greatest selling job ever facing a President" to get Congress and the American public to agree. Truman succeeded as Congress approved an increasing amount of economic aid to Greece, Turkey, and Western Europe. John Balfour observed there was by 1947 a "general realisation . . . that the United States dare not remain passive" with regard to the fate of non-Soviet Europe.[9]

Since the war's end, Balfour had watched the increasing number

8. Watson to Foreign Office, October 10, 1946, N 13250/971/38, in FO 371, 1946, PRO; Balfour to Foreign Office, August 29, 1947, N 10052/1380/38, in FO 371, 1947, PRO; War Department Memorandum, "Estimate of World Situation and Its Military Implications for U.S.," August 16, 1946, OPD 350.0575, in PODR-NA; Cabinet Meeting Minutes, March 7, 1947, in Connally Papers.

9. Blum, *The Price of Vision*, 537; Committee of Three Minutes, March 2, 1946, OPD 091, Russia 377 (TS), in PODR-NA; Kennan to State Department, April 22, 1946, in File 711.41/4–2246, DSR-NA; Joseph Harsch, "How To Get Tough with the Russians," *Christian Science Monitor*, March 6, 1946, p. 20; SWNCC Memorandum, April 1, 1946, in File 711.6/4–146, DSR-NA; War Department Memorandum, "Probable Russian Reaction to Withdrawal of British Armed Forces from the Middle East," March 7, 1946, OPD 092 (TS) Series III, in PODR-NA; Balfour to Foreign Office, July 17, 1946, N 9816/140/38, in FO 371, 1946, PRO.

of "sensible Americans" who favored a cooperative British and American effort in resisting Soviet expansion. He reported on the efforts made by the British Public Relations Service to convince Americans that Britain, the valiant ally in war, was also a vital element in the "establishment of an enduring peace." Kennan certainly agreed, telling the State Department that such a partnership was "necessary to assure peace" and that Britain was the logical ally to resist Moscow. Simultaneously, the State-War-Navy Coordinating Committee decided that to deny Moscow "hegemony" in Europe, the United States needed to provide Britain with all "feasible political, economic, and if necessary military support." [10]

Even as the committee made its recommendation, the military partnership was being formed. Secret talks between British and American military personnel were taking place to plan arms standardization and the exchange of intelligence and to consider joint strategic planning. By summer, Balfour reported that the Truman administration was "fully alive" to the need to support Britain and to resist Soviet expansion. However, he cautioned that American officials believed they still needed to show that they were not being "outsmarted by the British" to the American public. Balfour's view was supported by the Foreign Office's Russia Committee, which concluded in September that for the "immediate future" Byrnes would continue to avoid giving the impression that American policies were "influenced" by London. [11]

With or without public support, American policy makers throughout 1946 conducted a policy that provided "diplomatic opposition to Soviet aggression . . . economic support of only the countries which resist Soviet expansion . . . military opposition to Soviet expansion into areas vital" to the United States. An important part of that effort involved the "political, economic, and military support of the United Kingdom and the essential communications of the British Commonwealth." All that remained in 1947 was for the

10. SWNCC Memorandum, April 1, 1946, in File 711.6/4–146, DSR-NA.
11. Lord Inverchapel to Foreign Office, September 2, 1946, AN 2259/1/45, Balfour to Foreign Office, June 24, 1946, N 8694/97/38, both in FO 371, 1946, PRO; Robert M. Hathaway, *Ambiguous Partnership: Britain and America, 1944–1947* (New York, 1981), 238–47; Anderson, "Britain, the US, and the Cold War," 209–15, 263–75; Louis Galambus (ed.), *The Papers of Dwight David Eisenhower: The Chief of Staff* (New York, 1978), VII, 1157–58; Rothwell, *Britain and the Cold War*, 437.

Truman administration to make that policy part of the public record. That goal was accomplished by 1948 with the pronouncement of the Truman Doctrine and the establishment of the Marshall Plan. Examining American policy in 1948, Lord Inverchapel wrote that from the middle of 1946, throughout 1947, the American public had been "profoundly stirred" into supporting policies designed to contain the Soviets and build a stable and prosperous Western Europe.[12]

Soviet behavior in many ways duplicated that of the United States. To many Russian citizens, the shift from alliance to cold war also seemed abrupt. Throughout 1946 and 1947, the Russian media intensified its attacks on the West and Western statesmen, culminating in direct attacks on Truman, Attlee, Bevin, and other Western leaders. There also emerged within the Soviet Union a new emphasis on ideology and Russian patriotism, the *Zhadanovschina*. Those not fully supporting the shift in policy were discredited and purged from positions of importance. At the same time, the Soviet grip on Eastern Europe, including Hungary and Czechoslovakia, intensified, and new political, diplomatic, and military pressures were exerted in Korea and Germany and toward Greece and Turkey. The belief that Soviet policy was ideological and expansive appeared to be confirmed in October, 1947, with the formation of the Cominform. Clearly, the Soviet leadership was solidifying its hold on the peoples and territories within its sphere of influence so as to better resist the machinations of the West.

Since the disastrous London Conference, the Soviet press frequently had denounced capitalistic encirclement, reactionary Western warmongers, and the "Anglo-American bloc." But by the middle of 1946, the Soviet rhetoric sharpened. Prior to May, Britain was the principal target of Russian media abuse; after May, the United States received the majority of abuse. In turn, Britain was represented as a pawn and accomplice of the United States. The propaganda effort against the United States came as Secretary Byrnes assumed his firm stance at Paris. The Soviets "are really disturbed by American strength and the great changes in American policy,"

12. Rothwell, *Britain and the Cold War*, 433–34; Minutes of Russia Committee, September 24, 1946, N 12615/5169/38, Lord Killean to Sir Orme Sargent, August 17, 1946, N 11141/140/38, both in FO 371, 1946, PRO.

wrote a British observer; "they see this potentially dangerous America supported in all essentials by the British."[13]

By June, statements suggesting that Britain and the United States were planning a war against Russia were becoming frequent in the Russian press. Soviet commentator Ermashev stated that the "Anglo-Saxon *bloc*" intended to maintain a strong military capability with bases around the world to further American plans for world domination. Tarlé denounced the American "forced peace" and equated it with that imposed by Imperial Rome and Hitler's Germany.[14]

The image of the British and Americans working together against the Soviet Union was aimed largely at the Russian people. Soviet leaders sought public support for their policies and believed that the instruction of the public was one of the vital functions of the state. By early 1946, it became necessary, in the eyes of the Russian leadership, to inform the Russian people about the true nature of the West. The goal was to prevent the Russians from "regarding their late allies with sympathy" and to encourage support for governmental efforts to rebuild and strengthen the Soviet Union. Traditional Russian isolationism had been broken by the war, resulting in an infusion of Western ideas and culture. As the war ended, many Russians hoped for continued better relations with the West, especially the United States. As diplomatic relations with Britain and the United States soured, the Kremlin needed to reaffirm its Marxist-Leninist ideology, the innate hostility of the capitalist nations, and the resolve of the Russian people.[15]

The process began in February with the election speeches, but the theme of Western hostility and the necessity of ideological conformity clearly emerged only in midyear. British and American representatives in Russia closely followed the propaganda campaign and dispatched numerous telegrams home describing its rhetoric and consequences. To the American chargé d'affaires, Elbridge Durbrow, it was a "campaign for the psychological conditioning of

13. Hogan, "The Search for a Creative Peace," 274–77; Memorandum for the Secretary of Navy, March 17, 1946, in Forrestal Papers; Lord Inverchapel to Foreign Office, May 24, 1948, AN 1997/6/45, in FO 371, 1948, PRO.

14. FORD Paper, December, 1948, N 10521/1/38, in FO 371, 1948, PRO; Roberts to Foreign Office, September 7, 1946, N 1164/605/38, in FO 371, 1946, PRO.

15. Roberts to Foreign Office, June 7, 1946, N 7648/605/38, July 22, 1946, N 8409/605/38, both in FO 371, 1946, PRO.

the masses" and a "deliberate inculcation of xenophobia in the Soviet population." Roberts agreed that the Kremlin did not "intend
to have any 20th century Decembrist movement." He told the Foreign Office that it appeared that "the Central Committee of the
Party is thinking of intensifying . . . propaganda attacks on bourgeois ideas and philosophies."[16]

The educational effort was a success. Led by Andrei A. Zhdanov,
"correct" Soviet thought was reaffirmed and those holding "incorrect" ideas were discredited, purged, and sometimes reeducated.
In September, 1946, Roberts reported a 50 percent "turnover in Soviet and Party personnel" and that the last of the "Westerners,"
Maisky and Litvinov, had been removed from the Soviet foreign
service. Durbrow commented in October, 1947, that Soviet writer
Mikhail Zoshchenko, who had been a target of the "great ideological retrenchment" and had "disappeared from literary life," had reemerged writing "ideological orthodox" themes.[17]

Another result of the Soviet propaganda campaign was to generate periodic war scares. Roberts commented that it was "common
form in Moscow whenever international tension became more obvious than usual" for the Russians to have a "flutter of nerves." He
also noted that after a few days of nerves, the Soviet leadership
stepped in to "calm down the Soviet public opinion." This was the
pattern in March and September, 1946, when Western observers reported that the Russians were hoarding foodstuffs and assuming a
fatalistic attitude about impending war with the capitalistic West.
The March and September scares were immediately followed by assurances from Soviet officials that war was not going to take place
as long as the Soviet Union remained strong and a bulwark of
peace. Stalin gave two interviews with Western newsmen in October that received wide dissemination in the Soviet Union. In both
interviews, the Soviet leader stated that there was no danger of war
and that everyone needed to distinguish "between furor . . . and
real danger." Such statements calmed the Soviet people but did
nothing to reduce Soviet propaganda attacks on the United States
or Britain. Durbrow concluded that the assurances were merely a
"tactical maneuver . . . to strengthen elements in the USA advocat-

16. Roberts to Foreign Office, September 11, 1946, N 11501/605/38, November 19,
1946, N 14729/140/38, both in FO 371, 1946, PRO.

17. Roberts to Foreign Office, June 30, 1946, N 10049/605/38, in FO 371, 1946,
PRO; FR, 1946, VI, 773–76, 778–81, 806–808.

ing appeasement" and to drive a wedge betwen Britain and the United States. Bevin called the creation of a war scare and the following denials of war as "usual Communist" behavior and suggested that all the West needed to do in such cases was "to keep low and firm."[18]

Durbrow's evaluation of the war scare tactic reflected another central goal of the Russians' propaganda campaign—to split the British-American bloc. It is "more important for the Russians to split the Anglo-Saxons than to split the atom," wrote Geoffrey Wilson of the Northern Department. The Foreign Office firmly believed that although the Soviet propaganda campaign was meant to have some impact on the United States, its primary goal was to influence the British, especially the British left. Kiril Novikov told Ambassador Peterson that it was "unwise" for Britain to rely too much on the Americans because they were in an "expansionist frame of mind." He added that Moscow's desires were limited and reasonable and implied that Britain and the Soviet Union could work together. Novikov's assertions were dismissed by officials in the Foreign Office, who believed that the Soviet emphasis on the "inevitability of an American-Soviet clash" was designed to convince British opinion that it "would be wise to sit on the fence." Evaluating the effort, Thomas Brimelow concluded that while Russian claims of British and American war intentions were "absurd," some of the "poison sinks in and does us harm." Harm was particularly noticeable among those in the Labour party who sought a more socialist foreign policy that would make Britain independent of entanglements with capitalist America and more understanding of the needs of the Soviet Union. They suggested that Bevin be removed from office.[19]

The Soviet effort to present Britain and the United States as obstacles to an enduring peace was frequently supported by Soviet diplomacy. Throughout 1946 and 1947, Soviet actions toward Brit-

18. FR, 1946, VI, 774–78, 784–87, 790, 793–97; FR, 1947, (10 vols.; Washington, 1972), IV, 598; Roberts to Foreign Office, September 4, 1946, N 11644/605/38, Foreign Office Minute, October 17, 1946, N 14167/140/38, both in FO 371, 1946, PRO; Roberts to Foreign Office, October 3, 1947, N 11843/343/38, in FO 371, 1947, PRO.

19. Roberts to Foreign Office, September 16, 1947, N 11014/343/38, Paterson to Foreign Office, March 17, 1947, N 3299/343/38, both in FO 371, 1947, PRO; Rothwell, Britain and the Cold War, 277; FR, 1946, VI, 767–70, 786; Roberts to Foreign Office, June 30, 1946, N 10049/605/38, in FO 371, 1946, PRO.

ain, America, and post-war problems often seemed contradictory. For extended periods of time, the Soviets would reject all British or American solutions or compromises, acting as if Soviet policy was immovable; then, without explanation, they would reverse themselves and suddenly accept compromises and make concessions. This diplomatic action would be followed by a flurry of statements about the peaceful intentions of the Soviet Union, the need for the big powers to work together, and the need for Western statesmen to stop listening to reactionaries. It is unlikely that Soviet leaders believed such behavior would alter American or British policies, but it is possible that they hoped such actions would place restrictions on British policy.

By the middle of 1946, Bevin and the Attlee government faced what seemed to be an open revolt from those in the Labour party who wanted a more independent and socialist foreign policy. To demonstrate its desire for better relations with Moscow, the Labour party sponsored a goodwill trip by Harold Laski and other Labour party spokesmen to Moscow. In the Soviet capital, the delegation was wined and dined and treated to a personal greeting from Stalin, which was all designed to underline the desirability of closer relations between the British and the Soviets. At nearly the same time, the influential *New Statesman and Nation* ran a series of four articles attacking Bevin for not pursuing a socialist foreign policy and for following too much the anti-Communist policies of the United States. Further, Member of Parliament E. Cook, during a speech to his constituents, asked Bevin to "ensure firm friendship with the progressive forces throughout the world, and in particular with the USSR." His views, as part of the left wing, were to be expected; unexpected, however, was the view taken by the moderate Manchester *Guardian*. Following the meeting of the Council of Foreign Ministers in New York in November and December, at which the Russians had made several important concessions to Western views, the *Guardian* editorialized that the West should meet the "Russians halfway," taking the opportunity to "show the Soviet leaders that we really do appreciate their gestures and that it really does pay to cooperate."[20]

20. Jones, *The Russian Complex*, 128–29, 132–37; Dixon, *Double Diploma*, 241–42; Manchester *Guardian*, December 11, 1946, p. 16; Wayne Knight, "Labourite Britain: America's 'Sure Friend'? The Anglo-Soviet Treaty Issue, 1947," *Diplomatic History*, VII (1983), 268–69.

The Soviet attempt to modify British policy culminated with the offer to renegotiate the Anglo-Soviet Treaty of Friendship. First made privately to Field Marshal Montgomery during his visit to Moscow in January, 1947, the offer was repeated publicly a few days later. In the negotiations that followed, the Soviets made it clear that they sought a new treaty that would prevent either party from joining coalitions against the other. At the same time, the Soviet press emphasized Bevin's subordination to the United States and hostility toward the Soviet Union. General Mikhail R. Galaktinov wrote in *New Times* that the discussions between the British and the Americans on arms standardization amounted to British subservience "to the army, economy, and the industry of the United States." In Britain, the *Daily Worker* reprinted the article under the eye-catching headline, "ANGLO-U.S. ARMS STANDARDISATION PLAN A DIRECT THREAT TO BRITAIN'S INDEPENDENCE." Another Soviet writer, Polyak, directly attacked Bevin for "posing as a friend of the Soviet Union" and applauded the one hundred Labourites of the left wing who opposed Bevin's policies. According to a Foreign Office source, the attacks on Bevin had the Kremlin's highest approval. According to Molotov, "America was moving to the Right and Britain to the Left, and nothing could halt this progress."[21]

Ambassador W. Bedell Smith labeled the campaign against Bevin and British policy "crude, obvious, and hasty." He believed that it was prompted "by a sense of anxious urgency, a desire to split Anglo-American front before CFM decision on crucial German problem." Nevertheless, members of the Foreign Office and the State Department watched with apprehension as Labour Party discontent with British and American actions heightened following the announcement of the Truman Doctrine in March. Many within the center and left of the Labour party believed Truman's posture was harmful to the cause of peace and a perfect example of the United States' quest of economic and military interests. To Michael Foot, the speech indicated proof of "the American flag following the American oil magnates." The *New Statesman and Nation*, as well as the *Tribune*, deplored the tone of the message and advocated less

21. Knight, "Labourite Britain," 267–82; FORD Paper, N 1052/1/38, December 1947–January, 1948, in FO 371, 1948, PRO; Paterson to Foreign Office, February 4, 1947, N 1510/343/38, March 4, 1947, N 3299/343/38, Roberts to Hankey, February 5, 1947, N 2288/343/38, all in FO 371, 1947, PRO.

British dependence on the United States. In April, the center group, led by Richard Crossman and Foot, published *Keep Left*, which opposed Bevin's policies and suggested alternatives to eliminate or reduce American influence over British policy.[22]

The Soviet press depicted the revolt as a major attempt by progressives in the Labour party and throughout England to overcome reactionary warmongers like Churchill and Bevin. Roberts informed the Foreign Office that the Soviets thought they were backing a winner and that opposition to Bevin's policies would continue to grow. Officials in Washington were also worried about the seemingly growing strength of the left and center of the Labour party and their ability to restrict British policy. The American chargé d'affaires in London reported that British policy was being carefully constructed to protect Bevin "against the Labour Party rebels." Bevin personally stressed to H. F. Matthews, director of the Office of European Affairs, that despite the Russian effort a "wedge" could not be driven between Britain and the United States. The foreign minister's assurances reduced but did not end American concern that the Soviets might be successful in their campaign.[23]

By May, however, Durbrow concluded that the United States had "clearly captured [the] political warfare offensive" with congressional and world support for the Truman Doctrine. By the end of summer, the Soviets had suffered other major diplomatic setbacks as well. The United States' willingness to help rebuild Euope, according to Pierson Dixon, "not only put Europe back on its feet" but would cause Soviet leaders to "fear for their own positions and regime." Bevin had assumed control of the Labour party rebellion and fully supported the American plan of economic aid to Europe. The State Department and Foreign Office expected a major Soviet effort to regain the political initiative and reduce the diplomatic damage done by the announcement of the Marshall Plan. They foresaw renewed bitter attacks on the West and Western statesmen along with specific attacks on the Marshall Plan.[24]

22. Knight, "Labourite Britain," 268–73; *FR, 1947,* IV, 523–24, 525–26; Jones, *The Russian Complex,* 1252–59.

23. Knight, "Labourite Britain," 276–79; *FR, 1947,* IV, 526–28; Roberts to Hankey, February 5, 1947, N 2288/343/38, in FO 371, 1947, PRO.

24. Jones, *The Russian Complex,* 155–63; *FR, 1947,* IV, 262–63; Rothwell, *Britain and the Cold War,* 280–84, 439–44.

Western expectations were soon filled. An intensive anti-American press campaign began as soon as Molotov departed the Marshall Plan discussions. This was paralleled by an end to negotiations on the Anglo-Soviet Treaty of Friendship and an intensification of Soviet control over Eastern Europe. In November, strikes swept across France and Italy in opposition to American aid and influence. Roberts mildly commented that the Soviets were working "overtime" to stop and discredit the Marshall Plan.

Accompanying the verbal attacks on the Marshall Plan, which included vitriolic denunciations of Truman, Bevin, Attlee, and other Western leaders, was an internal propaganda effort designed to boost the Communist spirit. A campaign titled "The Pride of the Soviet Man" was launched to increase Soviet patriotism and the belief in the strength of the Soviet state. The Soviet media, and media services in Soviet-dominated regions, sought to underline a "new world outlook" based on the hostility of the West toward the Soviet Union and the ability of the Soviet Union to withstand Western aggression. Reflecting the new world view were the words spoken by the Soviet Ambassador to Romania on the anniversary of the October Revolution.

> The imperialists will not let go. They wish to encircle the Soviet Union with a twofold circle of military aggression. . . . We have shaken off the fetters of Czarist authority, we have defeated fourteen countries fighting us and counter-revolution. We have shaken off the cruel grip of fascism and German [and] Japanese imperialism. We shall also shake off the fetters now being prepared for us by imperialistic gangsters and warmongers. . . . No hand, not even one armed with the atomic bomb, will succeed in turning back the wheel of history. . . . Those who today are sowing the murderous winds of another war will reap the storm of revolution.[25]

Also reflecting the new world view was the formation of the Cominform. Its creation confirmed to Western observers that the Soviets were trying to recapture the diplomatic initiative while working from the assumption that the world was permanently di-

25. *FR, 1947,* IV, 563, 567, 592–94; Rothwell, *Britain and the Cold War,* 444–49, 452–56; FORD Paper, December 1947, N 10521/1/38, in FO 371, 1948, PRO; Roberts to Foreign Office, July 22, 1947, N 8791/343/38, August 11, 1947, N 9580/343/38, Holman to Foreign Office, November 6, 1947, N 12636/343/38, all in FO 371, 1947, PRO; Jones, *The Russian Complex,* 160–62,

vided into two hostile blocs. Ambassador Smith thought the formation of the Cominform "unmasked" Russian intentions and served
as "a declaration of political and economic war against the US and
everything [the] US stands for in world affairs." A Foreign Office
memorandum stated that the Cominform "denounced the very
idea of cooperation" and represented a "declaration of ideological
warfare." By October, 1947, the Soviet Union had put its house in
order, accepted the unity of the Western bloc, and officially announced its view that the world was divided into two camps: the
democratic and the imperialistic. The Soviet Union, of course, represented democracy.[26]

By the end of 1947, the United States and the Soviet Union clearly
were locked in an ideological confrontation. Both were presenting
images of a divided world, while seeking widespread domestic and
international support for their views. The London *Tribune* pointed
out that the "two continental powers were now in the open" and
hoped that the Labour party would follow a path independent of
both powers. The hope that Britain could resist the division of the
world into two blocs collapsed in early January, 1948, when Attlee
denounced the Soviet Union as the force of a "new imperialism"
that threatened world peace. On January 21, Bevin repeated the
message to Parliament, adding that it was necessary to organize
Western Europe to resist Soviet expansion. The last partner of the
Grand Alliance had joined the United States and the Soviet Union
in publicly accepting a divided world.[27]

In explaining his position to Commonwealth prime ministers in
October, 1948, Attlee stated that Britain had "carried forebearance
to the verge of risk" in dealing with the Soviets.[28] Forebearance,
however, would not have been the word chosen by the Foreign
Office to describe Britain's Russian policy from 1946 to 1948. Forebearance was a political word that suggested that British leaders
were not responsible for the failure of the Grand Alliance and that
they had repeatedly sought to find a working relationship with the
Russians. It did not express the frustrations felt by many within the

26. *FR, 1947*, IV, 595–611; FORD Paper, December 1947, N 19521/1/38, in FO 371,
1948, PRO; Jones, *The Russian Complex*, 160–63.

27. Jones, *The Russian Complex*, 150–66; 174–83.

28. Foreign Office Memorandum, October 4, 1948, N 10702/1/38, in FO 371,
1948, PRO.

Foreign Office over their inability to launch a propaganda and dip-lomatic offensive against the Soviets. Nor did the word refer to the primary reason why Britain was the last member of the Grand Al-liance to declare the cold war.

Unimpressed with the Moscow agreements of December, 1945, concerned about Soviet intentions in the eastern Mediterranean and the Middle East, and angered daily by Soviet propaganda aimed at Britain, members of the Foreign Office concluded in early 1946 that the Grand Alliance no longer existed and that a state of hostility existed between Britain and the Soviet Union. Brimelow wrote: "We are the target." Responding to the Soviets' anti-British posture, the Russia Committee's chief, Christopher Warner, wrote a lengthy memorandum, "The Soviet Campaign Against This Country and Our Response To It." Ruling out long-standing suspicions, Warner concluded that the dynamics behind Soviet policy were ideological. He suggested coordinating diplomatic, political, and economic policies to maximize British resistance to Soviet expansionism. He recommended that a large part of the counteroffensive be a global propaganda effort to emphasize the totalitarian nature of commu-nism and to expose the "myths" Moscow used to justify its policies.[29]

The cabinet considered the memorandum in May and rejected full implementation of its recommendations. Bevin reported to the Foreign Office that cabinet members believed that British propa-ganda should popularize "the achievements of our own political philosophy rather than attacking that of [the] Russians." The Russia Committee was disappointed and hoped that the cabinet would re-consider its decision.

The reasoning behind the decision rested upon three considera-tions. A minority, like the left wing of the Labour party, wanted a more socialist foreign policy and strongly objected to the anti-So-viet tone of the memorandum. They complained that Russia was being treated like an enemy. Their objections overlapped those cau-tioning that Warner's policies would serve to increase the strength of those opposing British policy toward Russia. They believed that the general public was not willing to accept the Soviet Union as an enemy and still believed that acceptable solutions could be found

29. Rothwell, *Britain and the Cold War*, 251–61.

to the problems facing the two powers. Lastly, most cabinet members worried that the Russian potential for harming British interests far exceeded the British capability to protect its interests. It was noted that the Soviet anti-British campaign was largely verbal, and, except in Eastern Europe and Iran, the Soviets had not attempted any overt or covert efforts to remove British influence.

The Foreign Office accepted two of the three considerations. It flatly rejected the idea that Britain should follow a more socialist foreign policy. Even in accepting the two cabinet considerations, however, the Foreign Office hoped for eventual approval of Warner's recommendations. The Russia Committee's chief, for example, agreed that relations with the Soviet Union could become "much worse quickly" and that such an event should "be avoided." However, he argued that there was little chance of improving relations and that there would be an eventual "showdown." In Warner's opinion, it was better to have the showdown at the present time, when the Russians were weak, than later, when they were stronger. R. M. A. Hankey, head of the Northern Department, was of a similar view, as were many within the Foreign Office. He admitted in autumn that the "tide [was] already turning" against the Soviets and that Britain would "be on safe ground" in continuing its defensive efforts. Nevertheless, he "earnestly" thought that Britain needed "to organize [its] world and set it on its feet."[30]

Members of the Foreign Office were also aware of the domestic considerations used by the cabinet and agreed that because center and left opposition was "very damaging" to British policy, every effort should be made to "harmonize with the line taken by the Ministers." However, they believed that British leaders could take a more positive stance toward the Soviet Union and help modify British public opinion. Statements by Labour party leaders protesting Soviet actions, British statesmen believed, would help break the self-imposed ban on anti-Soviet material in British newspapers and over the radio. "Strange as it may seem our Press Barons have imposed a ban on anti-Soviet news and views," concluded a Foreign Office study. The reason for the ban was the belief by editors that

30. Foreign Office Minute, May 24, 1946, N 6734/140/38, Foreign Office Memorandum, August 22, 1946, N 11451/140/38, October 17, 1946, N 14167/140/38, Foreign Office Minute, November 8, 1946, N 14146/605/38, all in FO 371, 1946, PRO; Foreign Office Memorandum, November 5, 1947, N 12653/343/38, in FO 371, 1947, PRO.

by printing anti-Soviet stories they would endanger cordial relations between the British and the Soviets. Such a policy had been
encouraged during the war but in mid-1946 Foreign Office officials
considered it harmful. It confused British public opinion and de-
prived British policy of support. Equally important, such a ban
could mislead the Soviets into miscalculating the British resolve to
resist Soviet expansion. British officials agreed that war would
come only as a result of Soviet miscalculation of the West's willingness to resist. To correct the problem, members of the Foreign
Office hoped that Labour party leaders might assume a "more positive attitude in exposing and replying" to Russian efforts to discredit Britain and weaken its position abroad. These leaders, however, preferred to await changes in the press and public opinion.
Throughout 1946 and 1947, members of the Foreign Office continued to recommend stronger anti-Soviet policies than the cabinet
was willing to approve.[31]

Although discouraged by the restrictions placed on their Soviet
policy, Foreign Office officials were by early 1947 increasingly confident that British official and public opinion was moving to support the correct policies. The cabinet, responding to apparent increased Soviet threats to British interests, was allowing a strong
propaganda campaign to be waged on the German question and in
the Middle East. Public opinion was also turning along the desired
path. This was not because of any British efforts, however; the shift
occurred largely due to Soviet actions at international meetings and
in Eastern Europe. It was becoming increasingly difficult for British
socialists and even Communists to explain and defend the harsh
realities of Soviet domination in Eastern Europe.[32]

On the diplomatic front, relations with the United States were
good. The Americans were assuming the task of restraining Soviet
expansionism, and the old fear that they would retreat into isolationism was fading. A new fear was replacing it: namely, that
American brusqueness and veneration of capitalism would gener-

---

31. Foreign Office Minute, May 14, 1946, N 6733/140/38, September 25, 1946, N
123400/140/38, Roberts to Foreign Office, June 30, 1946, N 10049/605/38, all in FO
371, 1946, PRO.

32. Jones, *The Russian Complex*, 159–79; Peter Weiler, "The United States, Inter-
national Labor, and the Cold War: The Breakup of the World Federation of Trade
Unions," *Diplomatic History*, V (1981), 2–4, 15–22; Foreign Office Memorandum,
November 5, 1947, N 12653/343/38, in FO 371, 1947, PRO.

ate too much of an anti-Soviet policy and see socialist Britain as an unreliable partner. Neville Butler, assistant undersecretary, wrote that "cooperation in military and intelligence matters [with the United States] . . . was a fragile plant" and that the center and left critics within the Labour party could cause it "to wilt." This fear was especially high when the Soviets sought a new treaty of friendship and when Labourites denounced the Truman Doctrine.[33]

The fear of American suspicion of Britain receded as Bevin assured the United States of Britain's support and as he fully supported the Marshall Plan. By mid-1947, Britain was busily putting its house in order, reorganizing its "world as quickly and as actively . . . without the Russians" as possible. At the same time, domestic opposition to Bevin's policies waned. The opposition had reached its zenith in April with the publication of the centrist pamphlet *Keep Left*. It was countered by a pamphlet titled *Cards on the Table*, by Bevin supporter Dennis Healey. His work not only justified Bevin's policies and supported the Truman Doctrine but attacked Soviet totalitarianism in Eastern Europe as well. It matched the type of strong campaign long advocated by the Russia Committee.

Healey's pamphlet was an attack upon those opposing Bevin's policies from within the Labour party. At the full party conference in Margate in 1947, Bevin also attacked, lashing out at his opponents and accusing them of stabbing him in the back and being appeasers of the Soviet Union. Bevin's speech crushed those who were finding it increasingly difficult to justify the Soviet Union's behavior in Eastern Europe and the country's withdrawal from the Marshall Plan. Throughout the first half of 1947, Labour party opposition to Bevin's policies shrank while support grew. By the time of the announcement of the formation of the Cominform in autumn, most members of the Labour party fully agreed with the London *Daily Herald's* view that Russia was the cause of European instability. Reflecting the opinion of the few who still denied the Soviets' aggressive intent, Harold Laski wrote: "I have the feeling that I am already a ghost in a play that is over."[34]

33. Rothwell, *Britain and the Cold War*, 343–49; Foreign Office Minute, December 12, 1946, N 16004/5169/38, in FO 371, 1946, PRO; Peterson to Foreign Office, June 20, 1947, N 66370/271/38, Balfour to Foreign Office, August 29, 1947, N 10052/1380/38, both in FO 371, 1947, PRO.
34. Jones, *The Russian Complex*, 151–74; Knight, "Labourite Britain," 268–72; McCagg, *Stalin Embattled*, 217–19, 223–25.

Laski was correct. The play, the image of positive relations between Britain and the Soviet Union, was over. The Labour party's leadership was finally ready to launch the publicity campaign long advocated by members of the Foreign Office. On January 3, 1948, the Foreign Office dispatched a series of telegrams to its major embassies, giving advance notice of the prime minister's speech scheduled for that day. The prime minister would be taking "a much stronger line than previous speeches . . . in regard to Communism and Russia," the telegrams said. The speech was just one of a series of "political broadcasts" that were scheduled. Herbert Morrison was to follow on the eleventh and Bevin the next week.[35]

The Soviet media vehemently attacked all three speakers. *Trud* stated, "Together with British monopolists, the Labour leaders are paving the path for American Imperialism, which is striving for world domination." Bevin was called a "traitor to the working class," and *Izvestia* asserted that officials in the British government were participating in a slander campaign against the Soviet Union. The Russian denouncements had little impact in Britain. The center and left critics had been either tamed or discredited. Communists and "fellow-travelers" were now being portrayed as "traitors." In October, the British Trades Union Congress claimed that British Communists took orders from Moscow, were in "servile obedience to the Cominform," and joined with other Communists in preventing stability in Europe. Having quieted domestic opposition, in January, 1948, Attlee and Bevin firmly placed the United Kingdom alongside the United States in resisting the expansion of Soviet power and influence. Attlee informed Commonwealth prime ministers that Britain was first supporting the main bastions of defense against Soviet expansion on the Soviet perimeter, and secondly, "exposing, preventing and combating Soviet attempts to penetrate or divide the non-Communist powers."[36] Clearly, Attlee accepted the fact of the divided world and sought to defend the non-Communist part. Britain had officially joined the cold war.

35. Jones, *The Russian Complex*, 174–84; Foreign Office Circular Telegram, January 3, 1948, N 482/2/38, Foreign Office Minute, January 24, 1948, N 1141/1/38, Attlee to Bevin, January 21, 1948, N 878/1/38, all in FO 371, 1948, PRO.

36. Foreign Office Memorandum, January 9, 1948, N 293/2/38, Foreign Office Minute, January 21, 1948, N 11412/1/38, Memorandum for Commonwealth Prime Ministers, October 4, 1948, N 10702/1/38, all in FO 371, 1948, PRO.

In moving from alliance to cold war, each of the powers had followed a similar path. Big Three diplomacy during the London conference revealed the strains, tensions, and divisions in the Grand Alliance. The powers' inability to implement the agreements reached at Moscow ended the Grand Alliance and began the process of staking out and defending territory while generating domestic support for pugnacious policies. By 1948, statesmen in all three countries viewed the events of the past two and a half years in much the same way—but in mirror images. "During this period," wrote one commentator, "two concepts have crystallized . . . one is of a democratic policy of cooperation of all powers, the recognition of the coexistence of various systems . . . the other is a policy of unrestrained expansion." The writer regretted that expansive policies had forced others to resist through self-protection.[37] The commentator was Russian, but he could have just as easily been American or British. All agreed that each power, against its original intentions, had been forced to adopt protective policies to safeguard vital national interests and to ensure the peace of the world. The Grand Alliance had collapsed. There were no victors, and no losers—only combatants.

37. Peterson to Foreign Office, March 23, 1948, N 3535/1/38, in FO 371, 1948, PRO; Elisabeth Baker, *The British Between the Superpowers, 1945–1950* (Toronto, 1983), 104–05; Weiler, "British Labor and the Cold War"; Roberts to Foreign Office, January 6, 1947, N 676/343/38, in FO 371, 1947, PRO.

Appendix: Provisions of the Communiqué of the Moscow Conference of the Council of Foreign Ministers, December 27, 1945

I. Preparation of the peace treaties for Italy, Romania, Bulgaria, Hungary, and Finland.

   A. The Italian treaty to be drafted by the United States, Great Britain, the Soviet Union, and France.

   B. The Romanian, Bulgarian, and Hungarian treaties to be drafted by the United States, Great Britain, and the Soviet Union.

   C. The Finnish treaty to be drafted by Great Britain and the Soviet Union.

   D. "Council of Foreign Ministers will convoke a conference for the purpose of considering treaties of peace with Italy, Rumania, Bulgaria, Hungary and Finland. The Conference will consist of the five members of the Council of Foreign Ministers together with all members of the United Nations which actively waged war with substantial military force against European enemy states."

   E. "The peace treaties will come into force immediately after they have been ratified by the Allied states signatory to the respective armistices, France being regarded as such in the case of the peace with Italy."

II. The Far Eastern Advisory Commission and Allied Control Council for Japan.

   A. The Far Eastern Advisory Commission will "formulate the policies, principles, and standards in conformity with which the fulfillment by Japan of its obligations under the terms of surrender may be accomplished."

   B. "The Commission in its activities will proceed from the fact that there has been formed an Allied Council for Japan and will respect existing control machinery in Japan, including the chain of command from the United States Government to the Supreme Commander and the Supreme Commander's command of occupation forces."

   C. "The United States Government may issue interim directives to the Supreme Commander pending action by the Commission whenever urgent matters arise not covered by policies already formulated."

   D. "There shall be established an Allied Council [for Japan] with its seat in Tokyo under the chairmanship of the Supreme Commander for the Allied Powers . . . for the purpose of consulting with and advising the Supreme Commander in regard to the implementation of the Terms of Surrender, the occupation and control of Japan."

   E. "In all cases action will be carried out under and through the Supreme Commander who is the sole executive authority for the Allied Powers in Japan. . . . His decisions upon these matters shall be controlling."

III. Korea.

   A. "With a view to the re-establishment of Korea as an independent state, the creation of conditions for developing the country on democratic principles and the earliest possible liquidation of the disastrous results of the protracted Japanese domination of Korea, there shall be set up a provisional Korean democratic government which shall take all the necessary steps for developing the industry, transport and agriculture of Korea and the national culture of the Korean people."

   B. "In order to assist the formation of a provisional Korean government . . . there shall be established a joint commission consisting of representatives of the United States command in southern Korea and the Soviet command in northern Korea. In preparing their proposals the Commission shall consult with the Korean democratic parties and social organizations."

C. "It shall be the task of the Joint Commission, with the participation of the Provisional Korean Democratic Government and of the Korean democratic organizations to work out measures also for helping and assisting (trusteeship) the political, economic and social progress of the Korean people, the development of democratic self-government and the establishment of the national independence of Korea."

D. "The proposals of the Joint Commission shall be submitted . . . for the joint consideration of the Governments of the United States, Union of Soviet Socialist Republics, United Kingdom and China for the working out of an agreement concerning four-power trusteeship of Korea for a period of up to five years."

IV. China.

A. The United States, the Soviet Union, and Great Britain "were in agreement as to the need for a unified and democratic China under the National Government, for broad participation by democratic elements in all branches of the National Government, and for a cessation of civil strife. They reaffirmed their adherence to the policy of non-interference in the internal affairs of China."

B. The United States and the Soviet Union "were in complete accord as to the desirability of withdrawal of Soviet and American forces from China at the earliest practicable moment consistent with the discharge of their obligations and responsibilities."

V. Romania.

A. "The three Governments are prepared to give King Michael the advice for which he has asked in his letter of August 21, 1945, on the broadening of the Rumanian Government. The King should be advised that one member of the National Peasant Party and one member of the Liberal Party should be included in the government."

B. A commission composed of A. Y. Vyshinsky, Averell Harriman, and Sir A. Clark Kerr to determine that those invited to participate in the government are "truly representative members of the groups of the parties not represented in the Government" and "are suitable and will work loyally with the government."

C. The Romanian Government "should declare that free and unfettered elections will be held as soon as possible on the basis of universal and secret ballot. . . . The reorganized government should give assurances concerning the grant of freedom of the press, speech, religion and association."

VI. Bulgaria.

A. "It is understood by the three Governments that the Soviet Government takes upon itself the mission of giving friendly advice to the Bulgarian Government with regard to the desirability of the inclusion in the Bulgarian Government of the fatherland front, now being formed, of an additional two representatives of other democratic groups, who (a) are truly representative of the groups of the parties which are not participating in the government, and (b) are really suitable and will work loyally with the government."

B. "As soon as the Governments of the United States of America and the United Kingdom are convinced that this friendly advice has been accepted by the Bulgarian Government and the said additional representatives have been included in its body, The Government of the United States and The Government of the United Kingdom will recognize The Bulgarian Government."

VII. Establishment by the United Nations of a Commission for the Control of Atomic Energy.

A. The United States, Great Britain, and the Soviet Union "have agreed to recommend, for the consideration of the General Assembly of the United Nations of a commission to consider problems arising from the discovery of atomic energy and related matters."

B. "The Commission shall proceed with the utmost dispatch and inquire into all phases of the problem, and make such recommendations from time to time with respect to them as it finds possible. In particular the Commission shall make specific proposals:

(a) For extending between all nations the exchange of basic scientific information for peaceful ends;

(b) For control of atomic energy to the extent necessary to ensure its use only for peaceful purposes;

(c) For the elimination from national armaments of atomic weapons and of all other major weapons adaptable to mass destruction;

(d) For effective safeguards by way of inspection and other means to protect complying states against the hazards of violations and evasions."

C. "The work of the Commission should proceed by separate stages, the successful completion of each of which will develop the necessary confidence of the world before the next stage is undertaken."[1]

1. *FR, 1945,* II, 815–24.

Bibliography

PRIMARY MATERIALS

Archival Materials

UNITED KINGDOM

Churchill College Library, Churchill College, Cambridge
    Bevin, Ernest. Papers.
    Lord Halifax Papers.
British Library of Politics and Economics, London School of Economics
    and Political Science, London
    Dalton, Hugh. Papers
Public Record Office, London
    Cabinet Papers, 1945.
    Chief of Staff Papers, 1945.
    Foreign Office General Correspondence, 1945–48.
Bodleian Library, Oxford University, Oxford
    Attlee, Clement. Papers.

UNITED STATES

Robert Muldrow Cooper Library, Clemson University, Clemson, S.C.
    Brown, Walter. Papers.
    Byrnes, James F. Papers.

Lilly Library, Indiana University, Bloomington, Ind.
    Berry, Burton Y. Papers.
Library of Congress, Washington, D.C.
    Bush, Vannevar. Papers.
    Connally, Tom. Papers.
    Davies, Joseph E. Papers.
    Feis, Herbert. Papers.
    Frankfurter, Felix. Papers.
    Hull, Cordell. Papers.
    Leahy, William. Papers.
    McCloy, Frank. Papers.
    Patterson, Robert. Papers.
    Sweester, Arthur. Papers.
    Swing, Raymond. Papers.
National Archives, Washington, D.C.
    Modern Military Branch
        General Records of Joint Chiefs/Combined Chiefs of Staff
        Manhattan Engineer District Files
        Plans and Operations Division of the Army General Staff Records
        Secretary of Navy Papers
        State-War-Navy Coordinating Committee Files
    State Department Branch
        Lot M 88; Council of Foreign Ministers Files
        Lot 59A, 1945
        Lot 52 M 45, 1945–46
        Herbert Freeman Matthews File
        Harly Notter Office Files
        Record Group 43, 1945
        Record Group 122, 1945
        Record Group 59, 1945–48
        Secretary's Staff Committee Records
        State-War-Navy Coordinating Committee Files
Firestone Library, Princeton University, Princeton, N.J.
    Baruch, Bernard. Papers.
    Dulles, Janet A. Papers.
    Dulles, John Foster. Papers.
    Forrestal, James V. Papers.
    Stevenson, Adlai E. Papers.
Franklin D. Roosevelt Library, Hyde Park, N.Y.
    Cox, Oscar. Papers.
    Hopkins, Harry L. Papers.
    Kilgore, Harley M. Papers.

Morgenthau, Henry L., Jr. Papers.
Roosevelt, Eleanor. Papers.
Smith, Harold. Papers.
Tugwell, Rexford. Papers.
Harry S Truman Library, Independence, Mo.
Acheson, Dean. Papers.
Ayers, Eben. Papers.
Clayton, William. Papers.
Clifford, Clark. Papers.
Connelly, Matthew. Papers.
Groves, Leslie. Papers.
McNaughton, Frank. Papers.
Official File.
President's Secretary's File.
Rigdon, William. Papers.
Rosenman, Samuel. Papers.
Ross, Charles. Papers.
Smith, Harold D. Papers.
Truman, Harry S. Papers.
United States Department of State, Suitland, Md.
Moscow Post Files
United States Department of State, Washington, D.C.
Lot 57 D 688, 1945–46.
Lot 57 F 103, 1945–46.
Lot 64 563, 1945–46.
University of Iowa Library, University of Iowa, Iowa City, Iowa.
Wallace, Henry A. Papers.
University of Michigan Library, University of Michigan, Ann Arbor, Mich.
Vandenberg, Arthur. Papers.
University of North Carolina Library, University of North Carolina, Chapel Hill, N.C.
Daniels, Jonathan. Papers.
University of Oklahoma Library, University of Oklahoma, Norman, Okla.
Hurley, Patrick J. Papers.
Sterling Memorial Library, Yale University, New Haven, Conn.
Acheson, Dean. Papers.
Stimson, Henry L. Papers.

Published Government Documents

Blakesee, George H. *The Far Eastern Commission: A Study in International Cooperation, 1945–1952.* Washington, D.C., 1953.

Ministry of Foreign Affairs of the U.S.S.R. *Correspondence Between the Chairman of the Council of Foreign Ministers of the U.S.S.R. and the Presidents of the U.S.A. and the Prime Ministers of Great Britain During the Great Patriotic War, 1941–1945*. 2 vols. Moscow, 1957.

Public Papers of the Presidents of the United States: Harry S Truman, 1947. Washington, D.C., 1963.

U.S. House of Representatives. Special Committee on Postwar Policy and Economic Planning. *Economic Reconstruction in Europe*. House Document 11, December 12, 1945. Washington, D.C., 1945.

U.S. Department of State. *Biographic Register of the Department of State, 1946*. Washington, D.C., 1947.

———. *Department of State Bulletin*. Vols. XII–XIV. Washington, D.C., 1945–46.

———. *Foreign Relations of the United States*. Annual volumes, 1944–47. Washington, D.C., 1959–72.

———. *Foreign Relations of the United States: The Conference of Berlin (The Potsdam Conference), 1945*. 2 vols. Washington, D.C., 1960.

———. *Foreign Relations of the United States: The Conferences at Malta and Yalta, 1945*. Washington, D.C., 1955.

Periodicals

Chicago *Tribune*, 1945–46.
Christian Science Monitor, 1945–47.
London *Times*, 1945–46.
Los Angeles *Times*, 1945–46.
Louisville *Courier-Journal*, 1945–46.
Manchester *Guardian*, 1945–47.
Newsweek, 1945–46.
New Times (Moscow), 1945–47.
New York *Herald Tribune*, 1945.
New York *Times*, 1945–48.
Public Opinion Quarterly, 1939–47.
Soviet Press Translations, 1945–47.
Time, 1945–47.
Twohey Analysis of American Editorial Opinion, 1945–46.
Washington *Post*, 1945–46.

Autobiographies and Diaries

Acheson, Dean. *Present at the Creation: My Years in the State Department*. New York, 1969.

Attlee, Clement R. *As It Happened*. New York, 1949.

———. *Twlight of Empire: Memoirs of Prime Minister Clement Attlee*. New York, 1962.

Beneš, Eduard. *Memoirs of Dr. Eduard Beneš: From Munich to New War and New Victory.* London, 1954.

Berle, Beatrice B., and Travis Jacobs, eds. *Navigating the Rapids, 1918–1971: From the Papers of Adolf A. Berle.* New York, 1973.

Bidault, Georges. *Resistance: The Political Autobiography of Georges Bidault.* New York, 1969.

Blum, John M., ed. *The Price of Vision: The Diary of Henry A. Wallace, 1942–1946.* Boston, 1973.

Bohlen, Charles E. *Witness to History, 1929–1969.* New York, 1973.

Bush, Vannevar. *Pieces of the Action.* New York, 1970.

Byrnes, James F. *All in One Lifetime.* New York, 1958.

———. "Byrnes Answers Truman." *Collier's,* April 26, 1952, p. 15.

———. *Speaking Frankly.* New York, 1947.

Campbell, Thomas M., and George C. Herring, eds. *The Diaries of Edward R. Stettinius, Jr., 1943–1946.* New York, 1975.

Conant, James B. *My Several Lives: Memoirs of a Social Inventor.* New York, 1970.

Connally, Tom, and Alfred Steinberg. *My Name is Tom Connally.* New York, 1954.

Dalton, Hugh. *The Fateful Years: Memoirs, 1931–1945.* London, 1957.

———. *High Tide and After: Memoirs, 1945–1960.* London, 1962.

Dilks, David. ed. *The Diaries of Sir Alexander Cadogan, 1938–1945.* New York, 1972.

Dixon, Pierson. *Double Diploma: The Life of Sir Pierson Dixon, Don and Diplomat.* London, 1968.

Eden, Anthony. *The Reckoning: The Memoirs of Anthony Eden.* Boston, 1965.

Francis-Williams, Edward. *A Prime Minister Remembers: The War and Postwar Memoirs of the Rt. Hon. Earl Attlee.* London, 1961.

Galambus, Louis, ed. *The Papers of Dwight David Eisenhower: The Chief of Staff.* Vol. VII of 9 vols. Baltimore, 1978.

Gladwyn, Lord. *The Memoirs of Gladwyn.* New York, 1972.

Groves, Leslie. *Now It Can Be Told.* New York, 1962.

Harriman, W. Averell, and Elie Abel. *Special Envoy to Churchill and Stalin, 1941–1946.* New York, 1975.

Hughes, H. Stuart. "The Second Year of the Cold War: A Memoir and Anticipation." *Commentary* XLVIII (August, 1969), 27–32.

Hull, Cordell. *The Memoirs of Cordell Hull.* 2 vols. New York, 1948.

Johnson, Walter, and Carol Evans, eds. *The Papers of Adlai E. Stevenson.* 3 vols. Boston, 1972.

Kennan, George F. *Memoirs, 1925–1950.* Boston, 1967.

Krock, Arthur, *Memoirs: Sixty Years on the Firing Line.* New York, 1968.

Leahy, William D. *I Was There.* New York, 1950.

Millis, Walter, and E. S. Duffield, eds. *The Forrestal Diaries.* New York, 1951.

Molotov, V. M. *Problems of Foreign Policy: Speeches and Statements, April, 1945–November, 1948.* Moscow, 1949.

Murphy, Robert. *Diplomat Among Warriors.* Garden City, N.Y. 1964.

Nicholson, Harold. *The Later Years, 1945–1962.* New York, 1968. Vol. III of Nigel Nicholson, ed., *Diaries and Letters.* 3 vols.

Strong, Lord. *At Home and Abroad.* London, 1956.

Szilard, Leo. "Reminiscences." *Perspectives in American History,* II (1968), 121–29.

Truman, Harry S. *Years of Decision.* Garden City, N.Y., 1955. Vol. I of Truman, *Memoirs.* 2 vols.

Vandenberg, Arthur H., Jr., ed. *The Private Papers of Senator Vandenberg.* Boston, 1952.

Oral History Collections

Columbia University Oral History Collection, Columbia University, New York, N.Y.

John Foster Dulles Papers, Princeton University, Princeton, N.J.

Jonathan Daniels Papers, University of North Carolina, Chapel Hill, N.C.

Oral History Collection, Harry S Truman Library, Independence, Mo.

SECONDARY MATERIALS

Books and Articles

Acheson, Dean. *Sketches from Life of Men I Have Known.* New York, 1959.

Adamthwaite, Anthony. "Britain and the World, 1945–9." *International Affairs,* LXI (1985), 223–35.

Alperovitz, Gar. *Atomic Diplomacy: Hiroshima and Potsdam.* New York, 1965.

Anstey, Caroline. "The Projection of British Socialism: Foreign Office Publicity and American Opinion, 1946–1950." *Journal of Contemporary History,* XIX (1984), 417–51.

Aspaturian, Veron V. *Process and Power in Soviet Foreign Policy.* Boston, 1971.

Baker, Elisabeth. *Britain in a Divided Europe, 1945–1970.* London, 1971.

———. *The British Between the Superpowers, 1945–1950.* Toronto, 1983.

Baldwin, Frank, ed. *Without Parallel: The American-Korean Relationship Since 1945.* New York, 1974.

Baram, Phillip J. *The Department of State in the Middle East, 1919–1945.* Philadelphia, 1978.

Bartlett, Christopher J. *The Long Retreat: A Short History of British Defence Policy, 1945–1970.* London, 1972.

Beal, John R. *John Foster Dulles: A Biography.* New York, 1974.

Beitzell, Robert. *The Uneasy Alliance: America, Britain and Russia.* New York, 1972.

Bell, H. C. F. *Lord Palmerston*. London, 1936.

Berge, Oscar. "The Big Three Off Guard." *New York Times Magazine*, December 8, 1946, p. 15.

Bernstein, Barton J. "The Quest for Security: American Foreign Policy and International Control of Atomic Energy, 1942–1946." *Journal of American History*, LX (1974), 1003–44.

———. "Roosevelt, Truman, and the Atomic Bomb, 1941–1945: A Reinterpretation." *Political Science Quarterly*, XL (1975), 23–69.

———, ed. *The Atomic Bomb: The Critical Issues*. Boston, 1976.

———, ed. *Politics and Policies of the Truman Administration*. Chicago, 1970.

Betts, R. R. *Central and South East Europe, 1945–1948*. Westport, Conn., 1971.

Bishop, Donald G. *The Administration of British Foreign Relations*. Westport, Conn., 1974.

Bishop, Robert, and E. S. Crayfield. *Russia Astride the Balkans*. New York, 1948.

Black, Cyril E. "The Start of the Cold War in Bulgaria: A Personal View." *Review of Politics*, XLI (1979), 163–202.

Blackmer, Donald L. M. *Unity and Diversity: Italian Communism and the Communist World*. Cambridge, Mass. 1968.

Boll, Michael M. *Cold War in the Balkans: American Foreign Policy and the Emergence of Communist Bulgaria*. Lexington, Ky., 1984.

Boyle, Peter G. "The British Foreign Office and American Foreign Policy, 1947–1948." *Journal of American Studies*, XVI (1982), 373–90.

———. "The British Foreign Office View of Soviet-American Relations, 1945–1946." *Diplomatic History*, III (1979), 307–20.

Brown, J. F. *Bulgaria Under Communist Rule*. New York, 1970.

Buhite, Russell D. *Patrick J. Hurley and American Foreign Policy*. Ithaca, N.Y., 1973.

Bullock, Alan. *Ernest Bevin: Foreign Secretary, 1945–1951*. New York, 1983.

———. *The Life and Times of Ernest Bevin*. 3 vols. London, 1960–83.

Campbell, John C. "Negotiating with the Soviets." *Foreign Affairs*, XXIV (1956), 305–14.

Campbell, Thomas M. *Masquerade Peace: America's U.N. Policy, 1944–1945*. Tallahassee, Fla., 1973.

Cantril, Hardley, and Mildred Strunk. *Public Opinion, 1935–1946*. Princeton, 1951.

Charlton, John. *Lancaster House*. London, 1957.

Chatham House Study Group. *British Security*. London, 1946.

Chubin, Shahran, and Sephr Zabin. *The Foreign Relations of Iran: A Developing State in a Zone of Great Power Conflict*. Berkeley, Calif., 1974.

Churchill, Winston S. *Triumph and Tragedy*. Boston, 1953. Vol. VI of Churchill, *The Second World War*. 6 vols.

Clemens, Diane S. *Yalta*. New York, 1970.

Cochran, Bert. *Harry Truman and the Crisis Presidency*. New York, 1973.

Coffin, Tris. *Missouri Compromise*. Boston, 1947.

Collier, Basil. *The Lion and the Eagle: British and Anglo-American Strategy, 1900–1950*. New York, 1972.

Curry, George. *James F. Byrnes*. New York, 1965. Vol. XIV of Robert H. Ferrell, ed., *The American Secretaries of State and Their Diplomacy*. 19 vols.

Dallek, Robert. *Franklin D. Roosevelt and American Foreign Policy, 1932–1945*. New York, 1979.

Davies, John Paton, Jr. *Dragon By the Tail: American, British, Japanese, and Russian Encounters with China and One Another*. New York, 1972.

Davis, Lynn Ethridge. *The Cold War Begins: Soviet-American Conflict Over Eastern Europe*. Princeton, N.J., 1974.

Davis, Vincent. *Postwar Defense Policy and the U.S. Navy, 1943–1946*. Chapel Hill, N.C., 1962.

De Carmoy, Guy. *The Foreign Policies of France, 1944–1948*. Chicago, 1970.

DeNovo, John A. "The Culbertson Economic Mission and Anglo-American Tensions in the Middle East, 1944–1945." *Journal of American History*, LXIII (1977), 913–36.

Dennett, Raymond, and Joseph E. Johnson, eds. *Negotiating with the Russians*. Boston, 1951.

Divine, Robert A. *Roosevelt and World War II*. Baltimore, 1969.

Donovan, Robert J. *Conflict and Crisis: The Presidency of Harry S Truman, 1945–1948*. New York, 1977.

Dulles, John Foster. *War or Peace*. New York, 1950.

Evans, Trevor. *Bevin of Britain*. New York, 1946.

Feis, Herbert. *The China Tangle: The American Effort in China from Pearl Harbor to the Marshall Mission*. Princeton, 1953.

————. *Contest Over Japan: The Soviet Bid for Power in the Far East*. New York, 1968.

————. *From Trust to Terror: The Onset of the Cold War, 1945–1950*. New York, 1970.

Ferrell, Robert H. *George C. Marshall*. New York, 1966. Vol. XV of Ferrell, *The American Secretaries of State and Their Diplomacy*. 19 vols.

Fischer, Louis. *Russia, America and the World*. New York, 1961.

————. *Russia's Road From Peace to War: Soviet Foreign Relations, 1917–1941*. New York, 1969.

Fitzsimmons, M. A. *The Foreign Policy of the British Labour Government, 1945–1951*. Notre Dame, Ind., 1953.

Francis-Williams, Edward. *Ernest Bevin: Portrait of a Great Englishman*. London, 1952.

Frankel, Joseph. *British Foreign Policy, 1945–1973*. London, 1975.

Friedman, Edward, and Mark Selden, eds. *America's Asia: Dissenting Essays on Asian-American Relations.* New York, 1961.

Gaddis, John Lewis. *The United States and the Origins of the Cold War, 1941–1947.* New York, 1972.

———. "The Emerging Post-Revisionist Synthesis on the Origins of the Cold War." *Diplomatic History,* VII (1983), 171–205.

———. *Strategies of Containment: A Critical Appraisal of Postwar American National Security Policy.* New York, 1982.

Gallup, George H. *The Gallup Poll: Public Opinion, 1935–1971.* 3 vols. New York, 1972.

Gamson, William A., and Andre Modigliani. *Untangling the Cold War: A Strategy for Testing Rival Theories.* Boston, 1971.

Gardner, Lloyd C. *Architects of Illusion: Men and Ideas in American Foreign Policy, 1941–1949.* Chicago, 1971.

Gardner, Richard N. *Sterling-Dollar Diplomacy: The Origins of the Prospects of Our International Economic Order.* New York, 1969.

Gati, Charles, ed. *Caging the Bear: Containment and the Cold War.* Indianapolis, 1974.

Gordon, Michael R. *Conflict and Consensus in Labour's Foreign Policy, 1945–1965.* Stanford, Calif., 1969.

Gormly, James L. "Keeping the Door Open in Saudi Arabia: The United States and the Dhahran Airfield, 1945–1946." *Diplomatic History,* IV (1980), 189–205.

———. "Plots and Tactics: The United States, Britain, Russia, and Rumania, 1944–1947." *Red River Valley Historical Journal of World History,* IV (1980), 269–92.

———. "Secretary of State James F. Byrnes: An Initial British Evaluation." *South Carolina Historical Magazine,* LXXIV (1978), 198–205.

Gowing, Margaret. *Britain and Atomic Energy, 1939–1945.* New York, 1969.

———. *Policy Making.* New York, 1974. Vol. I of Gowing, *Independence and Deterrence: Britain and Atomic Energy, 1945–1952.* 2 vols.

Halle, Louis J. *The Cold War as History.* New York, 1969.

Hammett, Hugh B. "American Non-Policy in Eastern Europe and the Origins of the Cold War." *Survey,* XIX (1973), 144–62.

Hammond, Thomas T., ed. *Witnesses to the Origins of the Cold War.* Seattle, 1982.

Harbutt, Fraser. "American Challenge, Soviet Response: The Beginning of the Cold War, February–May, 1946." *Political Science Quarterly,* XCVI (1981–82), 623–40.

Harsch, Joseph. "How to Get Tough with the Russians." *Christian Science Monitor,* March 6, 1946, p. 20.

Hathaway, Robert M. *Ambiguous Partnership: Britain and America, 1944–1947.* New York, 1981.

Herken, Gregg. *The Winning Weapon: The Atomic Bomb in the Cold War,
   1945–1950.* New York, 1980.
Herring, George C., Jr. *Aid to Russia, 1941–1946: Strategy, Diplomacy, the
   Origins of the Cold War.* New York, 1973.
————. "The Truman Administration and the Restoration of French Sov-
   ereignty in Indochina." *Diplomatic History,* I (1977), 97–117.
Hess, Gary B. "The Iranian Crisis of 1945–1946 and the Cold War." *Politi-
   cal Science Quarterly,* LXXIV (1974), 117–46.
Hewlitt, Richard G., and Oscar E. Anderson, Jr. *The New World, 1939–
   1946.* University Park, Pa., 1962. Vol. I of Hewlitt and Anderson, *A
   History of the United States Atomic Energy Commission.* 2 vols.
Hogan, Michael. "The Search for a Creative Peace: The United States,
   European Unity, and the Origins of the Marshall Plan." *Diplomatic
   History,* VI (1982), 267–86.
Hoopes, Townsend. *The Devil and John Foster Dulles.* Boston, 1973.
Ionescu, Ghita. *Communism in Rumania, 1944–1962.* New York, 1964.
Iriye, Akira. *The Cold War in Asia: A Historical Introduction.* Englewood
   Cliffs, N.J., 1974.
Jones, Bill. *The Russian Complex: The British Labour Party and the Soviet
   Union.* Manchester, 1977.
Jones, Roy E. "Reflections upon an Eventful Period in Britain's Foreign
   Relations." *International Relations,* XXXIX (1963), 236–52.
Kaiser, Karl, and Roger Morgan, eds. *Britain and West Germany: Changing
   Societies and the Future of Foreign Policy.* New York, 1971.
Kaplan, Lawrence, S. "Western Europe in 'The American Century': A
   Retrospective View." *Diplomatic History,* VI (1982), 111–24.
Kertesz, Stephen D. "Reflections on Soviet and American Negotiating Be-
   havior." *Review of Politics,* XIX (1957), 3–36.
King, F. P. *The New Internationalism: Allied Policy and the European Peace,
   1939–1945.* London, 1973.
Kirk, George. *The Middle East, 1945–1950.* London, 1954.
Knight, Jonathan. "The Great Power Peace: The United States and the So-
   viet Union Since 1945." *Diplomatic History,* VI (1982), 169–84.
————. "Russia's Search for Peace: The London Conference of Foreign
   Ministers, 1945." *Journal of Contemporary History,* XIII (1978), 137–63.
Knight, Wayne. "Labourite Britain: America's 'Sure Friend'? The Anglo-
   Soviet Treaty Issue, 1947," *Diplomatic History,* VII (1983), 267–82.
Kogan, Norman. *Italy and the Allies.* Cambridge, Mass., 1956.
Kolko, Gabriel. *The Politics of War: The World and United States Foreign Pol-
   icy, 1943–1945.* New York, 1968.
Kolko, Joyce, and Gabriel Kolko. *The Limits of Power: The World and United
   States Foreign Policy, 1945–1954.* New York, 1972.

Kovig, Bennett. *The Myth of Liberation: East-Central Europe in the U.S. Diplomacy and Politics Since 1941.* Baltimore, 1973.

Kuniholm, Bruce R. *The Origins of the Cold War in the Near East: Great Power Conflict and Diplomacy in Iran, Turkey, and Greece.* Princeton, N.J., 1980.

Lach, Donald, and Edmund S. Wehrle. *International Politics in East Asia Since World War II.* New York, 1975.

LaFeber, Walter. "American Policy-Makers, Public Opinion, and the Outbreak of the Cold War, 1945–1950." In *The Origins of the Cold War in Asia,* edited by Yonosuke Nagai and Akira Iriye. Tokyo, 1977.

———. "Roosevelt, Churchill, and Indochina: 1942–1945." *American Historical Review,* LXXX (1975), 1277–95.

Leffler, Melvyn P. "From the Truman Doctrine to the Carter Doctrine: Lessons and Dilemmas of the Cold War." *Diplomatic History,* VII (1983), 245–67.

Leigh, Michael. *Mobilizing Consent: Public Opinion and American Foreign Policy, 1937–1947.* Westport, Conn., 1976.

Lenczowski, George. *Russia and the West in Persia, 1918–1948: A Study in Big Power Rivalry.* Ithaca, N.Y., 1949.

Levering, Ralph B. *American Opinion and the Russian Alliance, 1939–1945.* Chapel Hill, N.C., 1976.

———. *The Cold War, 1945–1972.* Arlington Heights, Ill., 1982.

Login, I., and V. Ruzhikov. "Soviet-British Relations, Past and Present." *International Affairs, A Monthly Journal of Political Analysis,* III (March, 1974), 26–31.

Lundestad, Geir. *The American Non-Policy Toward Eastern Europe, 1943–1947.* New York, 1975.

McCagg, William O., Jr. *Stalin Embattled, 1943–1948.* Detroit, 1981.

McNeil, William H. *America, Britain, and Russia: Their Cooperation and Conflict, 1941–1946.* New York, 1953.

Manderson-Jones, R. B. *The Special Relationship: Anglo-American Relations and Western Unity, 1947–1950.* London, 1972.

Mark, Eduard M. "Allied Relations in Iran, 1941–1947: The Origins of the Cold War Crisis." *Wisconsin Magazine of History,* LIX (Autumn, 1975), 51–63.

———. "Charles E. Bohlen and the Acceptable Limits of Soviet Hegemony in Eastern Europe: A Memorandum of 18 October 1945." *Diplomatic History,* III (1979), 201–14.

Markham, Reuben. *Rumania Under the Soviet Yoke.* Boston, 1949.

Mastny, Vojtech. *Russia's Road to the Cold War: Diplomacy, Warfare, and the Politics of Communism, 1941–1945.* New York, 1979.

May, Ernest R. *"Lessons" of the Past: The Use and Misuse of History in American Foreign Policy.* New York, 1973.

May, Gary. *China Scapegoat: The Diplomatic Ordeal of John Carter Vincent.* Washington, 1979.

Medlicott, W. N. *British Foreign Policy Since Versailles, 1919–1963.* London, 1968.

Mee, Charles L., Jr. *Meeting at Potsdam.* New York, 1975.

Meeham, Eugene J. *The British Left Wing and Foreign Policy.* New Brunswick, N.J., 1960.

Merrick, Ray. "The Russia Committee of the British Foreign Office and the Cold War, 1946–47." *Journal of Contemporary History,* XX (1985), 435–68.

Messer, Robert L. *The End of an Alliance: James F. Byrnes, Roosevelt, Truman, and the Origins of the Cold War.* Chapel Hill, N.C., 1982.

———. "Paths Not Taken." *Diplomatic History,* I (1977), 297–320.

Morgan, Kenneth O. *Labour in Power, 1945–1951.* Oxford, England, 1984.

Mosely, Philip, ed. *The Kremlin and World Politics.* New York, 1960.

Nagai, Yonosuke, and Akira Iriye, eds. *The Origins of the Cold War in Asia.* New York, 1978.

Nogee, Joseph L. *Soviet Policy Toward International Control of Atomic Energy.* Notre Dame, Ind., 1961.

Northedge, F. S. *British Foreign Policy: The Process of Readjustment, 1945–1961.* New York, 1962.

Northedge, F. S., and Audrey Wells. *Britain and Soviet Communism: The Impact of a Revolution.* London, 1982.

Oren, Nissan. *Revolution Administered: Agrarianism and Communism in Bulgaria.* Baltimore, 1973.

Ovendale, Ritchie. "Britain, the U.S.A., and the European Cold War, 1945–1948." *History,* LXII (1982), 217–36.

Paterson, Thomas G. *On Every Front: The Making of the Cold War.* New York, 1979.

———. *Soviet-American Confrontation: Postwar Reconstruction and the Origins of the Cold War.* Baltimore, 1973.

———. "Presidential Foreign Policy, Public Opinion, and Congress: The Truman Years." *Diplomatic History,* III (1979), 1–18.

———, ed. *Cold War Critics: Alternatives to American Foreign Policy in the Truman Years.* Chicago, 1971.

Phillips, Cabell. *The Truman Presidency: The History of a Triumphant Succession.* New York, 1966.

Pollard, Robert A. *Economic Security and the Origins of the Cold War, 1945–1950.* New York, 1985.

Roberts, Henry L. *Rumania.* New Haven, Conn., 1951.

Rose, Lisle A. *After Yalta: America and the Origins of the Cold War.* New York, 1973.

Rothwell, Victor. *Britain and the Cold War, 1941–1947.* London, 1982.

Roy, M. N. *Men I Met.* Bombay, 1968.

Ruben, Barry. "Anglo-American Relations in Saudi Arabia, 1941–1945." *Journal of Contemporary History,* XIV (1979), 253–67.

Rubenstein, M. "The Foreign Press on the Atomic Bomb." *New Times* (Moscow). September 1, 1945, pp. 12–17.

Schneer, Jonathan. "Hopes Deferred or Shattered: The British Labor Left and the Third Force Movement, 1945–1949." *Journal of Modern History* LVI (1984), 197–226.

Schuman, Frederick L. *The Cold War: Retrospect and Prospect.* Rev. ed. Baton Rouge, 1967.

Sheehan, Michael. *Iran: The Impact of United States and Politics, 1941–1945.* Brooklyn, 1968.

Sherry, Michael S. *Preparing for the Next War: American Plans for Postwar Defense, 1941–1945.* New Haven, Conn., 1977.

Sherwin, Martin J. *A World Destroyed: The Atomic Bomb and the Grand Alliance.* New York, 1975.

Shlaim, Peter, Peter Jones, and Keith Sainsbury. *British Foreign Secretaries Since 1945.* London, 1977.

Shulman, Marshall D. *Stalin's Foreign Policy Reappraised.* Cambridge, Mass., 1963.

Smith, Gaddis. *American Diplomacy During the Second World War, 1941–1945.* New York, 1965.

Smith, Perry M. *The Airforce Plan for Peace, 1943–1945.* Baltimore, 1970.

Snyder, William P. *The Politics of British Defense Policy, 1945–1962.* Columbus, Ohio, 1964.

Sokolov, A. "Again on Democracy." *New Times* (Moscow). October 1, 1945, pp. 7–14.

Starobin, Joseph R. "Origins of the Cold War: The Communist Dimension." *Foreign Affairs,* XLVII (1969), 681–96.

Stephan, John J. *The Kuril Islands: Russo-Japanese Frontier in the Pacific.* Oxford, England, 1975.

Sulzberger, C. L. "The Four Who Speak for the Big Four." *New York Times Magazine,* August 21, 1946, pp. 7–9.

Shwadran, Benjamin. *The Middle East, Oil, and the Great Powers.* New York, 1973.

Taubman, William. *Stalin's American Policy: From Entente to Detente to Cold War.* New York, 1982.

Taylor, A. J. P. *Beaverbrook.* New York, 1972.

Theoharis, Athan G. *The Yalta Myths: An Issue in U.S. Politics, 1945–1954.*
    Columbia, Mo., 1970.
Thorne, Christopher. *Allies of a Kind: The United States, Britain, and the
    War Against Japan, 1941–1945.* New York, 1978.
Tolchenov, M. "The Atomic Bomb Discussion in the Foreign Press." *New
    Times* (Moscow). November 1, 1945, pp. 14–22.
Truman, Margaret. *Harry S Truman.* New York, 1973.
Tsou, Tang. *America's Failure in China, 1941–1950.* Chicago, 1963.
Tucker, Robert C. *The Soviet Political Mind: Studies in Stalinism and Post
    Stalin Change.* New York, 1963.
Ulam, Adam B. *Expansion and Coexistence: The History of Soviet Foreign Pol-
    icy, 1917–1967.* New York, 1968.
———. *The Rivals: America and Russia Since World War II.* New York, 1971.
Vyshinsky, Andrei Y. *The U.S.S.R. and World Peace.* Freeport, N.Y., 1969.
Walton, Richard. *Henry A. Wallace, Harry Truman, and the Cold War.* New
    York, 1976.
Ward, Jeremy K. "Winston Churchill and the 'Iron Curtain' Speech." *His-
    tory Teacher,* I (1968), 5–13.
Ward, Patricia D. *The Threat of Peace: James F. Byrnes and the Council of
    Foreign Ministers, 1945–1946.* Kent, Ohio, 1979.
Watt, D. C. *Britain Looks to Germany: British Opinion and Policy Towards Ger-
    many Since 1945.* London, 1965.
———. *Personalities and Policies: Studies in the Formulation of British Policy in
    the Twentieth Century.* Notre Dame, Ind., 1965.
Weiler, Peter. "The United States, International Labor, and the Cold War:
    The Breakup of the World Federation of Trade Unions." *Diplomatic
    History,* V (1981), 1–22.
Welch, William. *American Images of Soviet Foreign Policy.* New Haven, 1970.
Werth, Alexander. *Russia at War, 1941–1945.* New York, 1964.
Westerfield, H. Bradford. *Foreign Policy and Party Politics—Pearl Harbor to
    Korea.* New Haven, Conn., 1958.
Wheeler-Bennett, John W. *John Anderson, Viscount Waverley.* New York,
    1962.
Wheeler-Bennett, John W., and Anthony Nicholls. *The Semblance of Peace:
    The Political Settlement After the Second World War.* New York, 1972.
Windrich, Elaine. *British Labour's Foreign Policy.* Stanford, Calif., 1952.
Wolfe, Thomas W. *Soviet Power and Europe, 1945–1970.* Baltimore, 1970.
Woodhouse, C. M. *British Foreign Policy Since the Second World War.* New
    York, 1960.
Woodward, Sir Llewellyn. *British Foreign Policy in the Second World War.*
    3 vols. London, 1970–71.
Woolf, S. J., ed. *The Rebirth of Italy, 1943–1950.* London, 1972.

Wright, Theodore P. "The Origins of the Free Election Dispute in the
    Cold War." *Western Political Quarterly*, XIV (1961), 850–65.
Yergin, Daniel. *Shattered Peace: The Origins of the Cold War and the National
    Security State*. Boston, 1977.

Unpublished Materials

Anderson, Terry H. "Britain, the United States, and the Cold War,
    1944–1947." Ph.D. dissertation, Indiana University, 1978.
Cheriyan, C. F. "The United States and Korea: A Historical Study of Rela-
    tions, 1945–1960." Ph.D. dissertation, University Kerala (Triv-
    andrum, India), 1970.
Dunn, Keith A. "A Conflict of World Views: The United States, the Soviet
    Union, and Peace with Hitler's Former Allies." Ph.D. dissertation,
    University of Missouri, 1973.
Gormly, James L. "In Search of a Postwar Settlement: The London and
    Moscow Foreign Ministers Conferences and the Origins of the Cold
    War." Ph.D. dissertation, University of Connecticut, 1977.
Herken, Gregory. "American Diplomacy and the Atomic Bomb, 1945–
    1947." Ph.D. dissertation, Princeton University, 1974.
Lee, U. Gene. "American Policy Toward Korea, 1942–1947." Ph.D. disser-
    tation, Georgetown University, 1974.
Messer, Robert L. "The Making of a Cold Warrior: James F. Byrnes and
    American-Soviet Relations, 1945–1946." Ph.D. dissertation, Univer-
    sity of California, Berkeley, 1975.
Moore, Winfred, Jr. "New South Statesman: The Political Career of James
    Francis Byrnes, 1911–1941." Ph.D. dissertation, Duke University,
    1976.
Sylwester, Harold J. "American Public Reaction to Communist Expansion
    from Yalta to NATO." Ph.D. dissertation, University of Kansas, 1970.
Ward, Patricia D. "James F. Byrnes and the Council of Foreign Ministers,
    1945–1946." Ph.D. dissertation, University of Texas, 1975.
Weiler, Peter. "British Labor and the Cold War." Paper presented at the
    annual meeting of the Southern Historical Association, November,
    1983.

Index